PRACTICAL STEPS
FOR ALIGNING
INFORMATION TECHNOLOGY
WITH BUSINESS STRATEGIES

How to Achieve a Competitive Advantage

Bernard H. Boar
AT&T
Bell Laboratories

John Wiley & Sons, Inc.
New York • Chichester • Brisbane • Toronto • Singapore

Other Books by the Author

Abend Debugging for COBOL Programmers

Application Prototyping: A Requirements Definition Strategy for the 80s

Implementing Client/Server Computing: A Strategic Perspective

The Art of Strategic Planning for Information Technology: Crafting Strategy for the 90s

This text is printed on acid-free paper.

Copyright 1994 by AT&T
Published by John Wiley & Sons, Inc.

The opinions expressed in this book are those of the author and do not necessarily represent those of AT&T

Library of Congress Cataloging-in-Publication Data

Boar, Bernard H., 1947–
    Practical steps for aligning information technology with business
    strategy : how to achieve a competitive advantage / Bernard H. Boar.
        p.   cm.
    Includes bibliographical references.
    ISBN 0-471-07637-6 (acid-free paper)
    1. Strategic planning—Data processing.   2. Information
    technology—Management.   3. Management information systems.
    I. Title.
    HD30.28.B632   1995
    650'.0285—dc20
                                                    94-18522
                                                    CIP

Printed in the United States of America

10 9 8 7 6

In remembrance of my father, Irving Boar:
His memory is a blessing

On Strategy

A victorious strategy is not repeated, the configuration of responses to the enemy are inexhaustible. . . . Water configures its flow in accord with the terrain; the army controls its victory in accord with the enemy. Thus, the army does not maintain any constant strategic configuration of power; water has no constant shape. The end of an army's form is formlessness. One who is able to change and transform in accord with the enemy and wrest victory is termed genius.

—Sun Tzu, *The Art of War*

Contents

Author's Note

In this book, I will use the phrases *network computing* and *client/server computing* as synonyms. They refer to an information processing model wherein the servicing of computing requests is divided across multiple computers on a network. This is in contrast to traditional host-centered computing wherein all services are delivered on a centralized mainframe computer. I will also use the phrase *reach, range, and maneuverability architecture,* which refers to a specific way of designing an information technology environment to achieve the maximum freedom of action for the business. While one could create a network computing or client/server computing environment that doesn't meet the standards of a reach, range, and maneuverable architecture, such an action would be an appalling waste of I/T assets, evidence of glaring confusion, and an act of gross imprudence. We will therefore use the three labels as synonyms, unless a difference is explicitly noted.

Foreword

As we move through the turbulent 90s, it is becoming clear that we have migrated to a epoch of doing. People no longer want to listen or talk about business or information technology (I/T) strategy, they want to execute it. But the antecedent problem remains, exactly what are we to do? Execution for execution's sake is of little value; execution is the bottom line of strategy, but our actions must be deep, foresighted and purposeful; they must climax in the building of advantage.

At AT&T, we are acutely aware of the competitive fervor that characterizes our era, and of the importance of information technology as the preferred weapon of choice for winning the global wars of movement. We have never been content with what is, but the accelerating tempo of intense competition has made us even more starved for advantage-based change. It is toward that end that we have embraced business reengineering—not because it is faddish or new or because some guru recommends it, but because it provides a pragmatic context to renew our I/T resources in the service of the business. It provides a path for achieving perfect alignment between the business and the information technology assets.

We recommend this book because it is a book of action. It provides specific advice on how to reshape and remake the I/T organization. The advice is not only pragmatic and doable, it is built on sound strategic teachings. It therefore offers a rare find: deep and far-reaching strategy that is implementable. It delivers on the promise of reengineering. While one often feels that we are hopelessly adrift in an industry engulfed in chaos, there is a pathway to success. That pathway is built on vision and reason. Vision provides an end worthy of your extended commitment. Reason provides the means of obtainment. You will find substantial quantities of both in this book.

Norman R. Shaer
Director

Stuart A. Tartarone
Department Head

AT&T Bell Laboratories QUEST

Preface

If a poll were taken of information technology executives, whether they have the titles of Chief Information Officer (CIO), Chief Technology Officer (CTO), or Vice-President of Information Systems (VP/IS), for their favorite Broadway play of all time, I believe the answer would be unanimous, or nearly so. Without a doubt, the most common reply would be *Les Miserables*. Only a character with the endless trials and tribulations of a Jean Valjean played out against a background story of epic dimension could provide a play that the battered and weary information technology executive of the mid-1990s could completely identify with. Yes, *Les Miserables* would undoubtedly be the winner of such a poll.

As the mid-1990s unfold, the stress on the information technology (I/T) organization to deliver value for the business is accelerating. The business itself is under tremendous pressure from demanding customers, insistent stakeholders, and international competitors. The business needs to achieve unparalleled levels of customer satisfaction and competitive advantage. It is evident that the prerequisite or corequisite to achieving those ends is increasingly rooted in the novel and advanced uses of information technology. The information technology organization is on the hot seat, because the pressure cooker of global competition requires cost containment, value-added products and services, speed, adaptability, and customization; it demands the use of information technology to build and sustain advantage.

Specifically, the pressure points on the I/T organization are threefold:

1. *Business need:* the user organizations are demanding greater value from their I/T investment. In response to growing worldwide competition, the business needs to use I/T to build, sustain, and extend competitive advantage. The business is demanding more efficiency and effectiveness from the I/T organization. Most major strategic thrusts require the crafted use of information technology to succeed.

2. *Technology change:* I/T is changing at an unprecedented rate. There now exists a literal cornucopia of technologies to choose from and

integrate. With "one size fits all" traditional mainframe processing, the competencies that had to be nurtured were relatively few. This situation is changing dramatically, and the competency set that has sustained the I/T organization is rapidly becoming dated.

3. *Competition:* the internal I/T organizations are losing their historical monopoly status as the sole provider of information services. Besides the fact that users can now, more than ever, do it themselves, there is an army of outsourcers, system integrators, facility managers, and reengineers all competing for the user's business.

I/T management is thus caught between demanding business need, rapid technology change, and intense competition.

In my previous book, *The Art of Strategic Planning for Information Technology: Crafting Strategy for the 90s,* I recounted how the information technology organization could adapt and exploit the most modern strategic planning methods to develop a deep and far-reaching business strategy. The book made strategic business planning both relevant and accessible to the information technology professional. While the book provided some prescriptions to deal with selected challenges, for the most part, the book was descriptive—that is, it described the process of strategic planning for information technology and the various analytical concepts and tools that provide assistance to the strategist. Because strategy is a function of the specific time and circumstances of each business, the objective of the book was to teach strategic planning competency so that each organization could develop self-sufficiency and a tailor-made strategy in harmony with its special needs. The goal was not to provide "one size fits all" actions to be executed by all, but to provide the skills through which custom-made actions could be individually determined and developed. Public prescriptions of strategic therapy immediately devalue their efficacy. Anything that is public is replicable by all. It inevitably becomes the basis for creating a new baseline for competitive parity. True advantage must always be nonduplicable, so its source must be private and spring from within. Nevertheless, while all organizations may be given equal access to counsel, each proceeds in harmony with its own competence, vision, and hunger. So even that which is public can offer the basis of advantage, depending on the creativity of the individual implementation.

This book complements the previous book and applies its methods. While *The Art of Strategic Planning for Information Technology* was descriptive, this book is prescriptive. This book provides a generic analysis of the strategic situation and challenges that are common to many information technology organizations, and recommends specific strategic actions to be undertaken. While each I/T organization will need to customize and tweak the suggested actions to meet its own parochial circumstances, the challenges confronting the I/T community are of such monumental proportion that an overall analysis and action plan can be suggested—but with the caveat that it must be personalized. So while the previous book suggested how to do strategic planning, this book provides explicit guidance on what actions must be taken to accommodate the changes around us.

The selection of a framework for giving cogent advice is of prime importance. Information technology (I/T) executives are continually inundated with advice from gurus, academics, consultants, reengineers, and futurists. Advice is provided on a myriad of subjects. The areas of advice include, but are not limited to, I/T architecture, business reengineering, TQM for I/T, imaging, multimedia, electronic commerce, downsizing, CASE, mobile computing, outsourcing, client/server computing, artificial intelligence, fuzzy logic, on-line transaction processing, object-oriented technologies, UNIX, wireless communication, distributed database, on-line complex processing, executive information systems, vendor partnering, and open systems. A crisis will most likely materialize by the turn of the century, as the ratio of advice givers to receivers becomes 1:1, and by the year 2010 becomes 10:1. With so much clutter confusing the debate, it is critical to distinguish one's advice by targeting a primary need of the audience.

I have chosen to focus my advice on the theme of *strategic alignment*. Alignment is the most fundamental strategic concept, and identifies the ways in which multiple groups cooperate and collaborate to achieve a shared agenda. Our view of alignment is that the I/T organization must take actions to align itself perfectly with the needs of the business. When it does, it accomplishes a state of strategic fusion between the business and I/T. To achieve a state of perfect balance and harmony between the business and the I/T organization, the I/T organization will have to reengineer itself. Practices, procedures, and attitudes that have previously served the I/T organization well have become dated or even vestigial. The thrust of this book will therefore be to explain the overall strategic situation confronting the generic I/T community, and to suggest specific reengineering actions that the I/T community must take to respond to current and foreseeable circumstances.

This book should be of interest to those charged with developing information technology strategy. This should include members of the CIO staff, I/T architects, product planners, system designers, and business planners. It will not be of interest to application developers or system programmers who are interested in technology details unless they wish to expand their horizons and begin to understand the I/T business strategically.

Machiavelli, one of the most insightful strategists of all times, said,

My intention is to say something that will prove of practical use to the inquirer, I have thought it proper to represent things as they are in real truth, rather than as they are imagined. Many have dreamed up republics and principalities which have never in truth been known to exist; the gulf between how one should live and how one does live is so wide that a man who neglects what is actually done for what should be done learns the way of self destruction rather then self preservation.[1]

It is our objective to represent the situation as it is in reality and provide the means to self-preservation, rather than to self-destruction. Strategists must see and understand the world as it is, not as they wish it to be. It is always better to proceed with strategy founded on the most unbearable truth than to proceed with strategy based on reassuring but self-deceiving falsehoods. Strategy constructed on falsehood inevitably leads to a situation even more desperate and foreboding than the original one from which you had hoped to escape.

The recommended strategic moves may be difficult or controversial to enact, but such is the inevitable consequence of a time that demands intensive business reengineering. Strategy, to be of utility, must meet the standards of Sun Tzu, the master of strategy, who said,

When your strategy is deep and far reaching, then what you gain by your calculations is much, so you can win before you even fight. When your strategic thinking is shallow and near sighted, then what you gain by your calculations is little, so you lose before you do battle. Much strategy prevails over little strategy, so those with no strategy cannot but be defeated. Therefore, it is said that victorious warriors win first and then go to war, while defeated warriors go to war first and then seek to win.[2]

Strategy that meets Tzuian standards will be of enormous practical use, but it will not be accomplished painlessly. Then again, would you really have expected it to be a trivial effort? Did you imagine that advantage could suddenly be built on something that is effortless and petty?

Bernard Boar
East Brunswick, NJ
October 1994

NOTES

1. Machiavelli, *The Prince*, trans. George Bull (Penguin Books, 1961).
2. Sun Tzu, *The Art of War*, trans. Thomas Cleary (Shambhala Dragon Editions, 1988).

Acknowledgments

It is difficult to remember all the people whose knowledge and insights have influenced my thinking. For my thoughts on object-oriented technologies, I thank the Software Leadership Team at AT&T. Architecture has been an area of interest to me for years, and I have participated in and observed many efforts. There are too many to thank individually. I would, of course, like to thank the owners of market studies and other proprietary information who graciously gave permission to use their material. They are appropriately cited where used. Most of all, I would like to thank my wife and children, who not only provide constant support and encouragement for my writing, but who put up with the commitment I have given to it. Finally, a thank you to the Wiley production staff who devoted their time and skills to transforming my manuscript into a final book.

1

Introduction

1.1 PURPOSE

The purpose of this book is to provide the information technology strategist with specific advice on what actions can be taken to radically improve the efficiency and effectiveness of the Information Technology (I/T) organization. By *efficiency*, we mean the organization's productivity; by *effectiveness*, we mean its ability to meet the needs of its customers in a prompt, advantageous, and satisfying manner. The purpose of this book, therefore, is to aid the I/T strategist in developing strategic moves that will have a profound and sustaining effect on the ability of the I/T organization to add value to the business and, as a consequence, increase the reputation, prestige, and importance of the I/T function to the business.

If you listen to I/T executives and strategists as they bounce from one crisis to the next, their requests for advice can usually be summed up in five words: "What should I do now?" Of course, the timing of the request is a little late; what needed to be done for now, needed to have been done then—perhaps three years, two years, one year, or a few months ago. By definition, actions of a strategic nature are dramatic, require significant change and investment, and demand extended commitment. Strategic actions determine the character of a business in numerous dimensions and are not something that can be done "now," especially if they would need to be conceived, designed, and executed immediately. Things that can be quickly conceived of and executed are tactical in nature. They can stop the bleeding and hemorrhaging, or they can quickly cut costs, but fundamentally changing a business strategically takes forethought and time.

In my previous book, *The Art of Strategic Planning for Information Technology: Crafting Strategy for the 90s*[1] (referred to hereafter as *The Art of*), I presented a methodology for performing strategic business planning that was customized for the I/T function. The book described a complete three-step process for performing modern strategic business planning that encompassed the major steps of assessment, strategy, and execution. The methodology viewed the I/T organization as a strategic business unit. It included

1

technology planning, the traditional staple of I/T planning, but also took into account all major strategic areas, such as markets, suppliers, human resources, competitive advantages, positioning, critical success factors, and value chains. The goal of the book was self-sufficiency—that is, given that the particulars of each I/T organization are unique, although there are broad common drivers, the greatest benefit would be to teach I/T strategists how to develop strategies, rather than simply providing a one-time set of prescriptions.[2] Since time and circumstances continually evolve, one is much better positioned if able to revise strategy as times dictate, rather than being locked into a strategy conceived for a different time and circumstance.

While self-sufficiency is a admirable goal, it is a journey, not an event. The learning curve can be expedited with specific therapeutic advice. This book, consequently, complements my previous strategy book, *The Art of*, by executing part of the strategic planning process and providing specific actions that I/T strategists can customize to meet their organizational situations. Using *The Art of* as a reference methodology, this book will answer the I/T executive's lament, "What should I do now?"

It is my recommendation that the I/T strategist's overriding objective must be to achieve a state of strategic alignment between the business and the I/T organization. This will not be easy, and will require a major reengineering of the I/T organization. The I/T organization has spent nearly 30 years in a state of minimum alignment or intermittent alignment by accident, and the change from a position of gross misalignment to perfect alignment will require fundamental redesign. It is not so much that alignment needs to be reengineered as that it needs to be engineered for the first time. Reengineering the I/T organization will consequently be painful but necessary. This book will focus on two great themes:

1.   What is the nature of strategic alignment?
2.   What actions must be taken to reengineer the I/T organization to achieve a state of perfect strategic fit?

It is worth emphasizing that this view is framed within the idea that the I/T organization must adapt to accommodate and serve the business, not the converse, which is the traditional perspective of the I/T technologist. Most I/T technologists have never understood the simple truth that an art is practiced for the benefits of those for whom its services are intended, not for the benefit of the practitioner. Our entire thrust will therefore be to explain what strategic moves should be undertaken by the I/T organization for the paramount end of serving the customer of I/T services.

The problem of providing advice about change is not calling for change but selecting what to change to. Unless carefully designed, change can make things worse just as easily as it can make things better. Especially in an area like information technology, sooner or later, everything has only a past rather than a future. Our approach will therefore be to challenge many of the fixed beliefs of the I/T community through logic. Some of the resultant ideas may seem alien, but I ask that you suspend your normal defense mechanisms and skepticism and be open to possibility. As Descartes said, "Perhaps everything we believe is wrong. Perhaps."

Progress is possible only if there are people of action who have the courage to listen, reflect, discard, experiment, and finally trust their reason, their vision, and their instinct. Creative advances are always accompanied by a great outrage to some sacred custom, tradition, or belief; they are turbulent but exciting experiences. Do not be shy to confront the truth; change defaces what is, and what is will be staunchly defended. The mission of the I/T strategist to reengineer the I/T organization and reach a state of perfect strategic alignment with the business will not be easy, but it will be invaluable.

The most cynical statement I have ever heard about I/T management was as follows: "It is not so much that they don't have the strength of their convictions as that they have no convictions to have strength about." You will never achieve a state of alignment if you have no convictions. You will never get through the ordeal of reengineering if you have no strength. Strategists must have courage to affirm and confirm the actions that will be required.

Most people, when asked to characterize their business, will say that their company is in the *xyz* business, where *xyz* is chemicals, transportation, insurance, banking, lodging, entertainment, and so on. Information movement and management are certainly important to the business, but are adjunct to it. Perhaps, though, this view is antiquated and needs to be reversed. Perhaps all businesses are first and foremost in the information movement and management business. They all must collect, analyze, store, process, and disseminate information. The information value chain is often more lasting and of greater value than the transient hard products that they manage. Understood this way, the need for alignment and reengineering of I/T is obvious and glaring. Increasingly, I/T is the business.

1.2 STRATEGIC PLANNING AND STRATEGY

The purpose of this section is to review what we mean by strategic planning and strategy. The actions that will be recommended in the body of this book are neither isolated nor insular moves. Rather, they are integrated, and the context for that integration is a business strategy.[3] Since the language of strategy is constructed on common terms, it is important to establish careful definitions. Otherwise, everyone might read and assert agreement, when, in reality, they are agreeing to quite different ideas. This section will therefore attempt to lay a common foundation of strategic planning and strategy concepts.

The goal of strategic planning is to provide direction, concentration of effort, constancy of purpose, and flexibility, as a business continually strives to improve its position in all strategic areas. Historically, I/T organizations have done primarily technology planning that has been poorly linked to the business, if at all. With the increased pressures on the I/T organization in the 1990s—business demands for value-added solutions from I/T, accelerating technology change, and competition to in-house I/T sourcing—it is critical that the I/T organization use strategic planning methods to guide its evolution.

The raison d'être for strategic planning is rooted in the simple observation that all good fortune is but temporary. Machiavelli expressed this notion best when he said,

> Some princes flourish one day and come to grief the next without appearing to have changed in character or in any way. This I believe arises because those princes who are utterly dependent on fortune come to grief when their fortune changes. I also believe that those who adapt their policy to the times prosper, and those whose policies clash with the times do not. This explains why prosperity is ephemeral. If times and circumstances change, he will be ruined if he does not change his policy. If he changed his character to the times and circumstances, then his fortune would not change.[4]

Figure 1.1 illustrates the flow of Machiavelli's insightful advice. Strategic planning is necessary to prepare for the eternally recurrent challenge presented by forever changing times and circumstances.

Figure 1.2 illustrates the overall strategic planning model. The three primary steps are:

1. *Assessment:* the development of a clear and thorough understanding of the current and prospective business situation from both an internal and an external perspective.

2. *Strategy:* identifying the desired future state of the business, the specific objectives to be achieved, the strategic moves to be executed, and the enabling or supportive commitment and change management plans.

3. *Execution:* the process of executing the strategy and monitoring or tuning it as required by actual events and changing times and circumstances. Execution is a process of learning, discovery, and refinement.

Quality control and administration functions complete the planning process by attending to the quality of the strategy process and ensuring that the planning process is executed in an orderly, effective, and efficient manner.

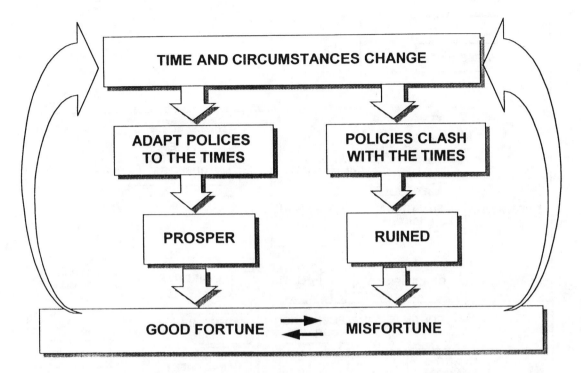

Figure 1.1 The Eternal Challenge. The eternal challenge dates your business idea and necessitates strategic planning. (Source: *The Art of Strategic Planning for Information Technology,* **Bernard Boar, John Wiley & Sons, 1993)**

Assessment

Assessment is the comprehensive analysis of the business, from both an internal and an external perspective, to reach conclusions on what requires strategic management focus and action. Assessment consists of five substeps, as follows:

1. *Business Scope Definition:* defines the key descriptors of the business. Table 1.1 itemizes the nine attributes that compose a business scope.

2. *Directives and Assumptions:* seeks to understand the strategic direction of the business and what priorities and constraints that direction places on the I/T function.

3. *Position Analysis:* identifies the state of one or more strategic areas. The position of a strategic area is normally expressed graphically. Position analysis forces convergence of understanding as to the

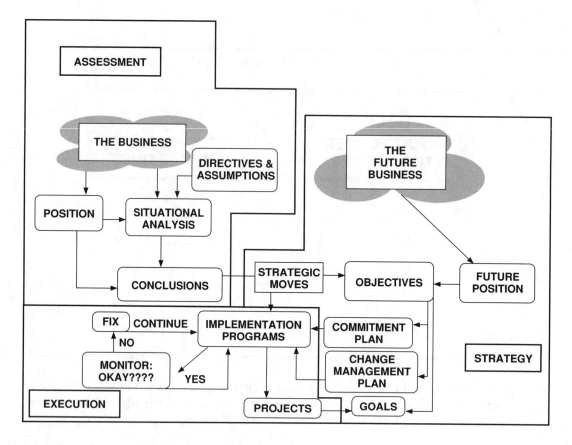

Figure 1.2   The Strategic Planning Model. The strategic planning process is divided into three primary steps. (Source: *The Art of Strategic Planning for Information Technology*, Bernard Boar, John Wiley & Sons, 1993)

state of the business by providing a shared view of "where we are." Typical position frameworks include Five Force Analysis, Capabilities Analysis, Market Segmentation, Core Competencies, and Product Maps.

4. *Situational Analysis:* collects information about all the strategic areas of the business for the purpose of developing conclusions about the state of the business. Situational analysis is very data intensive, and is best approached through the use of analytical models. Table 1.2 summarizes some common analysis methods.

5. *Conclusions:* comprise explicit statements identifying the situations requiring exploitative or remedial strategic action. They are

derived from the joint analysis of the preceding assessment sub-steps. Table 1.3 summarizes the structure of a conclusion.

Assessment takes place in multiple dimensions: current situation, projected futures, competitor situations, and ideal situation. At the end of the assessment step, the strategy team has a firm understanding of both the challenges confronting it and the logic of those challenges.

Strategy

Strategy consists of identifying the desired future state for the business, the specific objectives to be obtained, and the strategic moves necessary to realize that future. Strategy consists of six substeps, as follows:

1. *Future Business Scope Definition:* defines the key descriptors of the future business. This business scope may be an incremental or radical change from the current business scope defined in the Assessment step.

Table 1.1
Business Scope Definition. The business scope defines the essential character of a business.

Business Attribute	Definition
Vision	Business guiding theme
Mission	The purpose of the business
Values	Distinguishing beliefs—Ethos
Customer/markets	To whom we sell
Products/services	What we sell
Strategic intent	Long-term ambition of our efforts
Driving force	Primary determiner of products/ services and markets
Geography	Where we sell
Sustainable competitive advantage	Asset, capability or process that attracts us to our customers and deters our competitors

Source: Bernard H. Boar, *The Art of Strategic Planning for Information Technology* (New York: John Wiley & Sons, 1993).

Table 1.2
Analytical Methods. Situational analysis is best done through the use of a variety of analytical methods which structure and focus the analysis.

Analytical Method	Purpose
SWOT analysis	An analysis of business strengths, weaknesses, opportunities, and threats
Critical success factors	Identification of what the business *must* do well at to succeed
Root cause analysis	The analysis of a problem to discover the root etiology of the problem, as opposed to the superficial symptoms
Technology forecasting	The use of various forecasting methods, scenarios, "S" curves, Delphi technique, and timelines to develop forecasts of the future
Theory/Hypothesis	The generation of theories and associated hypotheses to explain what is or will be happening
Matrix analysis	Analyzing various strategic factors through matrices to discover relationships
Product analysis	Analyzing existing and new products from various perspectives—financial, competitive, market, risk
Value chain analysis	Tracing a product through the internal value chain to discover opportunities to improve the cost structure, value-added, or cycle time
Bottleneck analysis	Analyzing the value chain for bottleneck points
Benchmarking	Comparing selected strategic areas against other companies to discover shortcomings
Competitive analysis	Doing a strategic analysis of a competitor to understand relative deficiencies
Distribution channel analysis	Studying the distribution chain to discover improved ways of improving the effectiveness and efficiency of product/service distribution
Pivot position analysis	Analyzing strategic positions for the development of pivot positions, which allow for tremendous flexibility to deal with uncertainties
Gap analysis	Comparing where you are to where you would like to be for a given strategic framework

Table 1.3
**Conclusions. Conclusions identify the items that demand
strategic attention by management.**

Conclusion Attribute	Definition
Conclusion	A short, explicit statement that succinctly and clearly identifies a situation requiring strategic attention
Description	A one- to three-paragraph explanation of the conclusion
Etiology	An explanation of the root causes of the conclusion
Possible actions (strategic moves)	Examples of what actions may be taken to deal with the conclusion
Supporting evidence	Convincing arguments to support the conclusion

Source: Bernard H. Boar, *The Art of Strategic Planning for Information Technology* (New York: John Wiley & Sons, 1993).

2. *Future Positions:* identify the desired future strategic positions. These positions represent a strategic delta from the current positions identified in the Assessment step.

3. *Objectives:* identify specific measurable and dated objectives to be achieved in order to realize the future business scope and positions. Interim objectives are called *goals*.

4. *Strategic Moves:* are the specific actions to be taken to realize the objectives. Strategic moves are prescriptive, and represent initiatives that move the business from its current state to its desired future state. Table 1.4 summarizes the attributes of a strategic move.

5. *Change Plan:* is a subplan designed to preempt resistance to the strategy. The Change Plan anticipates resistance to change and details specific actions to be taken to minimize resistance and promote compliance with the strategy.

6. *Commitment Plan:* is a subplan explicitly designed to develop and sustain commitment to the strategy. The plan consists of both symbolic and substantive acts to convince the organization that the management team will, in fact, execute the strategy.

Table 1.4
Strategic Moves. A well-defined strategic move consists
of nine elements.

Strategic Move Attribute	Definition
Move	A brief and clear statement of the action
Description	A few-paragraph elaboration of the action
Owner	The individual in the organization responsible for making the action happen
Champion	The executive in the organization responsible for assisting the owner
Rationale	The business logic of the action
Priority	Relative importance of the action
Measurement	The way to measure that the action has been completed
Date	The date by which the action is to be concluded
Implementation program parameters	Rules, guidelines, and boundaries that the implementation owner should follow in implementing the action

Source: Bernard H. Boar, *The Art of Strategic Planning for Information Technology* (New York: John Wiley & Sons, 1993)

Strategy is the definition of both what is to be accomplished and the means of accomplishment. It determines the desired future to be achieved and how that future is to be realized. With few analytical methods available for assistance, strategy formulation is the most intellectually stimulating and challenging part of the strategic planning process.

Execution

Execution is the act of putting the plan into motion. The project management discipline is the heart of execution, through which implementation programs and projects are developed to move the business from its current business scope and set of strategic positions to the desired future. Throughout the execution process, monitoring and vigilance are maintained to tune and revise the strategy, as required, to remain in harmony with changing times and circumstances. Assessment, Strategy, and Execution are a trinity; strategic planning requires that each be done in turn and in order.

Schools of Strategy

Just as the I/T community is fractured into competing communities and special interest groups, the strategy community is likewise fragmented into different schools of strategy. The predominant school of strategy is the *design school*[5] (a.k.a. the rationalist school), with which this book is philosophically aligned. The design school believes that strategy is the deliberate consequence of forethought, experimentation, and design. Though the future is undeniably unpredictable, design school strategists subscribe to the belief that conscious actions can be taken to positively position for the future.[6] Sun Tzu described the design school when he says,

> Their victories in battle are not flukes. Their victories are not flukes because they position themselves where they will surely win, prevailing over those who have already lost.[7]

The design school believes that through analysis, perceptive insights, and experimentation, we can position for a successful future; we are not simply the hapless victims of a fickle fortune or fate.

The other schools provide a continuum of alternative views, as follows:

- *The emergent/learning school*[8]: takes the position that strategy is the by-product of the actual experiences and actions of the business. Strategy is not so much designed as it is an accident of actual events. In retrospect, one can package what has happened into a coherent story, but in reality, strategy amounts to a continual series of experiments and practical decisions; strategy is best understood as serendipity. A critic might take the view that the emergent school formalizes the practice of "muddling through."

- *The real-time (or interactive) school*[9]: takes the view that since the business world is changing so quickly, markets are in continual upheaval, and that in any case, the future can't be planned for, strategy must be done in real-time. As if playing a game of Nintendo, the strategist must react dynamically to each and every strategic stimulus and take appropriate corrective action. A critic might say that the real-time school is linguistic sophistry. It combines exciting words that make sense together linguistically, but that are nonsense semantically. Since strategic actions are actions of broad consequence and are not easily committed to or altered, it is logically contradictory to suggest that one can do strategy in real-time. The real-time school trivializes strategy and equates strategic actions to tactical actions.

- *The ready-fire-aim school*[10]: endorses action over planning. Its view is that companies get caught up in too much planning paralysis, and that learning is the essential element of good strategy. The thrust of strategy should therefore be to create extensive experimentation and discover empirically what works. The ready-fire-aim school is in direct contradiction with the teachings of Sun Tzu and Machiavelli, who certainly endorse adaptability, but see adaptability within the context of an overall guiding strategy.

- *The chaos school*[11]: takes the view that the business world is best understood under the rubric of chaos theory. The consequences of this view are somewhat confusing. Some chaos theorists suggest that because the business world is essentially a chaotic, nonlinear system, the hope of any predetermined strategy or mission is fruitless. Rather, one must position for flexibility and roll with the times. Other chaos theorists suggest that chaos can be modeled, and that the maturation of chaos theory will be improved prediction capability. This sub-school argues that nothing in this world is random; all apparent disorder and unpredictability are really the natural output of some deterministic processes. What is chaos is therefore determined by our level of understanding, not by the inherent nature of the subject matter. So while one chaos school views chaos as disorder, turmoil, and totally random confusion and turbulence, another chaos school views chaos as simply our shortcomings of knowledge. The consequence of this is that one school believes that chaos theory is reason to disband formal strategic planning methods ("why bother, it's all random"), while the other school believes that formal strategic planning will improve as the underlying chaos deterministic processes are mastered. As a whole, the chaos school is young and still emerging. It is one of the most interesting perspectives on strategy.

Figure 1.3 positions the various schools of strategy by the delineating dimensions of process formality and depth of strategic forethought. The following should be noted:

1. The design school's positioning includes ample room for experimentation, prototyping, learning, intuition, and trial and error. These actions are perfectly consistent with rational methods. The design school believes that while it can take positive actions to influence and anticipate the future, it does not suffer from the fatal conceit of believing that it can foresee or shape the future with exactitude. Like all the schools, the design school recognizes that strategy must be constructed on actions that enable the business to spontaneously reorder itself in sympathy with evolving times and circumstances.

2. The emergent school, the real-time school, and the ready-fire-aim school have rejected the idea that you can strongly influence your

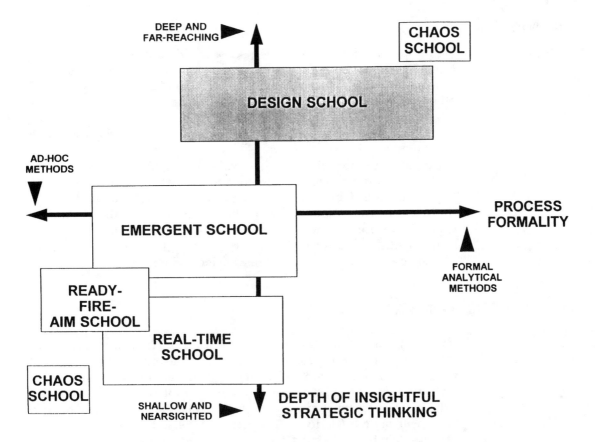

Figure 1.3   Schools of Strategy. The various schools of strategy can be positioned by the
dimensions of process formality and strategic forethought.

future by insightful deliberation leading to successful premeditated acts.

3. The chaos school is, itself, in a state of chaos. Depending on which chaos school analysis you accept, it either allows for the most rigorous design or concludes the hopelessness of trying to establish design.

If you're going to formulate strategy, it is important to understand both your own philosophy and the philosophy of your adviser. It is important to understand where the other guy is coming from. The advice given herein is based on the design school. The cardinal question for the student of strategy is "Do you believe that their victories were flukes, or do you believe that their victories were not flukes?" Which do you deem true?

Summary

Figure 1.4 summarizes the design school method of strategic planning. From Figure 1.4, it is clear what is meant by a *strategic action*. A strategic action is an action, initiative, or move that, individually or in concert with other actions, has the ability to move the business from a current position to a desired future position. A strategic action is an action of sufficient force and consequence to make a compelling difference to the future well-being of the business.

Strategic planning purposefully, with intent and forethought, moves the business from a state of potentiality to a state of actuality. The process requires the use of formal methods coupled with insight and sensitivity to the business. The future success of I/T organizations, as they struggle to cope with the forces of technology, business, and competitive change that swirl about them, will be more tightly associated with excellence, not in technology planning, but in strategic business planning.

1.3 STRATEGIC ALIGNMENT

If we are going to undertake major strategic thrusts to create a state of perfect alignment, a strategic fit between I/T and the business, it is necessary to have a clear and shared understanding of the nature of alignment. Otherwise, we may take actions, with the best of intentions, that instead of helping us escape our strategic quagmire, entangle us deeper in the misalignment tar pit. Clarity is hampered by colloquial definitions of the words. Therefore, we must take some time to uncover what strategic alignment between I/T and the business really means.

Basic Notions of Alignment

The basic notion of alignment is that when things are in a state of alignment, they naturally and harmoniously work together to accomplish a common end. There is neither friction nor drag between them; they perfectly complement and reinforce each other. Alignment has the basic property that those things in a state of alignment combine effortlessly as though they were one.

Basic alignment within a business is illustrated in Figure 1.5. Whether one looks at the business from a functional perspective (Figure 1.5a) or from a process perspective (Figure 1.5b), when a business is in state of alignment, all the functions or processes are linked together toward a common goal, the business scope. The business must, as a whole, be aligned with the needs of the marketplace, and must have its supplier chain aligned with itself. As shown in Figure 1.6, there are graduated

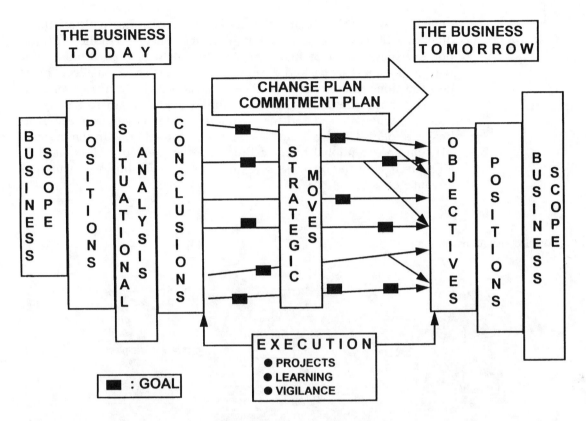

Figure 1.4   Strategic Planning Is Movement. The design school method of strategic planning is thoughtful and insightful movement of the business from its current state to a desired future state. (Source: *The Art of Strategic Planning for Information Technology*, Bernard Boar, John Wiley & Sons, 1993)

states of alignment. Any business must achieve at least a threshold state, or the misalignment will be so bad that it prevents the flow of products and services to the marketplace. Some businesses deteriorate to a state of chaos (Figure 1.7), where cooperation and collaboration are fleeting accidents. No business can survive at less then the threshold level. One popular view of strategy is that strategy is the movement of the business from its current state of (mis)alignment to a new and better state of alignment (Figure 1.8).

The final attribute of alignment involves the notions of *primary* and *secondary*. Of the functions or processes in alignment, one must define the direction for the others. For a business, the primary is always the customer. The secondary is composed of the business scope, internal functions, internal processes, and suppliers; all are in alignment with each other and with the primary, the marketplace. Aligning with anything other than the customer leads to but momentary success. For the I/T function to achieve a state of alignment with the business, then, it must align with the business scope, and through that business scope enable all business functions and processes to serve the customers in a superior manner.

So for those who understand the nature of alignment, there is no question as to who will lead and who will follow. The marketplace leads, the business follows, and I/T enables the business to align with the marketplace in an exceptional manner. But a question remains: How can I/T align itself with the business so as to convey to the business a unique advantage?

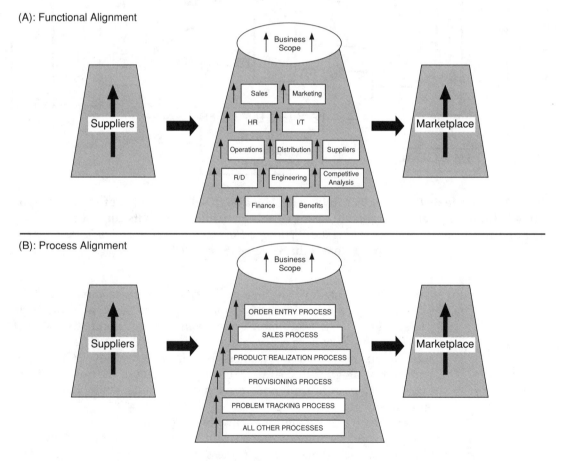

Figure 1.5   **Alignment. A business must be aligned internally as well as with the marketplace and its suppliers.**

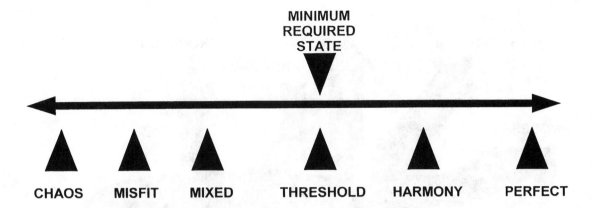

Figure 1.6   Graduated States of Alignment. Alignment is a continuous function with a few important data points.

Maneuverability

When one discusses alignment, one must concurrently discuss maneuverability. Maneuverability is the flip side of the alignment coin. Since a business must always be in fluid motion to respond creatively to environmental dynamics, alignment is not a static notion but one of movement. So when one speaks of alignment, one is also speaking implicitly of maneuverability.

The word *maneuver* has three common meanings:

1.   Simple movement.
2.   Purposeful movement to a superior position.
3.   Purposeful movement with speed and surprise to create a calculated disruption or dislocation. A dislocation is an action that

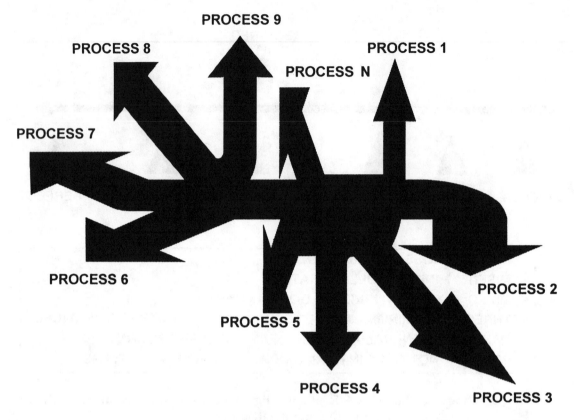

Figure 1.7   Chaos. If alignment disintegrates to a state of chaos, the business will be hopelessly unable to deliver products or services to the marketplace.

makes an opponent's advantage irrelevant and useless. It makes anything that formerly attracted customers null and void.

When we use the word *maneuver,* we intend it to mean all three things concurrently. In this way, *maneuver* is a word with rich meaning.

There are basically two alternative styles through which to conduct the battle for marketplace superiority:

- *Attrition:* success is achieved by taking a strong but fixed market position and attempting to "slug it out" for the marketplace. Through concentration of business assets against an inferior competitor, one attempts to win by exhausting the opponent's will and ability to compete. Through accumulated battling, the inferior combatant is worn down. The attrition fighter masses her forces

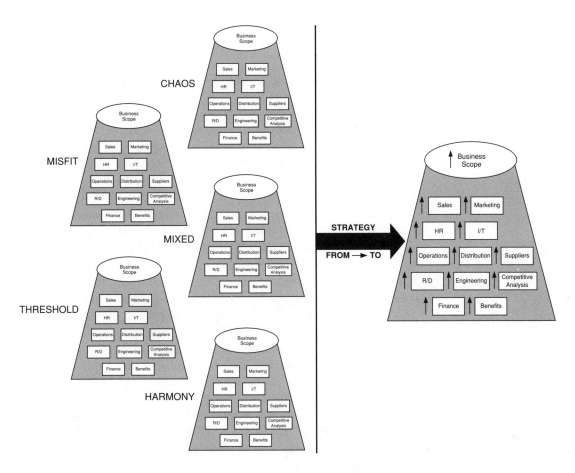

Figure 1.8   Strategy as Alignment. One view of strategy is that the thrust of strategy is to move the organization to an ever improved state of alignment, both internally and with the marketplace.

for pitched and decisive battles. This approach, to be successful, requires a stable market, clear superiority of assets (core competencies, processes, customer satisfaction systems, deep financial pockets, etc.), a mentality for "macho" confrontation, and an opponent who won't or can't maneuver against your head-on assault.

- *Maneuver:* success is achieved by moving to a new position from which you accrue a decided advantage, stinging the opponent and endlessly repeating the maneuver process until the accumulated impacts of the stings render the opponent unable to respond.

Sun Tzu said,

Maneuver means choosing the most advantageous way to go. Those who are good on the attack maneuver in the heights of the skies making it impossible for opponents to prepare for them.[12]

When you maneuver, you:

- Purposefully bring your assets to a chosen point of opportunity, a marketplace gap, which offers a disproportionate return for the effort. The best opportunities are those that offer nonsymmetrical risk to reward payoffs. The penalties for failure are finite, calculable, and absorbable, while the rewards for success are open-ended.

- Create a menace for the opponents, who must turn their attention from their agenda to your agenda. Even those who wish to ignore you can be made to turn their attention to you by a threat to something that is important to them.

- Create friction for your opponents by making them alter their plans, processes, initiatives, or alliances. Compounded friction from multiple maneuvers creates dysfunction and an inability to respond, which create future opportunities for more maneuvers.

- Continually attempt to raise the tempo and concurrence of the maneuvers. With each maneuver, the response period of the opponents lengthens, the quality of the response decreases due to their being rushed, and overall internal dissonance increases to the point that they are overwhelmed (systems break down, internal trust erodes, finger-pointing replaces focus on the marketplace, plans are useless, etc.).

- Cause your opponents to scramble about every which way, unsure of your next point of maneuver, while you proceed methodically with your plan. Rob them of their ability to make choices. If they spend all their time and energy chasing you, they will not have time to formulate and execute plans of their own.

- Overcome your opponents psychologically. By virtue of your speed, surprise, and nimbleness, overwhelm them emotionally and cause them stress, tension, fear of loss of honor and prestige, fear of being trapped, fear of personal failure and disgrace, psychological exhaustion, uncertainty, and despair due to inability to respond. Shatter their morale as you would attack their products.

- Rob them of their competitive advantages. Through radical and fundamental modification of the product/service value proposition, make the things that attracted customers repulse them.

- Improvise to take advantage of opportunistic situations that unfold as a consequence of the competitor's snarled responses. Maintain reserves in readiness to exploit gaps as they emerge.

- Lure your opponents out of their strongholds with the prospect of gain and then, and only then, confront them on a favorably lopsided playing field.

- Test your opponents through forays into their markets to discover where they are strong, where they are weak, and the nature of their response and their character. Use what you learn to design and calibrate your future maneuvers.

- Use deception, speed, surprise, and daring to stun and paralyze your opponents into inaction. Exploit the temporary advantage gained until they mass to counterattack, and then move swiftly to a new point of maneuver, thereby nullifying their effort.

- Focus your attention on satisfying your customers while your opponents focus on you.

Maneuver then is the art of creating marketplace dislocations (or breakpoints) that allow one to upset the marketplace status quo and create a newer and more advantageous marketplace order, while avoiding any direct confrontation with the opponent.

When you engage in maneuver warfare, your aim is to make your opponents overcome themselves. In response to each maneuver, your opponents must engage in a four-step response process:

1. Through market intelligence and data gathering methods, they must recognize that you have taken an action.

2. They must assess the implications of your maneuver and reach conclusions on its consequences.

3. They must prepare, design, and get approval for a response.

4. They must execute the response.

The speed and formality of each step will vary widely, but the sequence of steps is firm.

It is the express intent of maneuver to destroy the competition's ability to execute this sequence effectively and efficiently. As each maneuver gains in boldness, menace, tempo, and consequence, the competitor's processes began to unravel. Overlapping maneuvers cause intolerable friction, as the need to respond to new maneuvers overlaps and disrupts the response to prior maneuvers. Eventually, the competitor's ability to respond at all, or with quality and efficiency, is compromised by the accumulated turmoil you have created. All of this is done through indirection without costly direct confrontation.

There are three corollary ideas that are important to the design of maneuver actions:

- *Nonretaliation:* maneuvers may be explicitly designed to avert retaliation by competitors. Moving to a market position and avoiding competitive response can lead to the maximum profitability for the maneuver investment. The willingness of a competitor to respond to your action is a function of three variables, as follows:

  1. *Awareness:* the competitors must know that you have taken a threatening action. If your actions can be hidden, your action will not be easily discernible, so no response will be forthcoming.

  2. *Point of attack:* the competitors must feel threatened by where you attack in the marketplace. If you attack at the periphery of the market or a segment that they view as inconsequential, it will not be worthwhile for them to respond.

  3. *Difficulty of response:* the competitors must martial their forces and alter their plans to respond. The more difficult the means of response, especially if the point of attack is deemed of minor importance, the more inertia and lethargy will work to dissuade response.

  While nonretaliation-designed maneuvers can be quite profitable, they do not lead to the collapse of the opponent, which is the true objective of maneuver warfare. Nonretaliatory maneuver can be used to grow stronger, but eventually, if you wish to use the maneuver paradigm to overcome your opponents, you will have to make them turn their attention to you so that you can cause their processes to crumple in response to your actions.

- *Momentum:* the self-sustaining and cumulative negative effects of the maneuver actions on your opponents, as they compound disorder, is called *momentum.* Two complementary momentums are created: a momentum of confusion and chaos on the opponent and a momentum of success for yourself. Momentum is very important to maneuver warfare, and takes on a life of its own in defeating the opponent. In an ideal situation, the early maneuvers create such a self-sustaining and deteriorating state of momentum on the opponent that the opponent self-destructs and additional actions are not required.

- *Punch:* the mass of assets brought to the point of maneuver and the effort expended in applying them. In physics, force is defined by the equation $F = MA$ (force equals mass times acceleration). Punch is the force of the marketplace attack. In general, punch is increased in proportion to the cumulative success of the prior maneuver actions. Early on, the punch is sufficient only to draw your opponents' attention. As they collapse, the punch is made proportionally stronger to hasten their downfall.

Momentum and punch work very tightly together and are coupled notions. Imagine a strategic maneuver as a ball that is rolled toward an opponent. At the beginning, as though lying on a flat surface, the ball is rolled toward the opponent with minimum punch. As successive balls begin to have a deteriorating effect, self-defeating momentum commences. The momentum now has the effect of creating a virtual elevation for the newer balls. If the balls are rolled with the same punch as originally, they have a more deleterious effect by virtue of the virtual incline. The impact is much more harmful if the punch is increased. Of course, these new punches exacerbate the opponent's chaos and feed the momentum. So momentum and punch work together to optimize the impact of a maneuver strategy. The art of maneuver, then, is the design of punches with the minimum economy to create the greatest momentum.

All businesses must be able to maneuver at least minimally. If you wish to obtain some gain, you must be able to execute an offensive act. Conversely, even if you are content with the current marketplace situation, you must be able to maneuver defensively against more hungry competitors. Even if you wish to fight a war of attrition, your opponents may well choose to fight a war of maneuver, to which you must respond—or, better yet, you must maneuver to preempt their actions.

It is instructive to ask the question: "In a confrontation between an excellent attrition fighter and an excellent maneuver fighter, who will win?" In cases where either the attrition fighter or the maneuver fighter is clearly superior, the answers are fairly obvious. A capable attrition fighter will defeat an inept maneuver fighter, just as a sly maneuver fighter will best a fat and lazy attrition fighter. In the interesting case, the answer is probabilistic, but over time, I would side with the maneuver fighter. The reason for this is that cumulative battling with a capable maneuverer will bring frustration and emotional outbursts on the part of the attrition fighter. Accustomed to control, order, and doing it by the numbers, the attrition fighter will eventually be irritated by the onslaught of stings and disruptions and begin to react emotionally and without forethought to get revenge. The advantage that maneuver fighters have is that they are inherently better suited to the discomforts and open-ended nature of the game. The maneuver fighter is culturally at home with the indecisiveness and protractedness of the battle. It would therefore seem obvious that the best organization is one that, while asset-rich, big, and strong, can conduct itself in the marketplace like a fox. As a maneuver fighter grows successful, the challenge is not to convert into a bloated attrition fighter.

The obvious question is "What is the crown of creating dislocations?" Sun Tzu said, "Those who render others' armies helpless without fighting are the best of all."[13] He taught that the order of attack is the opponent's strategy, then her alliances, then her armies, and lastly her cities (seizes). The higher in this order that one can create a dislocation, the greater the ripple effect of disorder and chaos for the enemy. When you destroy an opponent's city, you annihilate only that target. When you destroy a critical element of your opponents' strategy, all their plans and preparations have become useless. So the height of dislocation science would be to compromise a strategic thrust of your opponents so that their plans, projects, training, alliances, products, preparations, competencies, processes, and so on are all in ruin. The higher in the order of attack that one can create a dislocation, the greater the multiplication of business problems caused for the opponent, and the greater the opportunities created for oneself.

Maneuverability is a very rich strategic framework for action, and should be implicitly understood as a corollary to alignment. Many of the best strategic planning frameworks, such as the Five Forces, Kano Methodology, and Strategic Thrust, all result in actions that demand maneuverability. It should therefore not be surprising that we will argue in the next section that the pinnacle of business to I/T strategic alignment requires I/T to maneuver dynamically in response to business requirements. Without friction, resistance, or drag, the I/T assets need to be brought to the selected marketplace opportunity at the chosen moment. In a global war of movement, where competitors maneuver around attrition fighters, success goes to those whose business systems, information resources, and decision-making support systems are the most reconfigurable. When I/T is the corporate lubricant of maneuverability, I/T achieves a state of strategic alignment.

An Aside

It is common in business strategy literature to dismiss military strategy as being inapplicable to business strategy. This is because their objectives seem to be quite different. The objective of military strategy is assumed to be to destroy, through violence, the opponent's ability or will to resist, while the objective of business strategy is to win in the marketplace by better satisfying customer needs. Competitors are actually a third party to business strategy, while in military strategy, they are the direct focus of your efforts.

The appraisal of maneuverability that we have just completed indicates the commonality of the two disciplines of strategy. The height of military strategy is "to win without fighting. Those who render others' armies helpless without fighting are the best of all."[14] The acme of military strategy is to create a state of such daunting military superiority that the opponent withdraws or surrenders without any physical combat.

Daunting superiority in business is often more economically achieved through indirection by way of splattering your opponent's cohesion than by predictably investing in your own competencies and capabilities. How can your opponents maintain a hold on the marketplace when the accumulation of your surgical chipping away at the gaps leaves their systems in a state of incoherence? If you choose the time and place of each encounter, do you not come well prepared, while they deplete themselves in rushed and inadequate responses? If you can make them fight by attacking what they must defend, or avoid a market encounter by leaving them no time to plan, are you not the puppeteer and they the puppets? This is accomplished through the art of maneuver. Is the goal to win through self-defeating price wars and feature versus functionality wars, or is it to win through finesse without impoverishing yourself? Military strategy and business strategy are therefore quite compatible, because when done correctly, they are both products of the intellect, not of brute force.

A Second Aside

Given what we have learned about alignment and maneuverability, it is very difficult to fathom why companies outsource I/T. If advantage springs from maneuverability, why would you turn your maneuverability assets over to mercenaries (outsourcers)? It would seem logical that only the most production operational components of I/T could be candidates for outsourcing. Although in the next chapter we will readily admit and analyze the threat that outsourcing presents to the typical in-house I/T organization, it would certainly seem to be strategic suicide to turn over the competencies of information movement to a third party in an era when wars of marketplace attrition are clearly being replaced by wars of global maneuverability.

Since outsourcing cannot be explained strategically, it must be that either corporate management has given up any hope of getting value from I/T, or the cost savings offered by outsourcing provide such tremendous short-term savings for a tactically driven business that they are irresistible. What will the company that has outsourced do when it finds that if the outsourcer is competent, the outsourcer will one day be able to hold it to ransom, or if the outsourcer is incompetent, the outsourcer will be the source of its ruin? When one chooses to outsource the basis of maneuverability for the business, one does freely to oneself what an evil fate did not.

A Final Aside

Through an understanding of the two basic styles of marketplace confrontation, attrition and maneuverability, the strategic rationale for the decline of the traditional mainframe host-centered computing environment is self-evident. Host-centered computing—as embodied in the IBM MVS operating environment, where associated presentation, processing, and data services all take place on one processor in one site—is a weapon of trench warfare. It is a weapon appropriate to wars of attrition. Network computing—a world of clients and servers where computing power or functionality is moved to where it is needed, when it is needed, and in units of how much is needed—is a weapon of the blitzkrieg. It is a weapon appropriate for wars of maneuverability. IBM's introduction of CMOS-based parallel mainframe host processors to replace the aging ECL processors will delay the inevitable, but will not stop the migration to distributed computing in all its varieties, because the issue is not cost but maneuverability. Host-centered computing is therefore in decline, not merely for all the routine reasons given, but even more fundamentally because it is the wrong weapon for the global war of movement for the 1990s and beyond.

I/T and Business Alignment

There are many ways to model I/T–business alignment. We will now review three representative models: a conceptual model, a four-stage model, and a five-stage model. All the models embrace an evolution in the impact of I/T to improve business effectiveness in the marketplace through business transformation.

- *Conceptual Model of I/T–Business Alignment:* Figure 1.9 illustrates three conceptual models of I/T–business alignment. All the models view the business and I/T as existing in parallel and needing to align perfectly at each level of decomposition. The optimum alignment of I/T and the business occurs when business strategy and I/T strategy are developed together, so that each can influence the other to maximum advantage. Misalignment at any level results in a dysfunctional relationship between I/T and the business.

- *The Four-Stage Model of I/T–Business Alignment:* The four-stage model suggests that as I/T improves its state of alignment, it moves through four stages of increasingly positive impact on the business, as follows:

    1. *Stage 1: Functional Automation:* I/T is used to individually automate functional business areas.

    2. *Stage 2: Cross-Functional Integration:* I/T is used to build systems shared across multiple functional organizations.

    3. *Stage 3: Process Automation:* I/T is used to build process-centric applications that transcend functional organizational boundaries.

    4. *Stage 4: Process Transformation:* I/T is used to fundamentally redesign processes and organizational structures to serve the customer.

- *The Five-Stage Model of I/T–Business Alignment:* The five-stage model suggests that as I/T improves its state of alignment, it moves through five stages of increasing positive impact on the business, as follows:

  1. *Stage 1: Localized Exploitation:* I/T is used to automate isolated business areas.

  2. *Stage 2: Internal Integration:* I/T is used to build common systems across functional organizations.

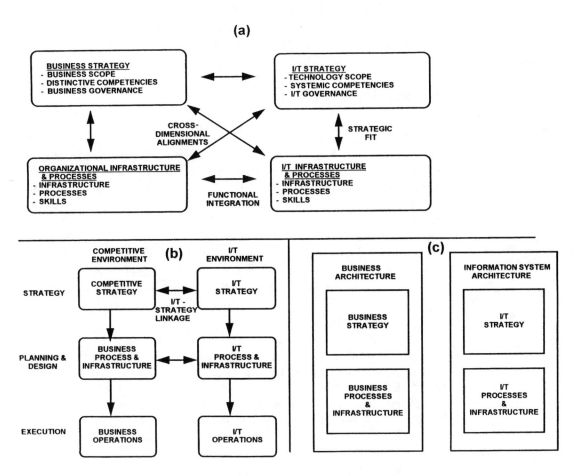

Figure 1.9   Conceptual Alignment Model. The conceptual alignment model illustrates how I/T both complements and enables the business by achieving perfect alignment at each level of decomposition. Source: (*a*) John Henderson, 1991; (*b*) J. McGee, *Managing Information Strategically* (New York: John Wiley & Sons, 1992); (*c*) G. Davis, *Managing Information* (Business One Irwin, 1990).

3. *Stage 3: Business Process Redesign:* I/T is used to build process-centric applications rather then function-centric applications.

4. *Stage 4: Business Network Redesign:* I/T is used to integrate business processes with suppliers and customers as one continuous system.

5. *Stage 5: Business Scope Redefinition:* I/T enables management to undertake novel business initiatives.

All these models present I/T–business alignment as an increasing ability of I/T to creatively alter the business. While these models are certainly adequate, we would suggest a different five-step model, which aligns I/T and the business in a perfect state of strategic alignment—a state where I/T conveys ideal competitive advantage to the business.

Perfect Strategic Alignment between I/T and the Business

We adduce that perfect strategic alignment between I/T and the business occurs when I/T can be used not merely to transform business processes, but also to create dislocations in the marketplace and, concurrently, the means of exploitation of those dislocations.[15] An act of dislocation creates such advantage that it upsets the balance of power in the marketplace and creates a new and more favorable marketplace for the designer of the dislocation. Dislocations can be understood by three dimensions, as follows:

1. *Point of Dislocation:* the point in the customer value chain or in the competitor's advantage where the dislocation is targeted.

2. *Power of Dislocation:* the strength of the dislocation shock created.

3. *Proximity of Dislocation:* the proximity of the competitor's home to the dislocation.

Francis Bacon said, "the folly of one man is the fortune of another. For no man prospers so suddenly and greatly as *by others' errors.*"[16] A perfect act of dislocation will attack a competitor's sustainable competitive advantage, destroy it completely, and be executed physically close to the competitor's home turf. In this way, the thing that is of primary marketplace value to the competitor is nullified in the most economical way. This breach of a competitor's stronghold causes devastating psychological demoralization.

The hub of a competitor's competitive advantage whose disruption will yield massive marketplace paralysis is referred to as the *center of gravity.* Your opponent's center of gravity may also be a critical vulnerability whose disruption will cause cascading failure. Invalidating your opponent's center of gravity through indirection is the climax of maneuver, and should be the long-term objective of your indirect maneuver actions. Developing a way to accomplish that will tax your strategic ingenuity to its limits.

The apogee of alignment occurs when I/T is sufficiently powerful and fused with the business, so that:

1. I/T is a primary participant in creating an attraction situation for customers.
2. The attraction is of such novelty and desirability that it creates a dislocation in the marketplace. Competitors are surprised, placed off balance, and confused as to how to respond; at best, they enter a state of paralysis.
3. I/T provides the means of exploiting the dislocating situation.

Perfect strategic alignment occurs when I/T is used to dynamically create and exploit business opportunities.

The five-stage model for the purposeful use of I/T to accrue perfect alignment is as follows:

1. *Stage 1: Functional Systems:* I/T is used to automate individual business functions.
2. *Stage 2: Cross-Functional Systems:* I/T is used to build systems that cross functional boundaries and permit the sharing of data.
3. *Stage 3: (Re)Engineering the Business:* I/T is used in novel ways to create processes in synchronization with business strategy. System boundaries include customers, suppliers, regulators, and any other trading partners.
4. *Stage 4: Imagineering the Business:* I/T is used as the cornerstone of radical restructuring of the business. Business advantage completely drives the selection and use of the most opportunistic technologies to infuse advantage into the business process.
5. *Stage 5: Create and Exploit Business Opportunities:* I/T has achieved a state of such power and maneuverability that it can be used by the business to create dislocations and corresponding exploitation of those dislocations in the marketplace. I/T can be used to force the competition to do something wrong; by exploitation of that mistake, the scales of the marketplace can be turned. The matter-of-course mayhem of the marketplace is imposed on the internal processes and plans of the competitors, causing the competitors to become inwardly focused while you accelerate the process of satisfying customer needs.

It is interesting to note that business opportunity creation is a higher rung on the alignment ladder than business reengineering. This is not a mistake. Dislocation design is like reengineering, in that the business design of the action is the intelligence of the act with I/T serving as the means of execution. It is different, however, in that business reengineering seeks to help you overcome your opponents through superiority of your business processes in delivering superior value to customers. Reengineering is about improving operations by the dimensions of speed, cost, or customer service. Dislocations seek to create a surprise imbalance in the marketplace so that your opponents, in their shock, confusion, and panic, *overcome themselves*. Dislocation is about upsetting the balance of power in the marketplace and creating a new and better status quo. Reengineering may make you invincible, but dislocations make your opponent vulnerable. Reengineering is a strategy of improving performance, while dislocation is a strategy for creating opportunities and growth. Sun Tzu said, "Destroy their countries artfully, do not die in protracted warfare."[17] What is more artful than creating a dislocation and then compounding your exploitation by the competition's thrashing and flailing efforts to respond? It is somewhat surprising that the advice community focuses on reengineering and ignores dislocation theory. Perhaps dislocation design will be next year's razzle-dazzle.

Maneuver also provides a way to attack process advantaged–based competitors. With maneuver initiatives, through the tempo of your actions and the points of attack, you deliberately strain and stress their processes to the point of collapse. When they reengineered them, they undoubtedly improved the processes' efficiency and effectiveness, but did they invest in agility? Maneuver is the competitive counterpunch to those who would attack you through superior processes.

Perfect alignment is achieved when I/T is used to throw competitors off balance, create the ability to take advantage of the resulting weakness, and exploit the situation. At this state of alignment, I/T is no longer a record keeper or process controller, it is the means of extended business success. But how does I/T become that powerful? How does I/T become powerful enough so that it can gracefully respond in mirrored movement to the abrupt starts and stops, jagged motions, twists and turns, and rapid accelerations and decelerations of the business as it responds to the marketplace?

Reach, Range, and Maneuverability Architecture

Information technology is the asset on which the enterprise constructs its business information systems. It may be rigorously defined as follows:

Information technology is the preparation, collection, transport, retrieval, storage, access, presentation, and transformation of information in all its forms (voice, graphics, text, video, and image). Information movement may take place between humans, humans and machines, and/or between machines. Information management assures the proper selection, deployment, administration, operation, and maintenance of the I/T assets consistent with organizational objectives.

I/T can reach a state of perfect strategic alignment when it achieves a reach/range/maneuverability architecture (see Figure 1.10) that has the following three attributes:

1. *Maximum Reach:* anyone or any processor, any time and anywhere, can access authorized I/T resources.

2. *Maximum Range:* all information objects (information, process, or services) can be shared.

3. *Maximum Maneuverability:* on top of the reach/range platform, applications are built with the attributes of modularity, scalability, adaptability, portability, openness, autonomy, flexibility, data accessibility, interoperability, information appliance connectivity, and maintainability.

We will later argue that the entire history of I/T can be understood as a continuous march, albeit with many turns and detours, to perfect reach, perfect range, and perfect maneuverability.[18]

Sun Tzu said,

A victorious strategy is not repeated, the configuration of responses to the enemy are inexhaustible. . . . Water configures its flow in accord with the terrain; the army controls its victory in accord with the enemy. Thus, *the army does not maintain any constant strategic configuration of power; water has no constant shape.* The end of an army's form is formlessness. One who is able to change and transform in accord with the enemy and wrest victory is termed genius.[19]

This is the most instructive Tzuian strategic imagery in this book. It is because the business must not "maintain any constant strategic configuration of power" that a reach, range, and maneuverable architecture is mandated. Only through reach, range, and maneuverability can the business processes achieve the requisite state of "formlessness."

Architecture is the overt I/T manifestation of "the strategic configuration of power." When I/T can dynamically alter its configuration in response to business requirements, then I/T can be used to attack everywhere and defend anywhere, so the strategic preparation of I/T will be complete. How will those whose architectures are fixed or only marginally malleable compete with your formless architecture? By virtue of the superior nimbleness of your I/T, your business will win even before the marketplace engagements occur. Reach, range, and maneuverability equal "the strategic configuration of I/T power." Architecture, as the strategic config-

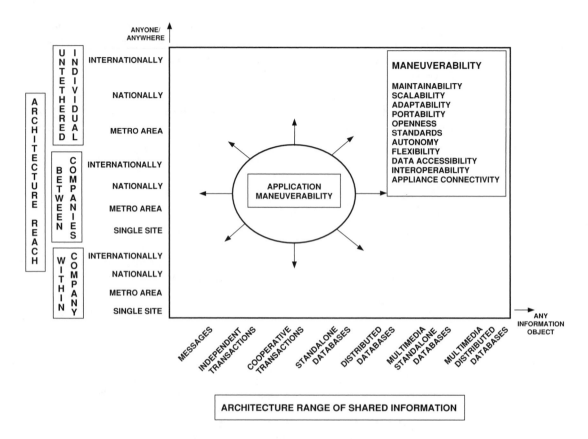

Figure 1.10   Reach, Range, and Maneuverable Architecture. I/T offers the maximum benefit to the business when it achieves perfect reach, perfect range, and perfect maneuverability. (Source: *Implementing Client/Server Computing: A Strategic Perspective,* **Bernard Boar, McGraw Hill, 1993)**

uration of I/T power, is the path to perfect business alignment and the consummate use of I/T to build sustainable competitive advantage. I cannot foresee or recommend any alternative path of equal merit.

There is a very important message in the reach, range, and maneuverability framework with regard to the continuing debate and hype over whether mainframes are dead and whether the future is client/server computing in all its flavors (distributed processing, peer-to-peer, network computing, etc.). What Figure 1.10 teaches us is that what is really important is not *an* architecture, but the ability to port applications effortlessly across architectures, as dictated by the continually changing intersection of business needs and technological possibilities. The end of I/T architecture is not an architecture, but an elastic continuum of architectures that bend and bow to business needs. The question of interest is therefore not whether mainframes are dead (why deny an application a mainframe if, for whatever reasons, it is the best solution?), or whether the future is client/server computing (after all, does architecture evolution end with client/server computing?), but whether you are developing an architectural framework that permits configuring and reconfiguring application architectures in perfect synchronization with business needs.

Understood this way, the act of posing the question of mainframe demise and client/server elevation is an admission of ignorance, because it demonstrates a tactical focus on particular architectures rather than a strategic understanding that what is important is the fluidity of architecture. The use of any single architecture is tactical; what is strategic is the ability to move across architectures as dictated by ever-changing times and circumstances.

Synthesis

Figure 1.11 shows the relationship between reach/range and maneuverability and the purposeful use of I/T. Perfect strategic alignment occurs when a reach/range/maneuverable architecture is achieved so that I/T can be used to create business opportunities. In the area below the arrow in Figure 1.11, I/T is being used at less than its maximum potential. In the area above the arrow, the designated use of I/T is not yet achievable. Perfect strategic alignment between the business and I/T, then, consists of the intersection of two notions: the business wish to use I/T to create and exploit business opportunities and the maturation of I/T to a state of maximum reach, range, and maneuverability.

Summary

Sun Tzu said, "The struggle is the struggle for advantage."[20] It therefore follows that the acme of alignment is a state where I/T can be used to create marketplace disruptions on demand; the business doesn't wait for fortuitous situations, it generates them. When I/T achieves a state of perfect strategic alignment (see Figure 1.11), the following occurs:

1. First and foremost, you satisfy your customer.
2. You place your competitor off balance; you do not wait, hoping that she stumbles, you cause her to stumble. This creates a situation ripe for exploitation.
3. You exploit the resulting state of imbalance, meeting or exceeding all customer expectations.
4. Your competitor, in a panic, reacts to your initiative. Rushed and harried, she creates responses of poor quality and incompleteness that further compound your advantage. Your competitor, inadvertently, becomes your ally against herself and pushes more customers to you through inept and defective responses.

5. You repeat the above in a series of premeditated and staggered dislocating actions. Optimally, your competitor is thrown into a state of confused punch-drunkenness as she struggles to respond to your carefully thought out dislocations and exploitations. The competitor is trapped in an endless and exhausting game of catch-up.

This is the dormant potential of information technology for the business. This scenario is not created out of nothing, it is created out of the consummate use of information technology.

It is important to recognize that in this consummate use, I/T is the chisel and the business organization is the sculptor. Just as in creating a beautiful sculpture, the chisel is only a tool of the sculptor; the business must understand the terms of how dislocations can be created and exploited, and then direct the use of I/T as the chisel to enact its marketplace insights. The logic of commanding the marketplace initiative rests with the business. I/T's value is as an opportunity-creation tool of the business.

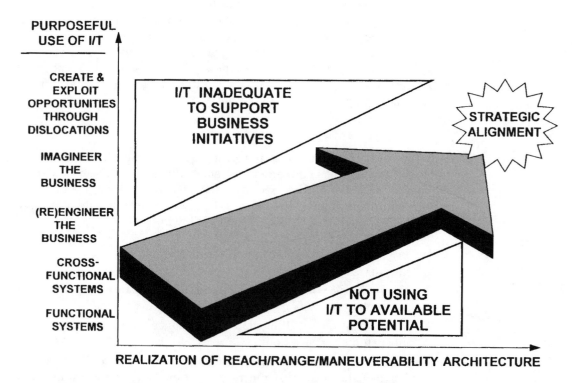

Figure 1.11   Strategic Alignment. Strategic alignment between the business and I/T occurs when I/T can be used to create and exploit business opportunities.

Sun Tzu summed up the strategic use of I/T 2,500 years ago as follows: "Overcome opponents by dispiriting them rather than by battling with them . . . overcome the opponents psychologically . . . cause them to lose spirit and direction so that even if the opposing army is intact, it is useless."[21] When you can do as Sun Tzu prescribes, you engage in a strategic seize of the marketplace.

We now understand strategic alignment as the state where one orchestrates errors for others and thrives on the resulting chaos. As Ed McCracken, CEO of Silicon Graphics, Inc., said, "the key to achieving competitive advantage isn't reacting to chaos, it's creating that chaos."[22]

Both the business and the I/T organization need to adopt marketplace styles, and these styles must be complementary. One may choose either a style of Position–Maneuver–Position (PMP) or Maneuver–Position–Maneuver (MPM). The former reflects the style of the attrition fighter, who takes a position, defends it vigorously and for an extended time, and then moves to a new position. The emphasis is on defending positions; movement is secondary. The latter reflects the style of the maneuver fighter, who moves to accrue advantage, fights from that advantage, and then quickly moves on to a new and better position before the competition counterattacks. The emphasis is on movement and temporary advantage. The era of PMP is being replaced by the era of MPM, and the I/T organization must adapt to this new reality or it will become irrelevant.

Those who deeply understand alignment comprehend that I/T–business alignment does not end with the mundane notion of a simple match or fit. Rather, as illustrated in Figure 1.11, alignment means that business processes have been elevated to the point where they can create marketplace dislocations, and I/T has been promoted to the point where it can enable those dislocations to occur. What we have in Figure 1.11 is a grand vision for I/T–business alignment. By reengineering both business processes and the enabling I/T infrastructure, we create a farsighted and pragmatic framework for action. It is this end state that we strive to achieve for information technology and the business. It is only at this end state that a position of strategic fusion is achieved between I/T and the business.

So properly conceived, we understand that alignment means that I/T permits business movement. The issues of strategy can be reduced to two simple questions of movement:

- *The Offensive Question:* Do I wish to attack, and if so, do I have the ability and how long will it take? The question of offensive marketplace action is a question of will, time, and ability.

- *The Defensive Question:* Do I wish to defend, and if so, do I have the ability and how long will it take? The question of defending your marketplace from the offensive thrusts of others is a question of will, time, and ability.

The purpose of I/T strategy, then, is to eliminate the questions of time and ability to attack or defend. I/T stands always ready, as the sword and the shield, to be used swiftly, depending on the will of the business. This is strategic alignment, and this is I/T for competitive advantage.

1.4 THE STATE OF I/T AND BUSINESS ALIGNMENT

Now that we have completed our requisite preparation in the preceding sections, we can address the question of interest: "What is the state of strategic alignment between I/T and the business as we navigate the mid-1990s?" After billions of dollars have been invested in information technology in the modern era alone (since the 1964 introduction of the IBM 360 architecture), are I/T and the business aligned or not? The answer to this question is crystal clear: The state of I/T–business alignment is poor.

The evidence to support this assertion is quite strong. Figure 1.12 summarizes the top strategic issues identified by business I/T executives. If you look at the most recent year alone, notice the following:

1. "Alignment" is the second most critical issue.
2. Building cross-functional systems and reengineering are identified as strategic issues, but the higher-rung objective of using I/T to create business opportunities through dislocations is not.
3. The strategic issues identified are fundamental issues—for example, the need to make data accessible, the need to speed application development, the need for an architecture, and the need for a strategic plan. How can the higher states of alignment be achieved if there is no architecture?

Tables 1.5 through 1.7 from other sources confirm the validity of these issues as the current points of executive strategic focus. Again, notice the glaring presence of alignment as a strategic problem in each. Could I/T with this set of issues possibly be used to create dislocations?

The situation is actually more ominous when you dissect Figure 1.12 horizontally. A horizontal analysis of Figure 1.12 betrays the following truths:

1. Every issue in the top eight in 1988 is still on the list.
2. Of the top ten 1993 issues, eight have been on the list since 1989.
3. Of the top seven issues, all have been on the list since 1989.
4. The top 1993 issue has been one of the top two since 1990.
5. Alignment, the second 1993 issue, has never been lower than fourth.

ISSUE	1993	1992	1991	1990	1989	1988
REENGINEERING	1	2	1	1	11	N/R
I/T BUSINESS ALIGNMENT	2	1	2	4	2	1
SYSTEM DEVELOPMENT	3	9	4	6	13	12
CROSS-FUNCTIONAL APPS.	4	6	3	3	7	N/R
UTILIZING DATA	4	4	5	7	6	7
COST CONTROL	6	11	11	10	14	17
I/T ARCHITECTURE	7	3	8	9	5	5
UPDATE OBSOLETE SYSTEMS	8	18	N/R	13	N/R	18
I/T STRATEGIC PLAN	9	10	6	5	4	2
CHANGE I/T PLATFORMS	10	N/R	N/R	N/R	N/R	N/R
INTEGRATE SYSTEMS	11	13	9	16	12	6
I/T HUMAN RESOURCE	12	5	13	11	8	8
DISPERSED SYSTEMS	12	15	19	N/R	16	13
CAPITALIZE ON I/T	14	19	20	N/R	17	N/R
I/T FOR COMPETITIVE ADVANTAGE	15	14	12	8	1	4
CONNECTING TO C CUSTOMERS & SUPPLIERS	16	20	15	19	N/R	N/R
LEADERSHIP SKILLS	17	7	10	N/R	N/R	N/R
EDUCATION MANAGEMENT	18	16	14	2	3	3
OPEN SYSTEMS	19	N/R	N/R	N/R	N/R	N/R
PROMOTING I/T	20	17	17	15	N/R	N/R

Figure 1.12   Top 20 I/T Issues. I/T–Business Alignment has persisted as a major strategic issue since 1989. (Source: CSC:Index.)

Table 1.5
CIO Magazine I/T Priority Items, 1992. The *CIO Magazine* priority items identify a similar range of strategic problems.

Number	CIO Priority Item
1	Align technology with business strategy
2	Implement state-of-the-art solutions
3	Provide and improve information access
4	Enhance customer service
5	Create links within the organization
6	Train and empower employees
7	Create links with external customers
8	Support business reengineering
9	Act as change agent/catalyst
10	Educate business units about I/T
11	Evaluate emerging technologies
12	Implement standard systems and architecture

Table 1.6
Network World Magazine I/T Priority Items, 1992. The *Network World* priority items identify a similar range of strategic problems.

Number	CIO Priority Item
1	Achieving interoperability among current systems
2	Moving to open computing
3	Improving communiations among departments
4	Aligning I/S and business goals
5	Implementing distributed processing
6	Reducing I/T expenditures
7	Consolidating standalone netwroks
8	Reengineering business processes
9	Centralizing procurement

Table 1.7
Datamation Key Issues. The 1994 list of key issues from *Datamation Magazine* reflect similar strategic concerns.

I/T Management Major 1994 Activities (Percent of Respondents)				
Issue	Critical	Very Important	Somewhat Important	Not Important
Use I/T to improve productivity	42	47	11	
Reengineering I/T to align with company strategy	35	38	13	13
Use I/T to improve company quality	32	54	14	
Reengineer business processes	32	38	22	8
Reduce I/T costs	17	33	36	14
Use I/T to develop competitive advantage	13	38	22	27
Create an information architecture	11	47	30	11
Keep up with emerging technologies	8	53	31	8
Selling I/T to top management	8	47	30	16

6. Two items from 1988 and 1989 that departed the list have returned.

7. The decline in importance of "I/T for Competitive Advantage" indicates the inability to deliver advantage through I/T.

8. "Open Systems" has finally made the list, yet open systems is a prerequisite or corequisite to escape the misalignment tar pit.

9. The 1993 list composes 81 percent of the issues ever listed during the six years.

10. The 1993 top ten issues have been in the top ten 77 percent of the time since 1988.

What is important here is that, for the most part, the problems are fundamental and persistent. Little, if any, strategic progress is ever made. It is almost as if the deck of problems is shuffled each year: out come the same strategic problems, but in a modified priority order. Strategic actions are of the highest consequence. Where is the progress? How could a business function like I/T with the chronic inability to solve strategic problems achieve strategic alignment?

In the interest of fairness, we must admit that the situation is actually much worst. Figure 1.13 illustrates strategic I/T issues from 1980 through 1987. Again, notice the presence of the current popular issues of strategic planning, data as a resource, software development, and alignment. If you look at Figure 1.14, it becomes obvious that almost all the top ten 1980 issues are still with us. So what we have is 13 years of essentially the same set of strategic issues unsolved. What we have is 13 years of strategic absurdity. Perhaps, as shown in Figure 1.15, in the year 2080 the key issues will be redefined as part of the American heritage and be a cause for celebration.

A Fall 1993 Fortune 1000 senior executive survey by Anderson Consulting further confirms the poor state of I/T. Of the executives polled, 81 percent ranked their organization's payback on I/T as "minimal" or "average." On a scale of one to five (five highest), Chief Executives rated I/T payback at 2.8, and Information Technology Executives rated it only .1 higher at 2.9. The consensus is that I/T, as a corporate asset, is run of the mill.

An impartial observer might conclude the following from the evidence presented:

1. Many of the problems identified as strategic by I/T executives since 1980 are fundamental issues.

2. Almost no substantive progress has been made in solving these problems since 1980.

3. I/T is, at best, a mediocre resource; it is average, and is therefore too low.

4. It is difficult to imagine I/T being used as a weapon of dislocation when its strategic house is in such persistent shambles.

It would not be unreasonable to conclude that CEO Rip Van Wrinkle could have gone to sleep in 1980 and awoken in 1994 and felt perfectly at home with the strategic I/T problems confronting the business.

An Aside

There is a growing backlash against network computing by the traditional mainframe community. It is interesting to wonder why, if host-centered computing was or is as wonderful as they would have us believe, the Figure 1.12 report card is so bad. With 30 years of presentation, processing, and data management on a central host architecture attended to by an elite group of data-processing experts, why are all the basics in such a state of strategic distress?

ISSUE	1987	1986	1984	1983	1982	1980
STRATEGIC PLANNING	1	1	1	1	1	1
COMPETITIVE ADVANTAGE	2	2	N/R	N/R	N/R	N/R
ORGANIZATIONAL LEARNING	3	3	6	6	N/R	8
IS ROLE & CONTRIBUTION	4	4	N/R	N/R	N/R	N/R
ALIGNMENT	5	5	7	7	N/R	9
END-USER COMPUTING	6	6	2	2	N/R	10
DATA AS RESOURCE	7	7	9	9	N/R	4
INFORMATION ARCHITECTURE	8	8	N/R	N/R	N/R	N/R
MEASURING IS EFFECTIVENESS	9	9	5	5	2	2
INTEGRATING DP, OA, & FA	10	10	3	3	6	N/R
SOFTWARE DEVELOPMENT			4	4	N/R	6
I/T HUMAN RESOURCE			8	8	7	7
DSS SYSTEMS			10	10	5	5
TELECOMMUNICATIONS					3	3
ROLE OF I/T MANAGER					4	N/R
EDUCATING MNGT					8	N/R
I/S CENTRALIZATION/ DECENTRALIZATION					9	N/R
EMPLOYEE JOB SAT					10	N/R

Figure 1.13   Top 10 I/T Issues. Alignment has been recognized as a major strategic problem since 1980. (Source: MIS Quarterly.)

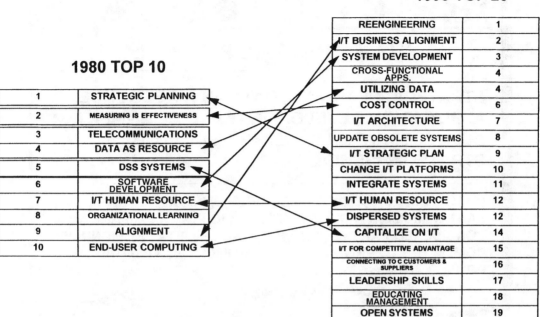

Figure 1.14   Stasis. Since 1980, there has been a remarkable constancy in the definition of the major strategic I/T issues.

Summary

The problem is not that I/T has strategic challenges—there will always be new opportunities that demand strategic change—it is that they are always the same problems. How can alignment be achieved when data is inaccessible, when development is too slow, when there is no architecture, when systems are obsolete, or when expenses are out of control? Figure 1.16 is our assessment of the current state of alignment and the gaps. It is obvious that even accomplishing reengineering will be quite a stretch for most I/T organizations.

We can explain this sorry situation in any of the following ways:

1. *Impossibility:* the problems that were identified as strategic are intractable. Due to technological constraints, conceptual constraints, engineering constraints, or human constraints, the problems are hopelessly immune to solution.

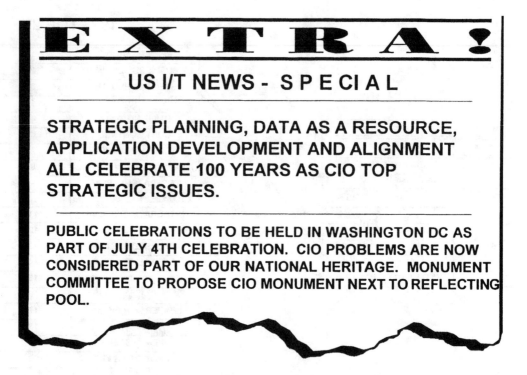

Figure 1.15   2080 I/T News Headline. Perhaps by the year 2080, when many of these strategic issues will be 100 years old, they will be redefined as cause for celebration.

2. *Tactical Focus:* I/T management has, for the most part, enjoyed a monopoly status for the last 20 years. As the keeper of the corporate information assets, they were free to do as they wished. What they wished to do was focus on tactical activities that accrued short-term benefits, rather then addressing the more critical I/T issues.

3. *Absence of Strategy:* viewing the world from essentially a technology perspective, I/T organizations equated business success to keeping the machines running and bringing in technology when and if they wanted. They really had no notion of strategic alignment, and even less notion of the commitment and change management that would be compulsory to attack these pressing strategic issues.

4. *A Curse:* one or more of the founders of computing made a pact with the devil or inadvertently disturbed a witches' Sabbath. In either case, a curse was placed on information technology so that it would forever offer improved price performance and strategic promise, but would in practice be a strategic dud.

As for me, I believe that the cause of the strategic failings is a little of each.

1.5 BOOK OVERVIEW

The remainder of this book will provide clear-cut advice to dramatically accelerate the achievement of a state of strategic alignment. What is particularly rewarding about following the I/T reengineering actions suggested herein is that they return incremental benefits. One does not have to wait for the finale to realize any profit. As one improves the reach, range, and maneuverability of the I/T architecture, each improvement permits the business to use I/T to better build advantage.

The advice given is focused; behind the architecture is a whole set of supporting positions that must also be achieved. As there is a potentially endless set of actions to choose from, we have performed a triage and selected only a few to focus on. While one can do almost anything well,

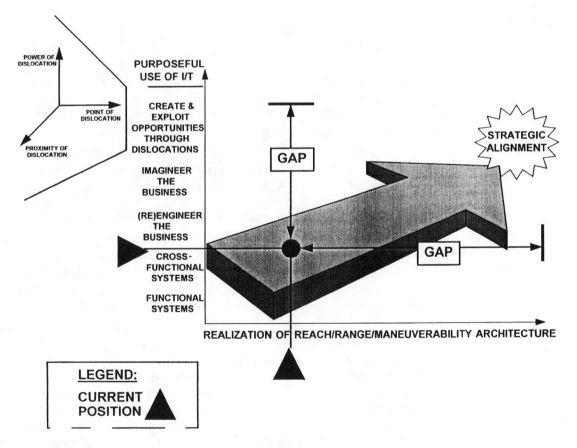

Figure 1.16   The State of I/T–Business Alignment. The state of alignment is meager.

one cannot do everything well. Focus is paramount for success. Reengineering the I/T organization is not a simple task, but it is preferable to extinction, which is the alternative.

There is an irresolvable dilemma and tension in strategy formulation between the demand for focus and the opposite but equal demand for completeness. In this book, I have fallen on the side of focus and limited discussions to the primary topics of architecture, planning, economy, application development, and management philosophy. In my other two books, *Implementing Client/Server Computing: A Strategic Perspective* and *The Art of Strategic Planning for Information Technology*, I discuss reengineering actions with regard to other important topics: core competencies, capabilities, human resource architecture, supplier relationships, organizational structure, product/service design, and customer satisfaction measurements. If one of these subjects is of more importance to your particular situation, I direct you to those sources for advice.

The structure of this book is as follows:

- *Chapter 2: The State of I/T Circa 1995*

    This chapter executes a small situational analysis. The I/T situation is reviewed from the perspectives of business demands, technology change, and competition. An approach built on using the current management approaches of Total Quality Management (TQM), business reengineering, ISO 9000, and the Balridge Award is presented.

- *Chapter 3: I/T Architecture*

    This chapter provides a thorough analysis of the importance of improving the I/T architecture. Topics covered include the rationale for an architecture, strategic repositioning to support an architecture, and a diagramming technique that allows one to unambiguously draw complicated reach, range, and maneuverable architectures.

- *Chapter 4: I/T Planning and Forecasting*

    This chapter presents a method for linking I/T forecasting and planning activities with the needs of the business. The material explains how a models-based approach can guarantee aligning new technology acquisitions with the strategic needs of the business units.

- *Chapter 5: The Economy*

    This chapter explains the importance of properly designing the business economy in which the I/T function operates. The I/T organization is engaged in two economic systems: an intereconomy system that governs transactions with the user organizations and an intra-economic system that governs internal transactions. Though often neglected, the careful design of these economic systems is crucial to creating an environment that spurs desired individual and organizational behaviors.

- *Chapter 6: Application Development*

  This chapter suggests three specific actions that must be taken to insure the timely and high-quality delivery of applications. Since what users want is applications, not database managers or telecommunication monitors or remote procedure calls or interactive debuggers, actions that expedite application delivery are crucial alignment efforts.

- *Chapter 7: Management Philosophy and Style*

  This chapter provides suggestions on management style and leadership. The reengineering changes that are being suggested can have a major impact on the I/T professional. This chapter provides a novel view of how management should oversee I/T and what associated actions are necessary to minimize change resistance and promote commitment to the new order.

- *Chapter 8: Finale*

  This chapter provides suggestions on how to support the suggested strategic moves by including in their implementation design certain key success attributes. Success enablers discussed include change management, commitment, bluffing, ownership, and learning.

These recommended actions are not only built upon sound strategic principles, but are eminently and refreshingly pragmatic. Accepting them does not require one to suspend critical judgment and engage in "journeys," "expeditions," or "quests" in search of highly desirable but elusive ideals. Instead, these recommendations provide practical and common-sense solutions to the major inhibitors of alignment.

It is most fortunate that our condition of misalignment is a consequence of misfortune and not of a malevolent fate. (Mis)fortune and fate are quite different, but often erroneously equated. *Fortune* is the unforeseen concatenation of events. *Fate* is destiny; it is the nemesis of freedom and represents a march of events, a curse, that must be fulfilled. Fate is to fortune as necessity is to contingency, as must is to may be. Misfortune, the clash of unanticipated and intersecting events, can be reversed and defeated through one's actions, but fate cannot be tricked or cheated. Even in Homer's *Iliad*, the Olympian gods could not alter the fate of the Trojans; how much less the ability of mere mortals to challenge inevitability.

In the following chapters, we will develop actions to change our state of misfortune and misalignment to a state of good fortune and perfect alignment. We will not accomplish this exchange by a twist of fate, but by carefully reasoned and purposeful strategic actions. We will accomplish this by understanding the goals of our efforts and committing to the initiatives required to reengineer us to a better tomorrow. Why succumb needlessly to an eternity of strategic failure and folly?

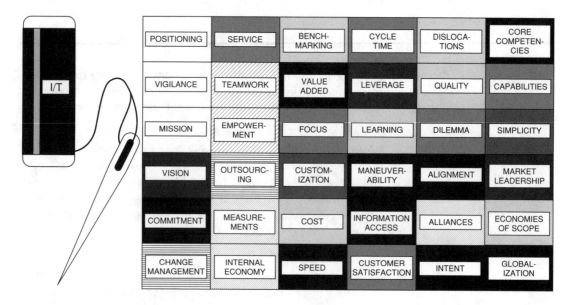

POSITIONING	SERVICE	BENCH-MARKING	CYCLE TIME	DISLOCA-TIONS	CORE COMPETEN-CIES
VIGILANCE	TEAMWORK	VALUE ADDED	LEVERAGE	QUALITY	CAPABILITIES
MISSION	EMPOWER-MENT	FOCUS	LEARNING	DILEMMA	SIMPLICITY
VISION	OUTSOURC-ING	CUSTOM-IZATION	MANEUVER-ABILITY	ALIGNMENT	MARKET LEADERSHIP
COMMITMENT	MEASURE-MENTS	COST	INFORMATION ACCESS	ALLIANCES	ECONOMIES OF SCOPE
CHANGE MANAGEMENT	INTERNAL ECONOMY	SPEED	CUSTOMER SATISFACTION	INTENT	GLOBAL-IZATION

Figure 1.17   A Patchwork of Advantage. The business needs I/T to be of sufficient power so that it can weave a patchwork of advantage.

1.6 CONCLUSION

There is really only one question that the I/T decision maker has to ask herself if she truly wishes to commence the expedition to alignment: "What is it that the business wants from me?" Does the business want cheaper and more MIPS? Does it want a LAN or routers, brouters, and bridges? Does it want the newest Intel microprocessor, or does it want object-oriented database management systems rather than relational database management systems? Do you think that the answer to the questions is rooted in technology?

What the business wants of I/T is to be able to weave a quilt of advantage. As shown in Figure 1.17, there are many different strategic themes that the business can select from to build a patchwork of advantage. What the business asks of I/T is that it should be robust and responsive so that it can convert a chosen set of themes into executable advantage. What it requires is that I/T never be a hindrance to strategic moves by the business, but that it provide the necessary information reach, information range, and information maneuverability so that the business can sow new advantages, sustain existing advantages, and contract the advantages of others. This is what the business asks of the I/T organization, and this is why a state of alignment is mandated.

Alignment is not just another strategic theme. Alignment is the fundamental strategic theme. While all the themes shown in Figure 1.17 offer

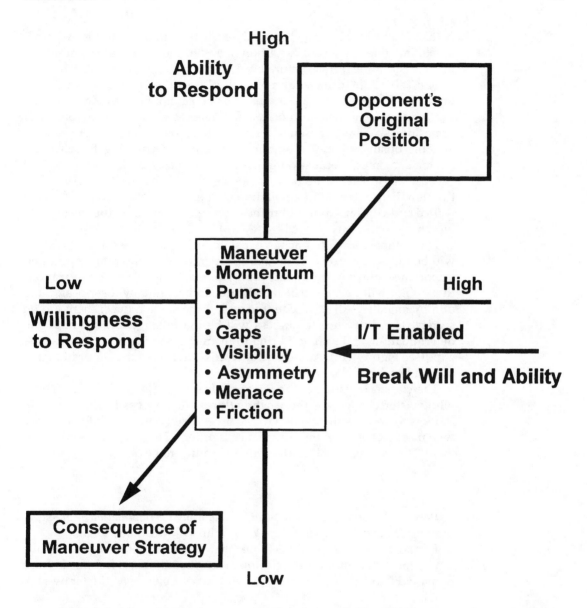

Figure 1.18   I/T as the Strategic Configuration of Business Power. I/T achieves perfect alignment when it can be used as the backbone of a maneuver strategy to move opponents from being able and willing to fight to being unable and unwilling to fight.

paths to success, the most elemental necessity is alignment. It is meaning-less to imagine successful execution of any of them if a state of misalign-ment exists at the infrastructure level.

Sun Tzu said, "In ancient times, skillful warriors first made themselves invincible."[23] When you are invincible, you cannot be threatened, so you can wait and choose the moment for dislocating and destroying your opposition. We have chosen to focus this book on alignment between I/T and the business because alignment is the underpinning for all other strategic themes, because alignment is the basis of invincibility, and because alignment is the basis for being able to win in the marketplace through dislocation and exploitation. Alignment means using I/T as the source and configuration of business power that permits the business to win through maneuver (see Figure 1.18).

I/T organizations that achieve a state of alignment with the business will be richly rewarded. They will prosper, grow in internal respect and importance, and not be threatened by outsourcing. Those organizations that do not will decline to a state of ruin and eventually disappear, relics of a bygone era. All have equal access to the same advice; there are no secrets. The difference to success will be the intelligence, commitment, determination, and zeal you bring to the reengineering effort to close the gaps (see Figure 1.16). Advice is but words; advice requires your imagina-tion and energy to become animated.

The classic Taoist text, *The Book of Balance and Harmony*, says, "Those who master change are those who address themselves to the times. To those who address themselves to the times, even danger is safe; for those who master change, even disturbance is order." The times demand align-ment. Do not tarry or be slothful; there is much to be done.

NOTES

1. Bernard H. Boar, *The Art of Strategic Planning for Information Technology: Crafting Strategy for the 90s* (New York: John Wiley & Sons, 1993).
2. For an example of another book that provides detailed prescriptive advice on why and how to implement client/server computing, see Bernard H. Boar, *Implementing Client/Server Computing* (McGraw-Hill, 1993).
3. See *The Art of Strategic Planning for Information Technology: Crafting Strat-egy for the 90s* for a complete strategic planning method designed explicitly for the I/T organization.
4. Machiavelli, *The Prince*.
5. The design school of strategy is often equated to the Harvard Business School. A good example of the design school themes can be found in M. Porter and C. Montgomery, eds., *Strategy* (Harvard Business Review, 1991).

6. Sun Tzu, Machiavelli, and B. H. Liddell-Hart are all precursors of the design school.

7. Sun Tzu, *The Art of War.*

8. The emergent school of strategy is best reflected in the writings of Dr. Henry Mintzberg. See his *The Rise and Fall of Strategic Planning* (The Free Press, 1993). Dr. Mintzberg, in a thorough analysis, identifies eleven schools of strategy: design, planning, positioning, cognitive, entrepreneurial, learning, emergent, political, cultural, environmental, and configurational.

9. See L. Perry, R. Scott, and W. Smallwood, *Real-Time Strategy* (John Wiley & Sons, 1993).

10. The ready-fire-aim school of strategy was formulated in *In Search of Excellence* by Tom Peters. In his later books, Peters acknowledged the failings of his *In Search of Excellence* strategy prescriptions.

11. Two books on the chaos school of strategy are R. Stacey, *The Chaos Frontier* (Butterworth-Heinemann, 1991) and H. R. Priesmeyer, *Organizations and Chaos* (Quorum Books, 1992).

12. Sun Tzu, *The Art of War.* Mao Tse-Tung summarized his Tzuian maneuver-based military tactics with the following slogan:

> When the enemy advances, we retreat!
> When the enemy halts, we harass!
> When the enemy seeks to avoid battle, we attack!
> When the enemy retreats, we pursue!

For an excellent book that explains the emergence of maneuver warfare as the dominant model of business conflict and competition, see Richard A. D'Aveni, *Hyper-competition* (The Free Press, 1994).

13. Sun Tzu, *The Art of War.*

14. Sun Tzu, *The Art of War.*

15. This view of alignment is based on military strategy, as presented in B. H. Liddell-Hart, *Strategy* (Meridian, 1991).

16. Francis Bacon, *The Essays* (Penguin Classics, 1985). Italics added.

17. Sun Tzu, *The Art of War.*

18. The notions of reach and range were introduced by P. Keen in *Shaping the Future* (Harvard Business School Press, 1991).

19. Sun Tzu, *The Art of War.* Italics added in this and subsequent references.

20. Sun Tzu, *The Art of War.*

21. Sun Tzu, *The Art of War.*

22. Ed McCracken, CEO Silicon Graphics, Inc., in *Harvard Business Review,* Nov.–Dec. 1993.

23. Sun Tzu, *The Art of War.*

2

The State of I/T Circa 1995

The purpose of this chapter is to provide a generic situational analysis of the pressures confronting the typical information technology organization. Strategy teaches the importance of assessment as the antecedent to action; one moves from where one is to where one wants to be. Without assessment, one proceeds without forethought, an assured prescription for strategic failure and folly.

The situational analysis is presented as follows:

- *2.1. Situational Analysis: The Business*
  This section analyzes the pressures that are affecting the business. It is the accumulation and culmination of these pressures that force the business to demand greater value from its I/T assets. The business must insist on being able to use I/T for competitive advantage, because few strategic business initiatives can be executed without capable I/T participation.

- *2.2. Situational Analysis: Technology*
  This section analyzes the technology changes that are affecting the I/T organization. It is argued that the I/T organization must shepherd itself through a change of technology eras. Failure to adapt to the new technological times and circumstances will result in an I/T organization whose products, services, competencies, and capabilities are increasingly irrelevant to the business.

- *2.3. Situational Analysis: Competition*
  This section analyzes the competitive changes that are affecting the I/T organization. For the first 30 years of commercial data processing, the internal I/T organizations enjoyed a virtual monopoly over all I/T resources. This monopoly is being eroded by competent and ambitious outsourcers, reengineers, facility managers, consultants, and systems integrators. Unless internal I/T organizations respond creatively to this competitive threat, they will discover that more and more of their once sacred and inviolate internal marketplace is being turned over to external I/T suppliers.

- *2.4. Four Great Miracles*
  This section discusses the critical importance of strategic indirection as a response to the aforementioned challenges. Specifically, it is argued that four popular management initiatives—Total Quality Management (TQM), International Standards Organization 9000 (ISO 9000), business reengineering, and the Baldrige Award—alone and together provide an almost miraculous context for responding to the situational analysis. We refer to the four of them as "miracles" because what would never have been initiated, let alone accomplished in business as usual, can be done under the "TQM/ISO 9000/business reeingineering/Baldrige" banner.

- *2.5. Conclusion*
  This section provides summary thoughts on the I/T situation in the mid-1990s.

All of the situational analyses are designed to be both concise and conclusive. The analytical dimensions of the business, technology, and competition are certainly not the only strategic dimensions that could be chosen for analysis. They are, however, three of the most critical ones, and they provide a strong sense of the problems confronting the archetype I/T organization. If you perform your own situational analysis, and you certainly should, you must be more complete and include other areas such as core competencies, supplier relationships, value chain analysis, and critical success factors.

2.1 SITUATIONAL ANALYSIS: THE BUSINESS

The archetype business in the mid-1990s will be under acute multidimensional stress. Since strategic responses reflect current and anticipated pressure points, it is reasonable to assume that the following macro forces will have significant impact in forming business demands on the I/T organization throughout this decade:

- Sluggish economy—an economic environment without sustained growth.
- Global competition—highly competitive and global markets.
- Health care crisis—the need to balance employee need for adequate health care against both soaring costs and regulations.
- Regulatory agencies—increased constraints and meddling by federal, state, and local government agencies.
- Environmental protection—increased attention to the impact of business decisions on the environment.

- Work force educational level and skills—the dilemma of a work environment that requires more educated employees with high-technology skills while a large part of the work force is barely functionally literate.

- Changing work force demographics—major shifts in work force composition in terms of age, gender, and ethnic diversity.

- Productivity growth—the need to make dramatic improvements in white-collar as well as blue-collar productivity.

- Product cycle time—the need to accelerate the evolution of existing products and create new products in synchronization with a transient market.

- Institutional influence—the growing influence of large institutional owners (pension funds and mutual funds) on corporate decisions.

- Quality—the "ante" to compete.

- Management style—transition to more participative and teamwork-oriented work environments.

- Marketplace volatility—the need to meet the requirements of customers who have increasingly fragmented needs and want customized products and services.

- Corporate volatility—the rise in the number of mergers, takeovers, divestitures, and alliances.

- Litigation—the increased tendency of society to solve its disputes through aggressive and expensive use of the legal system.

- Social responsibility—dealing with workplace problems relating to drugs, crime, and changes in the family.

- Cost pressures—relentless pressure to offer the highest-quality product at the absolute minimum cost.

Regardless of which problems are presented as the chief complaints, it is evident that the business will have no alternative but to insist on dramatic improvements from all functional organizations, and this will include continually escalated demands on the I/T organization. Business pressures will be the impetus for reengineering the I/T organization.

If you look back at the list of strategic vectors from which a business may build advantage (see Figure 1.17), it is evident that all can be served by extensive use of information technology. As itemized in Table 2.1, most strategic frameworks are also dependent on the novel use of I/T for successful implementation. Since the collection, preparation, presentation, and analysis of information are fundamental to all business processes and decision making, successfully overcoming the challenges of the mid-1990s cannot be done without information technology as a key business enabler.

What option is available other than using I/T to build and sustain advantage?

We therefore conclude that while all eras offer hurdles, the mid-1990s is the era of the high jump. The business will demand productivity and effectiveness from I/T, because it needs the maximum impact possible from information advantage on the business. If the internal organization does not deliver the information services required in a timely and efficient manner, and if it does not meet or exceed its customer's expectations, the business will look elsewhere. The ultimate voice that cannot be either silenced or ignored is the dissent or acclaim of the marketplace. Your customers' demands change. The logic of business demands on the I/T organization is thus as follows:

1. The business is engaged in a life-and-death struggle for advantage. In this era of exceptional business stress, the building and sustaining of advantage is inconceivably arduous.

2. The business insists that I/T contribute to the creation of advantage.

3. I/T must be able to be used to create superior customer satisfaction, enable the rapid creation and revision of business processes, create marketplace surprises, shift the rules of competition, and enable unprecedented business movement.

In this way, customers can be uncommonly satisfied and competitors can be induced to invest their time, energy, and resources elsewhere.

2.2 SITUATIONAL ANALYSIS: TECHNOLOGY

Many programmers started their careers coincident with the announcement of the IBM 360 architecture and have spent their entire careers evolving one skill set. For 30 years, these programmers learned and applied COBOL, JCL, TSO, IMS DB/DC, IEH utilities, IEB utilities, CICS, SORT, and the Linkage Editor. This period of a single set of technologies offered by one dominant vendor and incrementally evolved over decades is over.

The information technology field has gone from being a still-life painting to being a splatter painting. During this evolution, many I/T organizations found themselves being devalued as their skills atrophied and, in a last-ditch Alamo defense, positioned themselves as the staunch defenders of what was, rather than as the leaders of what will be. The dullness of the I/T organizations in adopting and applying new, emerging, and advantageous technologies has proven to be the primary reason for the

Table 2.1
Strategic Planning Frameworks. Many of the popular strategic planning frameworks require the rich use of I/T, either in doing the analysis or in implementing the conclusions.

Strategic Planning Framework	Framework Definition	How I/T Is Critical
Core Competencies	Build advantage through the leveraging of competencies into multiple products for multiple markets	1. Enable collaboration 2. Maximize reuse 3. Maximize speed of diffusion
Capabilities	Build advantage by optimizing the key business processes that deliver value to the customer	1. Minimize process cost 2. Enable process customization 3. Enable information sharing 4. Interlock with trading partners
Five Forces	Find a defensible position within the five forces of competition	1. Add information value to products 2. Raise barriers to market entry 3. Increase product differentiation
Critical Success Factors	Identify what the business must do well in order to succeed	1. Collect and analyze data to understand critical success factors 2. Support critical success factor implementation
Value Chain	Optimize the steps involved in moving a product from your suppliers to your customers	1. Increase speed 2. Reduce costs 3. Improve collaboration between steps
Kano Methodology	Identify customer satisfiers that will excite customers and deliver those satisfiers to customers	1. Enable market data analysis 2. Maximize speed of delivery 3. Enable customization
Business Reengineering	Radically alter business processes to improve price/performance, speed, or service	1. Maximize speed 2. Reduce costs 3. Add value through information

internal business user's dissatisfaction with the I/T organization and the concomitant emergence of I/T competition.

The I/T technology shifts that are causing this disruption can be explained by a four-level framework, as illustrated in Figure 2.1. The four levels are as follows:

1. *Level 1: Fundamental Technologies:* architecture evolution, price/performance, and miniaturization changes in base technologies (processors, memory, communication, etc.) provides an enabling infrastructure for radically new and exciting application technologies.
2. *Level 2: Enabling Technologies:* enabled by the fundamental technology shifts, a whole smorgasbord of feature- and functionality-rich

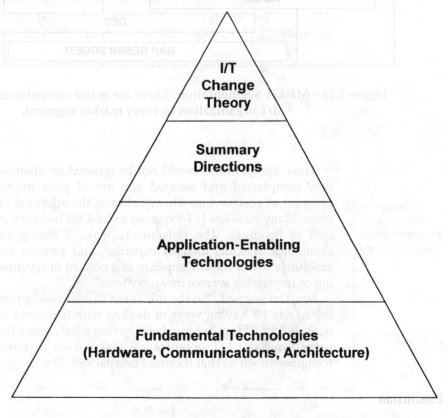

Figure 2.1   Technology Change. The unprecedented changes that are sweeping the I/T field can be understood through a four-level explanatory framework.

technologies has emerged that permit the business to reengineer itself in novel ways and accrue cost savings, robust capability, and/or maneuverability for maximum freedom of action.

3. *Level 3: Summary Directions:* all of the changes in I/T can be summarized by a small set of key direction vectors.

4. *Level 4: I/T Change Theory:* the evolution of I/T technology can be understood by a single theory, which asserts the inevitable thrust of I/T change as the continuing quest to achieve perfect reach, perfect range, and perfect maneuverability.

This four-level framework will now be explained in detail.

Level 1: Fundamental Technologies

Information technology has undergone continual evolution. The evolution of I/T can be understood as a series of overlapping waves. As shown in Figure 2.2, each wave has distinct characteristics:

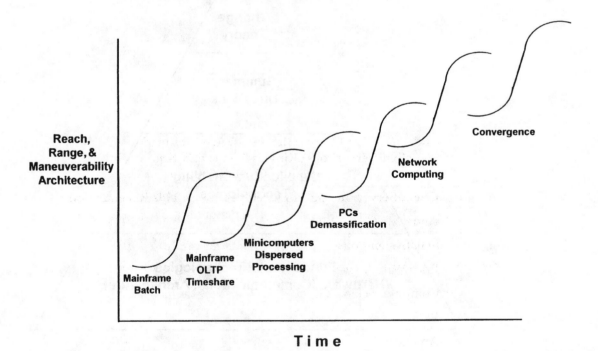

Figure 2.2   Computing Waves. The I/T industry continues to move among well-defined but overlapping computing waves with distinct characteristics.

- Different vendors have dominated the market during different cycles. IBM and the BUNCH (Burroughs, Univac, NCR, Cray, and Honeywell) led the initial two waves. Digital, Wang, Data General, and HP led the minicomputer wave. Compaq, Apple, Sun, Intel, Microsoft, and Novell have prevailed during the PC era. The network computing era will be dominated by those vendors offering superior interoperability, middleware, operational management, and shareability of data and network services.

- Each wave has had distinct characteristics. Table 2.2 summarizes some of the attributes that differentiate each period.

- The industry supplier structure has been radically transformed. In the early waves, as shown in Figure 2.3, the host vendor defined a proprietary environment; with the advent of network computing, different vendors provide each layer of the computing environment, based on who furnishes the maximum layer value.

- The convergent wave is just emerging. It is characterized by the convergence of the formerly discrete markets of information vendors, audio/video entertainment, publishing, computing, consumer electronics, interactive entertainment and education, office equipment, cable services, telecommunications, and personal communications into one contiguous and overlaid marketplace. Some examples of this convergence are as follows:

  - Bell South purchased 22.5 percent of Prime Management (cable system operator).

Table 2.2
Wave Attributes. Each computing wave has had differentiating attributes.

Wave	Input Medium	User Interface	Output Medium	Data Management	Programming Language	Storage Medium	Dominant I/T Asset
Batch	Punch Card	Paper	Paper	Record Files	Assembler, Cobol	Tape	Hardware
On-Line	CRT	Keyboard	CRT, Paper	Hierarchical DBMS	Cobol, PL/1	Disk	Data
Minis	Character Terminal	Keyboard	Terminal, Paper	RDBMS	Fortran, C	Disk	Data
PCs	Bit-Mapped Terminal	Mouse	Bit-Mapped Terminal	RDBMS File Managers	4GL, C++	Diskette	Software
Network Computing	Bit-Mapped Terminal, Multimedia	Mouse, Voice, Scanners	Bit-Mapped Terminal	DRBMS OODBMS	OO Programming Languages	RAID	Network Architecture

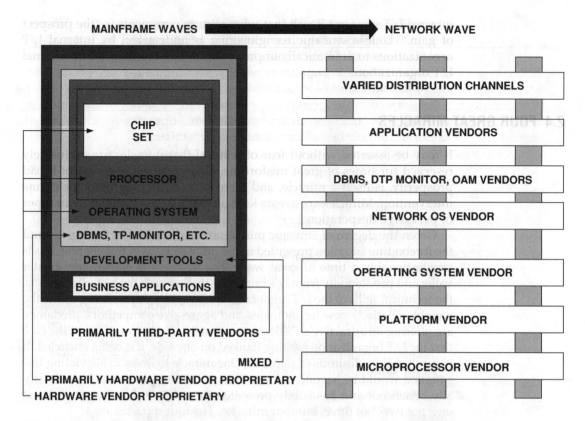

Figure 2.3 Computing Environment. With the evolution of I/T from host-centered computing to network computing, the supplier structure has been transformed from proprietary layers to best value and open layers.

- US West owns 25 percent of Time Warner (cable, media, and entertainment business).
- Sony owns CBS Records and Columbia Pictures.
- AT&T bought 20 percent of Sierra On-Line (interactive services).
- Oracle and US West plan to offer an Interactive Multimedia Information Server. Oracle will also provide multimedia server technology to Bell Atlantic.
- Matsushita owns MCA, Inc.
- Southwestern Bell bought Hauser Communications, a cable operator.
- NYNEX bought 12 percent of Viacom.

- AT&T and Paramount Communications will jointly provide interactive television programming (ITV).

In synchronization with the new opportunities provided by each wave, I/T architecture has also constantly evolved. As shown in Figure 2.4, the underlying architecture building blocks have undergone constant revision. Many I/T organizations have, unfortunately, frozen themselves in a technological rut with the technologies toward the front of the chains. They maintain unwavering dedication to practices that made them great in the past.

All of this change has been fueled by the incredible price/performance improvement of the basic computing technologies—that is, processors, memory, communications bandwidth, and so on. Table 2.3 summarizes some of the price/performance trends. Figure 2.5 illustrates the price/performance evolution of memory and processing chips.

Applications can only be as robust as the physical power of the underlying technologies permits. As we have seen, the basic technologies have gone through a continuous transformation over the years. This transformation has allowed for the building of more enticing application-enabling technologies that consume and exploit the power of the foundation technologies.

Level 2: Enabling Technologies

Application programmers primarily write code that handles four functions:

1. *Data manipulation:* the code to add, modify, retrieve, and delete records and the associated integrity checking and error recovery logic.
2. *Process logic:* the code that encapsulates and executes the business rules.
3. *Presentation logic:* the code that controls the interface to the input/output media and associated validation logic.
4. *Control logic:* the code that guides and routes a transaction through the application code.

The robustness of an application is not a function of this underlying application code, but of the enabling technologies that are made available to the application developer to exploit. Historically, there was a very limited and basic set of enabling technologies—for example, database manager, transaction manager, report writer, and query languages. This situation has changed radically.

Enabling technologies, which bring with them advantages, sit in an incestuous relationship with the fundamental technologies. The funda-

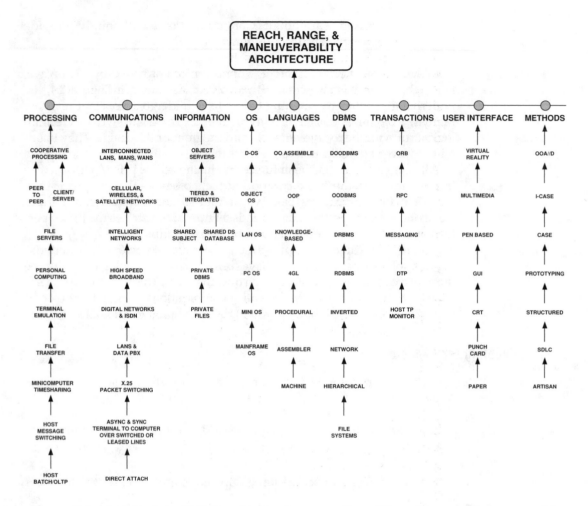

Figure 2.4   Architecture Building Blocks. In sympathy with each computing wave, different building blocks have emerged as the constructs of I/T architecture.

mental technologies permit the development of standardized and attractive enabling technologies, while the desirability of newer and richer enabling technologies pushes the research and development of the fundamental technologies. As shown in Table 2.4, there now exists a cornucopia of vibrant enabling technologies for the application developer to build upon. Through interfaces, the application can invoke these various technologies and, in consequence, accrue the advantages of increased price/performance, increased maneuverability, and/or increased feature/functionality.

Table 2.3
Price/Performance Trends. I/T technologies demonstrate consistent and incredible price/performance trends.

Technology	From	To	Trend
Microprocessor Transistor Density/Chip	1978	1996	from 29,000 to 3 Million
Microprocessor Transistor Density/Chip	1978	2001	from 29,000 to 100 Million
Microprocessor MIPS	1978	2001	from .5 MIPS to 800 MIPS
Microprocessor Clock Speeds	1978	2001	from 10 MHz to 250 MHz
PC/Mainframe Price Performance	1978	2001	700:1
DAT Storage	1989	1997	12 Times Increase Per Unit
DRAM Density	1970	2000	from 1 Thousand Bits/DRAM to 4096 Mbits/DRAM
$/MB DRAM	1970	2000	from $500 MB to 5 MB
PC Disk Form Factor	1991	1998	from 2.5" to .5"
MB/PC Disk Platter	1991	1995	12 Times Increase
Video Compression	1978	1993	Bandwidth Requirement to Carry Video Conference Signal Reduced from 6 Mbps to 80 Kbps

The I/T organization is thus caught in a squeeze. On one hand, it must maintain and extend its legacy systems and the associated technology. On the other hand, it must reeducate itself and retool itself to take advantage of all these new and more attractive technologies. It must do this while controlling costs, improving existing service, and dealing with the resistance to change exhibited by a technical staff that intimately associates its well-being with a decaying skill set. When one compounds this situation by the business pressures we have discussed and the threat of competition, it is obvious that the gifts offered by the enabling technologies have caught many I/T organizations unprepared. They are viewed, at best, as a mixed blessing that has created a threatening situation, rather than a rare opportunity for organizational renewal.

Level 3: Summary Directions

Rather than dealing with the details of microprocessor change, object-oriented programming, or architectural waves at a conceptual level, we can summarize the broad sweep of I/T movement by 16 key ideas, as follows:

Table 2.4
Application Enabling Technologies. The availability of newer and richer enabling technologies permits advantage to be infused into business applications.

Enabling Technology	Primary Competitive Business Advantage			Growth Factor		
	Maneuverability	Price/ Performance	Feature/ Functionality	From	To	Factor
Multimedia			X	1991	1996	20
Imaging			X	1991	1996	3
Optical Disk		X		1991	1994	1.5
E-Mail	X			1991	1995	5
Groupware	X			1991	1995	60
Workflow Software		X		1991	1996	1000
Video Conferencing		X		1991	2000	12
Pen-Based Computing			X	1991	1998	30
Wireless Communications	X			1991	1996	14
Voice Technologies		X		1991	1996	4
Electronic Commerce		X		1989	1995	7.5
AI			X	1989	1996	4.25
Object-Oriented Technologies	X			1991	1996	4
Massive Parallelism		X		1990	1994	4

I/T Directions	**From→To**
1. Diminution	Mainframe→Mini→PC
2. Digitalization	Analog→Digital
3. Mobility	Fixed Place Computing→Untethered Computing
4. Globalization	Local→Area→National→Global Computing
5. Electronic Commerce	Paper→Electronic Transactions
6. Customization	One Size Fits All→Cut & Paste
7. Engineering	Artisan Development→Software Engineering
8. Network Computing	Host-Centered Computing→Network Computing
9. Collaboration	Isolated Functional Systems→Inter/Intra Enterprise Systems

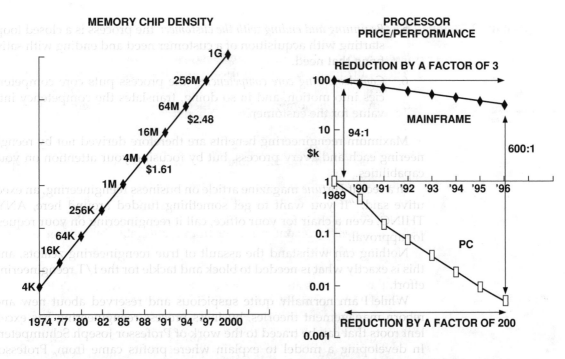

Figure 2.5   Microprocessor and Memory Price/Performance Trends. From 1985 to 1992, memory chips have improved price/performance by a factor of 8, while microprocessor price/performance has improved by a factor of 200.

10.	Broadband	Voice Data Communication Speeds→Giga-byte/Sec. Speeds
11.	Multimedia	Text Only→Information in All Its Forms (Voice, Animation, Graphics, Text, Images)
12.	Parallelism	Sequential Processing→Massive Parallelism
13.	Architecture	Kluge of Technology→Reach, Range, & Maneuverability Architecture
14.	Instantization	Slow Batch→Real-Time Data Access
15.	Price/Performance	Expensive Unit Costs→Incredibly Inexpensive Unit Costs
16.	Standards	Closed→Open

These notions capture the essence of the waves of transformation and innovation sweeping the I/T industry.

Level 4: I/T Change Theory

A *theory* is a systematically related set of statements, including some law-like generalizations, that is empirically testable. The purpose of a theory is to increase understanding through a structure capable of both explaining and predicting phenomena. A good theory has the following attributes:

1. It accounts for all relevant phenomena.
2. It has minimum conditions and constraints on its domain of explanation.
3. It has the absolute minimum number of postulates (Ockham's Razor).
4. It is falsifiable; one can infer from it a testable hypothesis that can prove it false.
5. It exhibits consilence. Consilence is the demonstrable property of a theory that is able, without amendment, to explain additional but related phenomena over time.

A theory, then, is concerned with concisely but precisely explaining a large set of events and facts. F. A. Hayek, the famous economist and philosopher, said, "Without a theory, the facts are silent." Theories bring order and meaning out of disorder and chaos.

We propose the following theory to explain the movement of the I/T industry (see Figure 2.6):

The I/T industry, as though pushed by an invisible hand and pulled by a powerful magnet, is constantly evolving in order to achieve a more perfect state of reach, range, and maneuverability. This manifest destiny of perfect reach, perfect range, and perfect maneuverability—joined with the traditional strategic vectors of speed, cost, value added, focus, leverage, surprise, simplicity, adaptability, and alignment—explains industry movement and change.

The gyrations, zigs, zags, dips, spirals, and other apparently chaotic motion of the I/T industry are, in truth, simply the competitive struggle to meet its fate while simultaneously conveying advantage to its players. New product announcements, entertainment industry and computer industry alliances, the rise of standards, the decline of IBM, the purchase of McCaw by AT&T, the immense promise of object-oriented technologies, the desirability of distributed database management, the industry preoccupation with middleware, the need for broadband communications, the rise of cellular communications, personal digital assistants (PDAs), and the decline of dumb terminals are all not independent asynchronous events: they are all explainable under this theory.

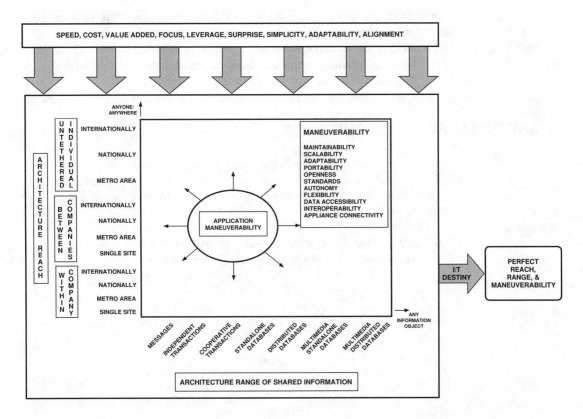

Figure 2.6   I/T Evolution Theory. The movement of the I/T industry is understandable as the quest to achieve perfect reach, perfect range, and perfect maneuverability, and concurrently to realize traditional strategic attributes.

You can test the consilence of this theory on a daily basis when you read the industry press, listen to vendor product pitches, or attend industry seminars.[1] You will find that most significant events are in harmony with this theory, or are attempts to block its inevitability because of proprietary interests. The irresistible march to perfect reach, perfect range, and perfect maneuverability may be delayed, but it will not be stopped, because it is required to achieve perfect strategic alignment (see Figure 1.11). I/T users will inescapably choose those vendors and solutions that permit them to achieve the most purposeful use of I/T.

Conclusion

The pace of change of the I/T industry is quickening. At whatever level of granularity you choose to comprehend the change, the conclusion is obvious: the I/T executive in the mid-1990s is confronted with a massive new set of technologies that must be integrated into her technology portfolio, and she must maintain or enhance the large embedded base of legacy systems while satisfying ever more demanding customers and fending off hungry and ambitious competitors. It is an epoch of action.

2.3 SITUATIONAL ANALYSIS: COMPETITION

For most of the first three decades of commercial data processing, the I/T organization flourished under an almost exclusive control of I/T resources. The following all conspired to create a most prosperous I/T monopoly:

- A dominant vendor, IBM, whose market position was solidified and enhanced by a strong centralized I/T function.

- A removed data center that housed and tended to the needs of very expensive mainframes.

- The growth of a technology elite, systems programmers and application developers, who solely understood the mysteries of computing.

Like any respectable monopolist, the I/T organization delivered I/T services when it wanted, how it wanted, and if it wanted. This era is in hopeless decay.

Sun Tzu said, "What attracts opponents of their own accord is the prospect of gain."[2] Driven by pressing business necessity and dissatisfied with the conservatism and technology-centric perspectives of the internal I/T organization, I/T outsourcing, in all its varieties, is flourishing. The internal I/T hegemony is rotting. This is demonstrated by the following:

1. Table 2.5 illustrates outsourcing contracts valued at greater than $.5 billion.

2. Figure 2.7 predicts that the U.S. professional services market and systems integration markets will grow at a compounded annual growth rate of 37 percent.

3. Figure 2.8 predicts that the U.S. systems integration and outsourcing markets will grow to $104.4 billion by 1999.

4. Figure 2.9 predicts the annual growth rates for the U.S. systems integration and outsourcing markets.

5. Figure 2.10 illustrates the historical growth of the worldwide I/T consulting market.

Table 2.5
Outsourcing Contracts. Outsourcing contracts greater than $500M
are not uncommon.

Client	Value	Vendor
Northern Telecom	$4B	CSC
General Dynamics	$3B	CSC
Xerox	$3B	EDS
McDonnel Douglas	$3B	ISSC
Continental Airlines	$2.1B	EDS
Lufthansa German Airlines	$2B	EDS
Australian Mutual Provident Society	$1.5B	CSC
Inland Revenue	£1.48B	EDS
British Aerospace	£1.32B	CSC
Kooperativa Forbundet	$1B	EDS
Mass. BC/BS	$800M	EDS
US Travel	$800M	EDS
Canadian Post Office	$750M	SHL-Systemhouse
Enron Corp.	$750M	EDS
Continental Bank	$700M	EDS
First City Bancorp	$600M	ISSC
Eastman Kodak	$500M	ISSC
Video Lottery Technologies	$500M	EDS
Amtrak	$500M	ISSC
National Car Rental	$500M	EDS
Bethlehem Steel Corporation	$500M	EDS

6. Figure 2.11 illustrates the positioning for growth by Arthur Anderson Consulting (AAC) and IBM Consulting. Table 2.6 shows how AAC has positioned itself as the leading client/server consultant and integrator. Figure 2.12 illustrates the consequences of these actions on AAC revenues.

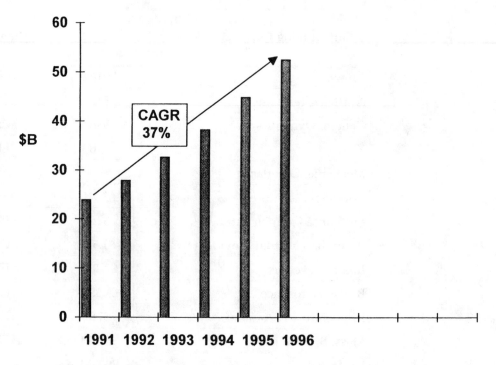

**Figure 2.7   U.S. Professional Services and Systems Integration Markets.
The four functions of development, consulting, implementation, and operations will demonstrate a combined compounded annual growth of 37
percent. (Source: Dataquest.)**

7.   Figure 2.13 shows the market segmentation interests of the major
players.

The composite business strategy of these competitors is as follows:

- Offer a seamless suite of services.
- Offer a complete end-to-end set of services.
- Offer global capabilities for global clients.
- Maintain double-digit revenue growth.
- Be perceived as a leader through "thoughtware" and I/T blueprints.
- Increase market penetration through aggressive reference marketing, demonstration centers, and high industry visibility, and sell at
the highest levels of the client business.

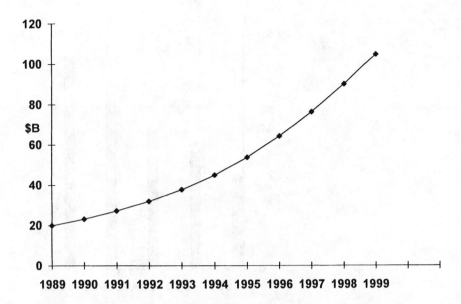

Figure 2.8   U.S. Systems Integration and Outsourcing Markets. This market is predicted to grow over ten years from a $19.9B market to a $104.4B market. (Source: Frost & Sullivan.)

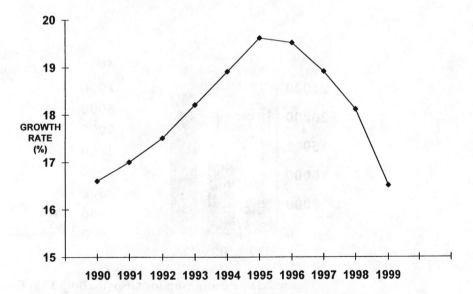

Figure 2.9   U.S. Systems Integration and Outsourcing Markets Growth Rates. The minimum growth rates for these markets is predicted to be 16.5 percent. (Source: Frost & Sullivan.)

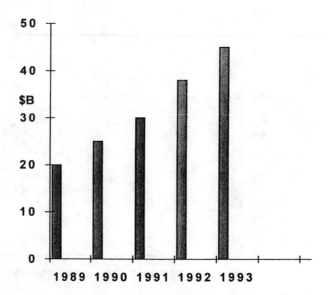

Figure 2.10   Worldwide MIS Consultant Expenditures. I/T consulting expenditures have demonstrated consistent growth. (Source: G2 Research.)

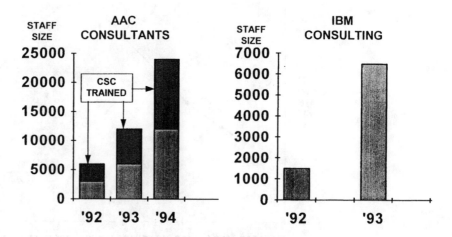

Figure 2.11   Positioning for Growth. Both IBM Consulting and AAC are positioning themselves for tremendous growth. (Source: Newspaper Reports.)

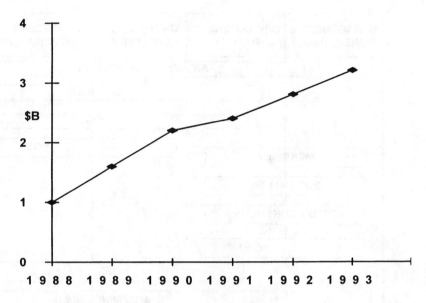

Figure 2.12   AAC Revenue Growth. AAC is thriving.

Table 2.6
Anderson Client/Server Revenues. AAC has made as much from
client/server consulting as the next six firms combined.
(Source: Gartner Group.)

Client/Server Integrator/Developer	1992 Revenue ($M)
Anderson Consulting	$435
SHL Systemhouse	$119
Price Waterhouse	$85
Computer Sciences Corp.	$80
EDS	$70
American Management Systems	$50
Technology Solutions Co.	$45

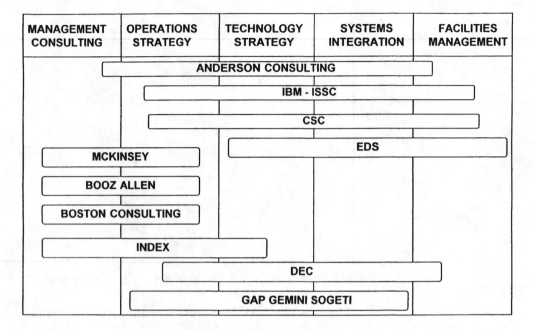

Figure 2.13   Market Segmentation. There are major competitors to the internal I/T organization in every market segment.

These competitors should not be ignored or dismissed, regardless of how complacent and assured you are of your internal position. The prospect of cost savings always attracts the attention of senior management. Many business I/T expenses exceed the industry average of 2.5 percent of revenues. The outsourcers make a strong case that through economies of scale, focused expertise, and process leverage, they will absolutely lower the I/T expense as a percent of revenue while maintaining or improving service measurements.

Sun Tzu warned, "So the rule is not to count on opponents not coming, but to rely on having ways of dealing with them; not to count on opponents not attacking, but to rely on having what cannot be attacked."[3] They have come; the I/T organization that wishes to remain vibrant must reengineer itself so that it cannot be attacked.

Conclusion

The conclusion from this evidence is obvious even to those suffering from the most heightened levels of denial. A large and capable outsourcing industry has emerged to close the gap between business user needs and internal I/T services. Recall that what attracts opponents is "the prospect of gain." Unless strategic reengineering is undertaken by internal I/T organizations to dramatically improve alignment, there will be no internal I/T organization.

2.4 FOUR GREAT MIRACLES

It may be asserted without fear of rebuttal that miracles are exclusively reserved for times of great misfortune. Good fortune, a period of broad prosperity, is itself a miracle, and there is no additional need for divine intervention. Miracles are events kept on the bench for relief only in times of pervasive desperation.

Given the degree of strategic misalignment discussed in Section 1.4 and the foreboding situation presented in the prior sections of this chapter, this is unquestionably a time of great want. The business is demanding greater value and productivity from I/T but is dissatisfied with the historical results, the technical skills of the I/T organization are rapidly depreciating under the weight of entirely new technologies, and aggressive competitors, predators, are offering an attractive substitute to internal I/T services. It is not the case that the I/T organization is being flanked on one side: it is being encircled. It is surely a time desirous of miracles. One miracle to assist in alleviating this situation would be beyond our worthiness, but the Divine has been unusually beneficent and has subtly presented the astute I/T manager with not one, not two, not three, but four miracles. The four miracles are

- The Baldrige Award (Baldrige)
- Business Reengineering (reengineering)
- Total Quality Management (TQM)
- International Standards Organization 9000 (ISO 9000)

Though normally perceived exclusively as quality initiatives, these individually and together provide the needed miracle of indirection. They provide a context and a mask through which "they" will let the change-oriented reengineering-possessed I/T executive do what otherwise "they" would never let be done. They provide the camouflage of indirection to pierce the layers of organizational resistance to change and enable the necessary reengineering of the I/T organization to reverse its misfortune.

Indirection

Indirection is the strategic theme that acknowledges that in overcoming resistance, especially when there is a deep psychological, skill-based, and temporal commitment to the status quo, the most economic approach is not to attack the resistance head-on but to flank it, chip away at it, or in any other way artfully reduce it piece by piece until the resistance disintegrates of its own accord. Indirection has as its aim the absolute minimization of direct confrontation. Indirection asserts that the shortest distance between two points between which there are numerous resistance barriers is not a straight line but a jagged or circular line, carefully drawn to melt the resistance slowly and almost unknowingly, rather than to challenge it directly.

The best description of the art of indirection is provided by B. H. Liddell Hart:

> The history of strategy is, fundamentally, a record of the application and evolution of the *indirect* approach. . . . Throughout the ages, effective results have rarely been attained unless the approach has had such *indirectness* as to insure the opponent's unreadiness to meet it. The *indirectness* has usually been physical and always psychological. In strategy, the longest way 'round is often the shortest way home. . . . In most campaigns, the dislocation of the enemy's psychological balance has been the vital prelude to a successful attempt. . . . To move along the line of direct expectation, consolidates the opponent's balance and thus increases his resistance. . . . All conditions are more calculable, all obstacles are more surmountable than those of human resistance. . . . The soundest strategy in war is to postpone operations until the moral disintegration of the enemy renders the delivery of the mortal blow both possible and easy.[4]

The attempt to reengineer the I/T organization will encounter monstrous resistance, because many will interpret the necessary changes as a threat to their well-being. Some will resist overtly, but most will resist through benign neglect. In either case, each of the necessary reengineering moves will encounter fortified barriers. Sun Tzu taught that "indirect methods will be necessary to secure victory."[5] As shown in Table 2.7, you will have to manage the reactions of your allies as well as your enemies. But what are your indirect methods to be?

The Four Miracles of Indirection

The Baldrige Award, reengineering, TQM, and the ISO 9000 standard provide the instruments for indirection. Using them as the focus of attention, the call to arms, and the banner for action, the painful but necessary I/T reengineering actions can be undertaken. It is one thing to resist reengineering of the I/T organization's economic system from one of medieval fiefdoms to a modern 20th-century free economy, but a whole different thing to resist reforming economic processes such as budgeting, charge-

Table 2.7

Reactions to Reengineering. It should be anticipated that there will be an incredibly wide variety of reaction from the I/T community on the need to reengineer.

	New Technology Enthusiast	New Technology Hopeful	The Faithful	The Old Guard	Technology Moderates	Technology Cynics	Technology As Toys	Technology Anarchists
Attitude toward Status Quo I/T Environment	What is old and getting older	Dissatisfied but it works	As it has been has been pretty good—for us	As it has been it will be and as it will be it has been	Things can always be better	Vendor junk	These toys aren't fun anymore	Things are too routine
Desire to reengineer (intellectual commitment)	Can't wait	Strong but concerned about complexity of change	Will listen but but but …	Never is too soon	Yes, but we need cost/benefit analysis	Ambivalent	Do I get to play?	Lots of opportunities for empowerment
Will to reengineer (action commitment)	When do we get started?	Okay, but I want a solid plan	But but but but …	Over my dead body	Need plan with measurable results and milestones	New vendor junk	As long as I get to play	Computing power to the people

back, and project selection when they are but a minor part of a grand TQM initiative. It is one thing to hamper efforts to redesign technology selection and support processes, but a whole different thing to resist absolutely necessary reforms to meet Baldrige requirements. It is one thing to refuse to maintain formal engineering drawings of client/server architectures because the complexity of I/T necessitates the maturation of the I/T profession from artisan to engineer, but a whole different thing to say "no" if the drawing maintenance is required to meet and maintain ISO 9000 certification. Let Baldrige, TQM, reengineering, and ISO 9000 take the direct heat and cloak your true intent.

The resistance to the actions proposed in the following chapters will be intense. While change theorists propose all types of theories to explain organizational resistance to change, I believe that a parable related in the movie *The Crying Game* provides the essential explanation:

> A frog and a scorpion were sitting at the edge of a pond. The scorpion said, "Mr. Frog, I wish to get to the other side of the pond, but I can't swim. Will you carry me on your back?" The frog replied, "Mr. Scorpion, if I carry you on my back, you will sting me and I will surely die." The scorpion answered, "If I sting you, I will drown also; why would I do that?" The frog thought about it, said okay, and took the scorpion on its back. Halfway across the pond, the frog felt a searing pain, realized that it had been stung, and said to the scorpion, "Mr. Scorpion, why did you sting me? You've killed us both!" The scorpion, as it was about to drown, said, "I couldn't help myself—*it's my nature.*"[6]

So it is with most people. Regardless of the situation, the explanations of necessity, and the various attempts at preparation, counsel, and assurances, they will resist. They will resist because *it is their nature.*

Each of the tools of indirection will now be reviewed.

1. ISO 9000

The ISO 9000 standard series is a set of five standards intended to establish and maintain documented quality procedures. It is aimed at manufacturing companies and covers the areas of planning and design, production and delivery, and support. Most countries that adopt the ISO 9000 standard give it a national identity. In the U.S., the standard has been reincarnated as the ANSI/ASQC Q90 series. In Europe, it has been renamed the EN 29000 series. Table 2.8 summarizes the standard. As more countries, companies, and trading communities adopt the standard, conformance will become mandatory. Obviously, extensive I/T support will be required to implement ISO 9000 compliance programs, and that I/T

Table 2.8
The ISO 9000 Standard. The ISO 9000 standard provides distinct quality systems of varying stringency for different applications.

ISO 9000 Standard Number	ISO 9000 Standard Name	ISO 9000 Standard Description
9000	Quality Management and Quality Assurance Standards—Guidelines for Selection and Use	Explains basic quality concepts, defines key terms, and provides guidance on using and tailoring the other standards.
9001	Quality Systems—Model for Quality Assurance in Design/Development, Production, Installation, and Servicing	Covers all elements listed in ISO 9002 and 9003, as well as addressing design, development, and servicing.
9002	Quality Systems—Model for Quality Assurance in Production and Installation	Addresses the prevention, detection, and correction of problems during production and installation.
9003	Quality Systems—Model for Quality Assurance in Final Inspection and Test	Addresses the requirements for detection and control of problems during final inspection and testing.
9004	Quality Management & Quality System Elements—Guidelines	Provides guidance for the development of a quality system.

support will also need to meet quality standards. ISO 9000-3 specifically addresses quality guidelines for software engineering.

2. TQM

TQM is an approach to operating a business that relies on maximizing business success through maximizing customer satisfaction. TQM is a continuing process for excellence; it is not a temporary fix or an event. TQM asserts that the entire management system must be built upon data-driven analysis and decision making, development of a quality culture, focus on customer satisfaction, and empowerment of employees.

The key principles of TQM are as follows:

• Customers and their evolving needs shape and reshape the business.

- Quality products and services have their origin in quality systems and processes.
- Quality is at the core of the business, and is the basis for any and all sustainable competitive advantage.
- Quality is achieved through continuous efforts at improvement.
- Quality requires measurement, in general, and statistical quality control, in particular.
- Quality requires employee empowerment.
- Quality leaders lead through example and commitment.
- Quality provides the only enduring means to achieving the business objective of profit maximization. Maximum profitability for the firm is a by-product, an accident, of quality.
- Quality provides a convergence point for the normal competing self-interests of employees, shareholders, and customers. Quality provides a nonzero-sum game where everyone can win by sharing the economic fruits of quality products and services to satisfied customers.

TQM has achieved unparalleled broad acceptance and spawned an entire industry of self-proclaimed experts. The unquestionable gurus of TQM are

- *Dr. W. Edward Deming:* the author of *Out of Crisis*. Dr. Deming is revered for his work in reforming Japanese manufacturing methods. He urges the use of statistical process control and is famous for his 14 points of quality management.
- *Mr. Joseph M. Juran:* one of the founding fathers of quality-centered management. He is a strong advocate of the notion of internal customers, customer/supplier relationships, supplier management, and formal problem-solving techniques.
- *Mr. Kaoru Isikawa:* the developer of the quality circle concept and the creator of a form of cause/effect diagramming known as the fishbone diagram.

TQM has been the dominant management theory for at least the last five years. Under its banner, much can be accomplished, and much of that requires the use of quality I/T.

3. Business Reengineering

Business reengineering is the radical rethinking and redesign of business processes to achieve dramatic breakthroughs in speed, cost, and service.

The unchallenged father of business reengineering (a.k.a. business process redesign or business process reengineering) is Dr. Michael Hammer, the author of *Reengineering the Corporation*. Business reengineering is built on the following notions:

- Start with a clean slate—don't be encumbered by all the sludge that has accumulated over the years.
- Rethink/redesign—don't tinker or modify; annihilate and build anew.
- Aim for orders of magnitude of improvement—don't settle for double-digit percent increases.
- Infuse the processes with the novel use of I/T to automate and accrue the time, cost, or service advantages.
- Drive reengineering by continual senior management involvement.

Reengineering usually embraces process redesign, job redesign, organizational restructuring, management oversight systems, revised culture, and the extensive use of I/T to enable the reengineered process.

Prime candidates for business reengineering are the key *capabilities* of the business. This strategic framework asserts that the focus of strategy is the nurturing of the primary business processes and practices that deliver value and satisfaction to the customer. Strategic focus should concentrate on enabling the infrastructure to support robust capabilities and selecting which capabilities to compete on.[7] A capabilities perspective asserts that the logic of competition is not with whom to compete, nor with what to compete, nor for whom to compete, but *how* to compete. Success therefore depends on transforming key processes into strategic capabilities that consistently provide superior value to the customer. A capability has six attributes:

1. *Speed:* the process can quickly respond to customer demands and the incorporation of a stream of new ideas and technologies—the capability must be maneuverable.
2. *Process consistency:* the process can unfailingly produce a product that meets or exceeds customer expectations.
3. *Agility:* the process is highly malleable to accommodate unique customer requirements—the capability must deal with market fragmentation.
4. *Cross-functionality:* the process crosses multiple business areas in its execution.

5. *Beginning and ending with the customer:* the process is a closed loop, starting with acquisition of a customer need and ending with satisfying that need.

6. *Complementing core competencies:* the process puts core competencies into motion, and in so doing, translates the competency into value for the customer.

Maximum reengineering benefits are therefore derived not by reengineering each and every process, but by focusing your attention on your capabilities.

In a recent *Fortune* magazine article on business reengineering, an executive said, "If you want to get something funded around here, ANYTHING, even a chair for your office, call it reengineering on your request for approval."

Nothing can withstand the assault of true reengineering zealots, and this is exactly what is needed to block and tackle for the I/T reengineering effort.

While I am normally quite suspicious and reserved about new and reborn management theories, business process reengineering has excellent roots that can be traced to the work of Professor Joseph Schumpeter.[8] In developing a model to explain where profits came from, Professor Schumpeter postulated a *routinized* market economy where, with boring regularity, business produced standardized products and consumers consumed in known quantities and styles. Eventually, such an economy would achieve a state of stasis where all profits would be driven out. There would be no profitability, because all the producers would have copied each other and competition would have driven out any margin due to the absence of differentiation and value added. Professor Schumpeter then postulated that what prevents this from happening and permits new profits to materialize is innovation, or *entrepreneurship*. Entrepreneurship alters the status quo and injects novelty and new value into a business, and thereby permits the business to command profit margin by virtue of its innovations. Profit is a symptom of an imperfection, and that aberration is entrepreneurship.

Business reengineering should be understood as an entrepreneurial activity within Professor Schumpeter's model. It is a welcoming of innovation. Rather than the normal resistance to change and novelty, business reengineering aggressively embraces innovation. In doing so, it provides the business with new profit opportunities. Professor Schumpeter said, "The function of entrepreneurs is to reform or revolutionize the pattern of production by exploiting an invention or, more generally, an untried technological possibility for producing a new commodity or producing an old one in a new way, by opening up a new source of supply of materials or an outlet for products, by reorganizing an industry, and so on." The essential traits of an entrepreneur are total commitment, perseverance and determination toward a focused goal, an all-encompassing drive to succeed, pragmatism, problem-solving ability, calculated risk-taking, and the ability to bounce back quickly from adversity. Are these not the same marks of a reengineer? So business reengineering is not so much a new concept as it is a new instance, a recycling, of the Schumpeterian driver of business profits, *entrepreneurship*.

4. The Baldrige Award

The Malcolm Baldrige Quality Award was authorized by the U.S. Congress in 1987. It is given annually to organizations that convince examiners that they have outstanding quality management principles and practices—that is, companies that have successfully implemented TQM. The specific purpose of the award is public recognition of the importance of quality to competitive success, acknowledgment of exceptional quality achievements, and publicizing and disseminating the message about quality.

The winners are selected through a three-stage review process. Seven categories of quality characteristics covering leadership, information and analysis, planning, quality assurance, human resources, and customer satisfaction are evaluated. Winning the Baldrige has become an obsession with some companies. Winning before one's competitors is viewed as a critical component of competitive advantage. Baldrige has become a high-stakes game in the battle for advantage. I/T is integral to Baldrige success.

Trouble in Quality Paradise

Although quality is absolutely needed, and all the efforts are well intentioned, the results are mixed. Consider the following:

- Experts tell us that 50 to 70 percent of reengineering projects fail to achieve their goals. In all fairness, this is not as bad as it appears. If reengineering initiatives are really entrepreneurial acts, one should anticipate the normal dear failure rates that accompany the undertaking of high-risk economic activities.
- TQM has been criticized for ignoring results in favor of process. Identical criticism has been leveled at ISO 9000.
- Wallace Company, a 1990 Baldrige winner, filed for Chapter 11 bankruptcy in 1992. In 1992, Wallace was acquired by Wilson Industries.
- Florida Power & Light, after winning the 1989 Japan Deming Award, dismantled its quality bureaucracy, and its CEO resigned.

- Applications for the Baldrige award have dropped by 20 percent between 1991 and 1994.

- Ritz-Carlton Hotels, which was the first hotel chain to win the Baldrige Award in 1992, reported that fewer than half of its 30 hotels were profitable by the first quarter of 1994. In an interesting reversal of the standard quality slogan, the *Wall Street Journal* article said, "But quality costs."

- Consultants suggest that only 20 to 30 percent of quality initiatives yield tangible results.

- There is substantial debate over what "quality" is.

- The gurus are sometimes in radical disagreement. Some preach benchmarking, while others feel that it is a step backward. Some preach zero defects, while others more versed in statistical quality control argue that zero defects contradict normal expected statistical variations. Some are strong advocates of objective setting, while others are opposed. Some favor rallies, slogans, and rewards to promote quality, while others are against material remuneration.

Whether these four methods are as beneficial as claimed by their adherents, suffer from statistically expected flaws, or are false paths to salvation is quite irrelevant to our immediate purpose. The simple and undeniable truth is that all four of these quality approaches have received and continue to receive unmatched executive endorsement, funding, and attention as the path to competitive superiority. Under the banner of any and all of them, anything can be done, and that is our interest. Baldrige, TQM, ISO 9000, and business reengineering provide the miracle of indirection for our I/T reengineering efforts. While they take the brunt of any resistance, and few can stand up to them, behind them we can do what never has been done before. Tom Peters summarized the point very nicely: "The answer is not TQM and it is not reengineering—even though one aspect of reengineering is terribly important, which is that it is a convenient and best-selling handle for finally destroying the remnants of functional bureaucracy."[9] Use TQM, reengineering, Baldrige, and ISO 9000 as a means of indirection to your ends. Use them for what they really are, a context and a call for action. Use them as the linchpin of your maneuver strategy.

2.5 CONCLUSION

A new period of business challenges is emerging, due to the proliferation of competitors, the fragmentation of markets, the acceleration of product life cycles, and the globalization of business. Against this hard business reality, the I/T organization is caught in its own quagmire of growing technological obsolescence and the emergence of intense competition for the internal corporate market. It is becoming a war of all against all, a war of movement, a war for advantage—and the power weapons of this war are information technology.

The U.S. Marine Corps publishes a manual that summarizes its doctrine of warfare. The manual is crisp, clear, and direct. It covers in 30 pages the subjects of military theory, strategy, tactics, leadership, and training. The only thing more remarkable than its conciseness is its crystal clarity of thought. The manual is called *Warfighting*. The marines are not confused about their nature; they are warriors.

The typical business is, fortunately, not engaged in fighting wars. It is, however, becoming engaged in a global battle for markets. As the basis of conflict shifts from wars of attrition to wars of maneuver, victory will go to those who better align I/T with the business. Winning will go to those who master *I/T Fighting*—the use of I/T to enable dramatic maneuverability by the business in order to elongate, build, and sustain competitive advantage.

Table 2.9 summarizes the problems confronting the I/T executive by use of the root cause analytical method. The symptoms are all the persistent critical issues that linger unresolved forever (see Figure 1.12); the immediate problems are the issues of business pressure, technology change, and competition that were reviewed in this chapter. However, the root cause of our sorrows is the absence of strategy. It is at the root that therapy will have to be provided.

Table 2.9
Root Cause Analysis. The cause of the sorrows and afflictions
of the I/T organization are rooted in the absence of strategic
I/T–business alignment.

Root Cause Analytical Model	I/T–Business Analysis
Symptoms: External Signs and Indications of a Problem	Figure 1.11 Recurrent Critical Issues
Immediate Problem: Malfunctioning Part, System, etc.	1. Business Demands on I/T 2. Technology Change 3. Competition
Root Cause: Ingrained and Systemic Failure	Absence of I/T Strategy Aligned with the Business

Table 2.10
**Management Theories. There is no shortage of theories on how to
attack management problems.**

Management Theory	Summary Description
Management by Objectives	Set specific measurable goals and evaluate performance based on goal realization.
Matrix Management	An organizational structure where an employee has multiple bosses.
Decentralization	Push out decision making to the line.
Product Life Cycles	Manage products through predictable stages.
Zero-Based Budgeting	Start each year's budget fresh.
One-Minute Management	Balance praise and criticism in 60-second doses.
Management by Walking Around	Spend extensive personal time with customers, suppliers, and employees.
Competitive Strategy	Focus on competition.
Quality	Adopt TQM quality circles and strive for Baldrige.
Management of Chaos	Build a highly malleable organization to deal with the unknown and unknowable.

The ravaged I/T executive who wails, "What do I do now?" in reaction to this situational analysis may get more advice than she ever wanted. Table 2.10 lists selected fashionable management theories that have come and gone over the last 30 years. They seem to follow a fairly predictable life cycle, as shown in Figure 2.14.[10] The standard stages are

- *Idea:* a new idea is born, researched, and reported.
- *Cult:* a small group of true believers nurtures, evangelizes, and refines the idea.
- *Popular acclaim:* the idea spreads and is labeled a panacea, and a community of "internationally recognized experts" suddenly appears.

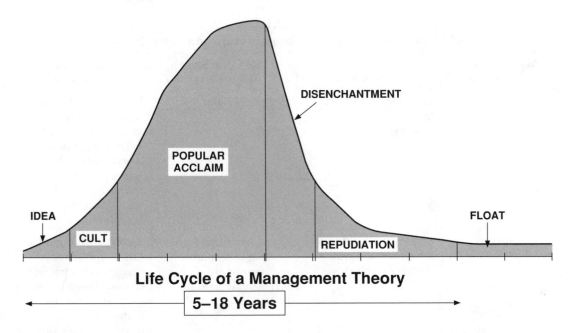

Figure 2.14   Management Theory Life Cycle. Management frameworks seem to follow a predictable life cycle. (Source: Joe A. Bailey, "The Rise and Fall of Educational Panaceas," *NSPI Journal* 10:7.)

- *Disenchantment:* there is nothing new to be said, and failures begin to surface.
- *Repudiation:* a tidal wave of negative comments surface. The idea is cast aside, but a new theory sitting in the cult stage awaits.
- *Float:* some zealots remain loyal and the ideas are periodically resurrected or rediscovered in modified forms.[11]

This model may be somewhat dated. I recently attended a seminar session called "Business Reengineering Magic." Perhaps, after the "popular acclaim" stage, a new stage called "mysticism" is needed for truly extraordinary panaceas.

Why management theories come and go is difficult to discern. Is the advice inherently shallow and nearsighted, or is the advice excellent but the execution second-class? Perhaps even the best of advice is doomed to this cycle. After all, a public theory available and executed by all inevitably yields only parity, not advantage. Table 2.11 provides a quick synopsis of the state of the most popular management and technology

Table 2.11
Fad Status. Some fads have a bright future and some do not.

Management Technology Fad	Short Description	Life Cycle Stage (Figure 2.14)	Long-Term Assessment
Empowered teams	Employees, assembled into teams, run the business.	Popular acclaim.	Will survive, but not without a resurgence of strong traditional individual leadership. As commonly presented, it contradicts the leadership teachings of Sun Tzu and Machiavelli.
Team building	Employees go off into the woods to develop teamwork and trust.	Disenchantment—benefits of corporate intramurals are increasingly hard to justify.	Too expensive and too little—three days of therapy is not enough. Careful design of the internal economic system will do more to develop cooperation than a month of jumping off trees into each other's arms.
Liberation management	Reinventing the corporation based on: 1. Delighting customers 2. Market focus 3. Competencies 4. Teams	Cult.	Will be replaced in 2–3 years by new theory and repudiation of this theory, as have been all of Tom Peter's other book-based theories.
Outsourcing	Contracting with an independent vendor to manage part or all of the I/T assets.	Late popular acclaim/ early disenchantment.	Not even good nonsense.
Reengineering	Radical redesign of business processes.	Height of popular acclaim—mutations such as "rapid reengineering" and "quantum leap reengineering" are appearing for those who can't wait.	Long-term winner—entrepreneurship is always in fashion.
Total Quality Management—Baldrige Award	Obsession with customers, process, and measurement.	Disenchantment.	Nobody ever really understood what it meant. Baldrige Award applications are down and two big Baldrige winners (Federal Express and Xerox) hit hard times.

Table 2.11 (*Continued*)

Management Technology Fad	Short Description	Life Cycle Stage (Figure 2.14)	Long-Term Assessment
Client/Server Computing	Networking of computers	Between cult and popular acclaim—the old guard will not surrender without a fight.	Big winner for next 20 years in all its variations—i.e., distributed processing, dispersed processing, network computing, peer-to-peer computing, downsizing, etc.
Object-Oriented Technologies	Software design and construction by the building of reusable parts.	Cult.	Big winner—promotes software from artisan to engineering discipline.
CASE	Automated support for application development.	Repudiation.	It doesn't work.
SAA	IBM'S architecture for making IBM computing environments inter-operate.	Float.	*Question:* What do you get when you put a blanket on an elephant? *Answer:* An elephant with a blanket on it.
Data warehousing	Creation of a highly accessible and non-redundant data environment to enable decision support applications.	Early popular acclaim.	Long-term winner
The structured revolution	Use of various structured techniques to enable application development.	Float.	Premier example of I/T hubris—a grand pretense of knowledge.
Credibility management	Management must be built upon trust-worthiness and believability.	Idea.	1995 roll-out
Open-space agendaless meetings	No predetermined speakers, topics, or structure. People gravitate to tableless round seating arrange-ments to discuss things they care about.	Cult.	An important agenda item for your next meeting.

fads currently being inflicted upon the overwhelmed I/T executive.[12] A cynic would view the parade of management theories as a history of swindles that demonstrate an eternal victory of hope over experience.

I believe that a large part of the problem with the rapid turnover in management theories is that they are really not theories at all, at least not in the scientific meaning of the word. In science, a theory goes through two stages, discovery/development and justification/defense. Though most often associated with the use of induction, theories may be discovered or developed in any way. What is important is that regardless of how they are formulated, at the end of the discovery step there exists a statement of explanation and prediction with as few constraints as possible. The theory carefully postulates a firm, constant, and repeatable cause (C) and effect (E) relationship—that is, "If C, always E."

Having completed development, that theory now moves to the stage of justification and defense. This is generally done in one of two ways: the citation of numerous phenomena that confirm the theory, or attempts at falsification wherein the theory is subjected to severe testing to see whether it holds up under its own implications. If a hypothesis generated from the theory is shown to be false, then the theory is compromised, and either a new theory has to be developed or additional limiting constraints are put on the theory.

Most management theories appear to be the product of generalization from limited induction. Having been discovered, they are promoted as general truths with the minimum constraints and maximum application possible. This creates the widest possible market for the management theories. Unfortunately, they rapidly succumb to falsification even under modest testing. As evidence of contradictions in practice mounts, a theory's proponents weave, bob, dance, and clutch like a boxer with a glass jaw to explain away the falsification—anything to avoid taking the punch and admitting that the induction was wrong, that insufficient constraints were put on the theory, or that the cause-and-effect relationship is not universal. Last-ditch efforts by a theory's most staunch proponents to defend its honor culminate either in insulting those who "didn't do it right," or in putting so many "and causes" (If C and C_1 and C_2 and C_3 ... and C_n, always E) that the conditions become impossible to fulfill (or the additional causes are themselves so valuable that it becomes impossible to know what is truly the driving cause). Eventually, a combination of punches (falsifications) is just too much, and the theory becomes overwhelmed by all the counterevidence. So most management theories are not scientific theories, they are ideas somewhere in the space defined by random acts of working, apparent good logic, wishful thinking, misunderstood cause and effect, extraordinary hard work, excellent leadership and vision, and oversimplification of reality.

One should anticipate a flood of new management theories (with endless mutations) as we move through the 1990s. Having taken seriously the biblical injunction "to be fruitful and multiply," the management consulting industry has grown in the triple digits between 1982 and 1992 in terms of number of consultants, number of consultancies, and consulting revenues. All of these consultants, attempting to differentiate themselves, will become theory machines—after all, what they peddle is advice. It should therefore be anticipated that:

1. There will be significant growth in the number of new theories and mutations of these theories.
2. There will be a decrease in the efficacy of the average theory. The growth in consultants will exceed the growth in deep and far-reaching thinking.[13]
3. There will be a decrease in the life cycle period for the average theory (see Figure 2.14). This will be due to both the decrease in quality and the need to increase the tempo for new theories to generate new business in response to the horde of consulting competitors.

Business decision makers will consequently have to be even more selective and discriminating in choosing what theories to adopt.

It is my perspective that the immediate situation requires neither extraordinary nor sophisticated responses; it requires merely common sense and pragmatism. It requires doing five fundamental things to realize alignment and the use of indirection to deflect resistance. The strategic moves that will be presented in the following chapters are conceptually simple, but they are not easily done, because 30 years' worth of gross misalignment is not easily altered, and because sooner or later, all problems reduce to people problems, and there is the eternal problem of their *nature*. You must be strong and resolute, for it is your task to lead them. Your task is almost holy: you must raise them out of darkness, you must lead them on an exodus out of misalignment.

NOTES

1. Some would suggest that the market failure of the first generation of hand-held personal data assistants (PDAs) contradicts this theory. Nothing could be farther from the truth. The first generation of PDAs (Apple Newton MessagePad and AT&T EO) failed because of a combination of price, feature/functionality, quality, and most important, poor and expensive communications (i.e., reach). Since one would expect a PDA to be the

embodiment of reach, the absence of this feature made the product an uncompelling purchase.

2. Sun Tzu, *The Art of War.*

3. *Ibid.*

4. B. H. Liddell Hart, *Strategy.* Italics added.

5. Sun Tzu, *The Art of War.*

6. From *The Crying Game.*

7. See G. Stalk, P. Evans, and L. Shulman, "Competing on Capabilities," *Harvard Business Review* 3–4 (1992).

8. Joseph Schumpeter, *Theory of Economic Development* (Harvard Business University Press, 1962).

9. Tom Peters, "Unconventional Wisdom," *CIO Magazine* 7:6. For an excellent defense of TQM, which asserts that TQM not only is the answer but provides a far superior management paradigm to the traditional rational economic model of individual and business behaviors, see Robert Grant, Rami Shani, and R. Krishnan, "TQM's Challenge to Management Theory and Practice," *Sloan Management Review* (Winter 1994).

10. From Joe A. Bailey, "The Rise and Fall of Educational Panaceas," *NSPI Journal* 10:7. For an interesting example of a panacea moving from popular acclaim to disenchantment, read "Deming's Luster Dims at Florida Power & Light," *Journal of Business Strategy* 14:5 (Sept.–Oct. 1993). The article documents Florida Power & Light's retreat from Deming-based quality. As the Florida Power & Light spokesperson said, "It's easy to get sucked into the latest and greatest management fad." The diplomatic retreat is all the more instructive since Florida Power and Light is the only American winner of the Japanese Deming Award. Also see "Report Card On TQM" in *Management Review* (January 1994) for a grading of TQM.

11. Float is the management theory equivalent to the "Jason Returns" movie genre. No matter how or how often you kill the theory, it keeps coming back!

12. For an excellent analysis of management fads, see R. Eccles and N. Nohria, *Beyond the Hype* (Harvard Business School Press, 1992).

13. For an excellent example of this, see "The Transgenic Enterprise" in *Information Week,* 21 Feb. 1994. The theory postulates that "By their nature, reengineered processes are trapped in an architecture of formalism" and that "we must move beyond self-limiting reengineering to a transgenic enterprise that is modeled on genetic engineering concepts. We must move beyond reengineering into the post-reengineering age, which will be the transgenic enterprise age." I believe that this theory will traverse the theory life cycle (see Figure 2.14) in record time.

3

I/T Architecture

The purpose of this chapter is to analyze the reengineering required to implement a reach, range, and maneuverability architecture. There is no target for I/T reengineering more important than the successful design and implementation of the new I/T architecture. It is the most important component because, as has been previously argued, it is through the malleability of the architecture that the business is able to achieve the maximum advantage by creating marketplace dislocations (see Figure 1.11). Without the implementation of an I/T architecture that is constantly stretching to achieve greater reach, range, and maneuverability, strategic alignment between the business and I/T will always remain elusive.

An I/T architecture is a set of principles, guidelines, and rules that guides an organization through acquiring, building, modifying, and interfacing I/T resources throughout the enterprise. I/T resources include hardware, software, communications equipment and protocols, application life cycle development and maintenance methodologies, application enabling technologies (DBMS, TP-Monitor, middleware, user interface, etc.), modeling tools, and I/T organizational structure. With the migration to network computing environments, an I/T architecture most importantly defines, communicates, and demonstrates the adaptability, interoperability, scaleability, and portability of applications and their subcomponents across the architecture. An architecture should preserve application investments as it evolves. As is true with any engineering discipline, an I/T architecture demands a formal and rigorous diagramming methodology to communicate architectural structure.

The concern and focus on architecture is a recent event; it is a consequence of the movement to network computing. Under the proprietary host-centered computing model (Figure 2.3a), the vendor took complete responsibility for architectural integration. The third-party after-market (DBMS tools, utilities, operations software, etc.) was careful to maintain compatibility, and there was little architectural concern for the I/T organization. After all, architecture meetings were very short in those days; all the applications, for the most part, looked exactly the same. They ran on a vendor's big mainframe, ran under the same operating system, used the same DBMS, used the same TP-Monitor, were written in COBOL, and used synchronous communication to a full-screen dumb terminal. What was there to discuss other than sizing issues?

This has all changed with the migration to network computing. Reach, range, and maneuverability architectures are open architectures; they are software-based, heterogeneous, built on standard service interfaces, and require the rigorous definition of the architectural components. To gain the benefits of the emerging advantage technologies discussed in Section 2.2, it is necessary to design an architecture that is adaptable, interoperable, portable, scaleable, and open. It is necessary to create an architecture that can reshape itself as necessary to continually accept new technologies and meet the made-to-order needs of each individual user, while maintaining overall I/T integration throughout the enterprise. It is necessary to design an architecture that can go through continual metamorphosis. This is the responsibility of the I/T organization and is of the highest priority.

The issues surrounding implementation of an I/T will be presented as follows:

- *3.1. The Business Logic of an I/T Architecture*
  This section reviews the business logic of implementing a robust I/T architecture. The rational for I/T architecture starts and stops with strategic alignment.

- *3.2. The Problems of I/T Architecture*
  This section analyzes some of the alternative approaches currently prescribed for modeling I/T architectures and analyzes their short-comings. It concludes, as is true for any serious engineering discipline, that I/T architecture requires a rigorous diagramming technique to enable communication and specificity.

- *3.3. Diagramming I/T Architectures*
  This section presents a state-of-the-art methodology to draw reach, range, and maneuverability architectures. The diagramming technique provides a strict way to draw the essence of a network computing architecture, and to eliminate many of the prevailing communication problems involved in maintaining I/T architectures. The diagramming technique also serves an educational purpose in explaining precisely what an architecture is.

- *3.4. Extensions to the Diagramming Technique*
  This section suggests additional actions that should be taken based on the diagramming technique to improve the asset value of the I/T architecture.

- *3.5. Implications for I/T Architecture*
  This section analyzes the implications of the architecture on I/T processes and other business areas.

- *3.6. Summary*
This section summarizes the most important points of this chapter.

In each era of computing (see Table 2.2), different I/T assets have risen to prominence. For the foreseeable future, the eminent asset will be architecture.

In Milton's *Paradise Lost,* Mulciber was the architect of Hell. After the fallen angels were cast out of Heaven, Mulciber, in response to the command of Satan, built Pandemonium, a great meeting hall for the devils in Hell. If you do not build a carefully engineered network computing architecture for your business with ample forethought and rigor, you too will create an architectural Hell. Design your network computing architecture carefully, or you may be remembered as your organization's Mulciber.

3.1 THE BUSINESS LOGIC OF I/T ARCHITECTURE

It is becoming obvious that as the 1990s unfold, successful information technology organizations will migrate from being technology-centric to being business-centric. Rather than starting with new and exciting information technologies and then trying to rationalize how the business may use them, they will start with business requirements and search for information technologies that will directly address a business-driven need. Nowhere is the need for a business-centric approach more required than in justifying and winning consensus for an information technology architecture.

Figure 3.1 illustrates a typical I/T architecture for the 1990s. It represents an evolution from the host-centered computing model that has dominated computing for the past 30 years to a client/server architecture, characterized by distributed intelligence and extensive networking, that moves all aspects of computing (i.e., presentation, processing, and data management) to the most advantageous point in the business. Attempts to justify such an architecture from a technology-centric approach will inevitably fall on deaf ears. To win approval for a corporate computing architecture, what is needed is a rationale that explains the business logic of such an investment.

This section will review the business logic of an information technology architecture by answering five key questions:

1. What is the purpose of a business strategy?
2. How is that purpose realized?
3. How does an I/T contribute to that purpose?
4. Where does I/T architecture fit in?
5. What are the business implications of an I/T architecture?

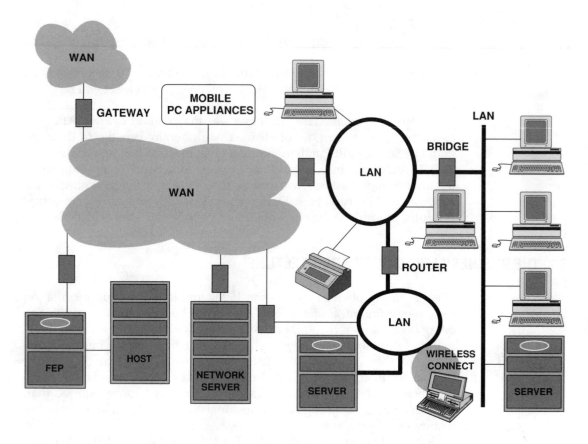

Figure 3.1   I/T Architecture of the 1990s. The I/T architectures of the future will be networks of networks. (Source: *Implementing Client/Server Computing: A Strategic Perspective*, Bernard H. Boar, McGraw-Hill, 1993)

It is our aim, in answering these questions, to first establish a set of business goals and then show how I/T architecture is critical to achieving those goals. In doing so, we are business-centric: I/T architecture exists only to fulfill the mission of the business.

Business Strategy

The eternal struggle of business is the struggle for advantage. Business strategy focuses on

1. *Building new advantages* that increase customer satisfaction and create distance from competitors.

2. *Elongating existing advantages* that increase customer satisfaction and create distance from competitors.

3. *Reducing/eliminating* the advantages of competitors.

The purpose of business strategy is the nurturing of advantage. The business with more advantages wins; the one with fewer advantages loses. It really is that simple. Advantage can be realized through infinite combinations of strategic moves. Typical ways of building advantages are

- *Alignment:* getting multiple organizations to collaborate toward a shared agenda.
- *Benchmarking:* comparing oneself against the best in class and appropriately redesigning work processes based on that comparison.
- *Bottleneck analysis:* searching for bottlenecks in the movements of products from your suppliers through yourself to your customers and eliminating them.
- *Capabilities/processes:* building highly agile and fast processes to deliver and support your products and services.
- *Critical success factors:* understanding what you must do well to compete and focusing on doing those things exceptionally well.
- *Economy design:* designing an internal business economy for the exchange of goods and services that stimulates positive customer-focused behaviors.
- *Learning system:* establishing a set of formal and informal learning events that keeps management abreast of changing market requirements.
- *Human resource architecture:* building a set of human resource systems that stimulates winning staff behaviors.
- *Organization structure:* designing an organization structure that promotes sensitivity to customer needs.
- *Strategic intent:* defining a long-term ambition for the business.
- *Competencies:* developing a set of core competencies that can be leveraged into multiple products to serve multiple markets.

These are not the only ways to build advantage, but they certainly are common, and they are a representative sample.

While there are many ways to build advantage, all advantages can be classified into five categories:

1. *Cost advantage:* the advantage results in your being able to provide products/services more cheaply.

2. *Value-added advantage:* the advantage creates a product/service that offers some highly desirable feature or functionality.

3. *Focus advantage:* the advantage more tightly meets the explicit needs of a particular customer.

4. *Speed advantage:* the advantage permits you to service customer needs more quickly than others.

5. *Maneuverability advantage:* the advantage permits you to adapt to changing requirements more quickly than others.

Sun Tzu said, "The one with many strategic factors on his side wins. . . . The one with few strategic factors on his side loses. In this way, I can tell who will win and who will lose."[1] If an action does not lead to development of a winning advantage, it is of no strategic interest.

The culmination of advantage is the building of a set of sustainable competitive advantages (SCAs) for the business. An SCA is a resource, capability, asset, or process that provides the enterprise with a distinct attraction to its customers and a unique advantage over its competitors. An SCA has seven attributes that are itemized in Table 3.1. Without a well-designed set of sustainable competitive advantages, a business engages in a continual life-and-death struggle for marketplace survival, since there is no compelling reason to choose that company's products or services.

In summary, the key ideas to this point are that:

1. The purpose of strategy is to build advantage.

2. Advantage can be built in many ways.

3. Advantage is classifiable into five categories.

4. The culmination of advantage is the creation of sustainable competitive advantage (SCA).

It would therefore be reasonable to infer that any asset or resource that can be used to build advantage is of interest to the business.

Information Technology and Advantage

Information technology is of interest to the business because it offers a rich variety of technologies that can be used to lower costs, add value, deliver focused products or services, infuse speed into processes, and create maneuverability. Table 3.2 provides examples of ways in which specific information technologies can offer advantage. Given the fierce global competitiveness of business today, information technology offers an unusually fertile area from which to construct advantage for the business.

Table 3.1
Sustainable Competitive Advantage (SCA). A company's
sustainable competitive advantages defines the basis
of winning for an extended period.

Attribute	Definition
1. Customer Perception	The customer perceives a consistent difference in one or more critical buying factors.
2. SCA Linkage	The difference in customer perception is directly attributable to the SCA.
3. Durability	Both the customer's perception and the SCA linkage are durable over an extended time period.
4. Transparency	The mechanics/details of the SCA are difficult for competitors to understand.
5. Accessibility	The competitor has unequal access to the required resources to mimic the SCA.
6. Replication	The competitor would have extreme difficulty reproducing the SCA.
7. Coordination	The SCA requires difficult and subtle coordination of multiple resources.

However, as shown in Figure 3.2, there is a significant constraint to converting the potential of I/T advantage into practical reality. The decline of "one size fits all" host-centered computing, coupled with the emergence of so many opportunistic but diverse technologies, has created a mess. When one reflects on Figure 3.2, it becomes obvious that the problem is not the raw availability of advantageous technologies, the problem is integrating them so that they collaborate with each other to build instances of advantage and, through interoperability, to compound advantage. An I/T architecture is necessary to transmute the potential of isolated I/T technologies into cooperative practical applications.

The attributes of the host-centered computing environment and the client/server computing environment are quite different, as illustrated in Table 3.3. In the host-centered environment, the vendor provided architectural coherence. In the client/server computing environment, the advantage is built upon diversity, but you need to provide architectural coherence and order, or your I/T environment will quickly degenerate into chaos.

Table 3.2
Information Technologies and Advantage. Information technologies
are of interest because they convey advantage.

Information Technology	Business Advantage
Open Systems	Maneuverability
Distributed DBMS	Data Access
Object-Oriented	Leverage
Wireless Communications	Information Reach
Client/Server	Maneuverability
Pen-Based	Focus
Electronic Commerce	Speed
Multimedia	Focus
Groupware	Alignment
CASE	Cost
AI	Leverage
Prototyping	Cost
Massive Parallelism	Cost
E-Mail	Alignment
Video Conferencing	Alignment
Mobile Computing	Information Reach
Voice Processing	Cost
EIS/DSS	Value-Added
RAID	Cost
Virtual Reality	Value-Added

The culmination of an I/T architecture is the creation of a reach/range/
maneuverability architecture, as illustrated in Figure 1.10. The business
needs to build systems on an architecture that has the following three
attributes:

1. *Maximum reach:* anyone (or any processor), anywhere, any time can
   access the I/T assets.

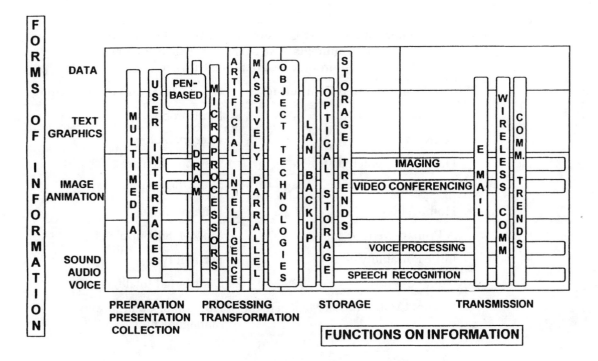

Figure 3.2   Technology Proliferation. There is tremendous growth in the availability of desirable technologies, but they are not integrated.

2. *Maximum range:* any information object (data or process) can be shared.

3. *Application maneuverability:* on top of the reach/range platform, applications are built to maximize maneuverability.

Only when a state of such architectural flexibility is achieved can all the advantageous technologies be linked together to create endless permutations of applied I/T advantage for the business.

As illustrated in Figure 1.11, when increased reach, range, and maneuverability are realized by the architecture, the purposeful use and value of I/T to business success increases dramatically. The supreme advantage that I/T can achieve is to be used to create and exploit business opportunities in the marketplace. That is, an I/T functional capability permits the business to offer a distinct product or service that excites and attracts customers. This is done in a differentiated manner, which creates distance from any competitor's ability to offer a similar or superior service. As an

Table 3.3
Comparison of Host-Centered and Client/Server Computing
Environments. The characteristics of the two
environments are radically different.

Host-Centered Computing	Open Client/Server Computing
Uni-Processor	Multiprocessor
Self-Contained	Interoperability
Hardware-Centered	Software-Centered
Proprietary	Open/Standards
Homogeneous	Heterogeneous
A Primary Vendor	Mix/Match Suppliers
Little Portability	Portability
Dumb Client	Distributed Intelligence
Vertical Configuration Management	Horizontal Configuration Management

I/T architecture evolves from low reach/range/maneuverability to high reach/range/maneuverability, it permits the transmutation of advantageous information technologies from a state of potential advantage to directed purpose for the business.

Business Implications

It is therefore evident that a powerful I/T architecture that sits as the framework through which individual I/T technologies are integrated is not an arcane add-on or an optional extra. Specifically, if advantage is to be accrued by converting the potential of I/T to realize advantage, then:

1. Processes must be developed and executed to maintain an architectural blueprint.
2. New product development and existing product evolution must remain in harmony with the architecture.
3. Processes must be developed to maintain the architecture in synchronization with changing time and circumstances.

Architecture success is as much process-driven as it is content-driven.

Summary

The purpose of strategy is to build advantage. While advantage can be built in many ways, all the ways can be generically classified by the dimensions of cost, value added, focus, speed, and maneuverability. Advantage culminates in the building of sustainable competitive advantages, which ensure marketplace success. I/T is of interest to the business because it is a fertile ground from which to build advantage. The emerging set of distinct I/T technologies is incredibly opportunistic but, as presented, yields I/T chaos. This preempts the building of advantage through I/T. Architecture is therefore necessary to provide an orderly framework through which to accrue I/T advantage and preempt chaos. A reach/range/maneuverability architecture is the culmination of I/T architecture; it positions the business to achieve a perfect state of strategic alignment between I/T and the business, wherein I/T can be used as a strategic weapon to create dislocations and opportunities in the marketplace.

3.2 THE PROBLEM WITH ARCHITECTURE

While there is broad recognition of the need for an enterprise-wide I/T architecture, there is no agreement on exactly what an I/T architecture is or how one portrays (models) it. This confusion is a serious barrier to the expeditious implementation of a reach, range, and maneuverability environment within corporations. If you can't reach a consensus on what something is or how to visualize it, how can you talk about it, plan for it, implement it, or manage it?

The architecture advice community can be partitioned into two camps that are hierarchically related. The first group is concerned with architectural frameworks. Architectural frameworks are high-level structures that define the overall contents and boundaries of an architecture. They focus on settling the global question of what an architecture is and exactly what must be done to have an architecture. They navigate in the clouds at the overview level. The second group is concerned with the details of architectural drawings, and may be referred to as the architecture diagramming community. This community provides guidance on how to create specific models of the architectural items defined within the frameworks. This group is concerned with developing drawing models that unambiguously communicate the contents of a framework cell. This group is focused on modeling the nitty-gritty of each architectural element. We will now review representative samples from each group and attempt to reach some conclusions on the efficacy of the current state of advice.

Architectural Frameworks

Architectural frameworks are overall high-level structures that define what an architecture should embrace, but often do not go into any detail of how to complete the framework item by item. Tables 3.4, 3.5, and 3.6 are examples of three leading frameworks that serve as blueprints for architectures. Architecture equates to completing each matrix cell. Figure 3.3 illustrates a different approach to defining architecture, in which the composition of an architecture is portrayed as a data-entity diagram.[2]

Though the frameworks are quite different, they do share some critical common attributes:

- They define the entire domain of an I/T architecture.
- High-level explanations are provided for how to complete the contents of the architecture, but they often fall short on exact methodologies to complete cells.
- The frameworks are holistic: they do not view architecture as only a technical issue, but equally embrace nontechnical issues.
- Because the audience for frameworks is usually higher-level executives, the emphasis is on concepts. When details are provided, they are usually provided on executive-level issues such as "values" or "principles."

Architectural frameworks are very important in identifying the architectural problem, but are often deficient in providing detailed methodological advice on how to model the implementation of the selected framework. It is also clear that unless one does a lot of extra work, the frameworks are not easily reconciled with each other.

Table 3.4
I/T Architecture Framework I. This framework sees I/T architecture as the definition of 16 items. (Source: CSC/Index.)

	Inventory	Principles	Models	Standards
Infrastructure				
Data				
Applications				
Organization				

Table 3.5
I/T Architecture Framework II. This framework sees I/T architecture
as the definition of 30 items. (Source: IBM/Zachman.)

	Data	Function	Network	People	Time	Motivation
Scope						
Enterprise Model						
System Model						
Technology Model						
Components						

Table 3.6
I/T Architecture Framework III. This framework sees I/T architecture
as the definition of 27 items. (Source: Gartner Group.)

	Values	Principles	Processes	Standards	Buy List
Executive Direction		N/A	N/A	N/A	N/A
Organization Architecture	N/A			N/A	N/A
Application Architecture	N/A				
Data Architecture	N/A				
Services Layer	N/A				
Facilities Layer	N/A				
Platform	N/A				
Network	N/A				

Architecture Diagramming Methodologies

The diagramming community focuses on the problem of how to complete the cells of the architecture frameworks. Many of the cells in Tables 3.4 to 3.6 are fairly self-explanatory and do not require elaboration. For some rows such as "Data" in Tables 3.4 and 3.6, there already exist robust data diagramming methodologies to be applied. There is, however, no well-accepted diagramming technique for modeling processing architecture, and this is the core architectural problem with modeling network computing environments. It is our thesis that the shaded areas in Figure 3.4 encompass the processing model of the architecture, but that there does

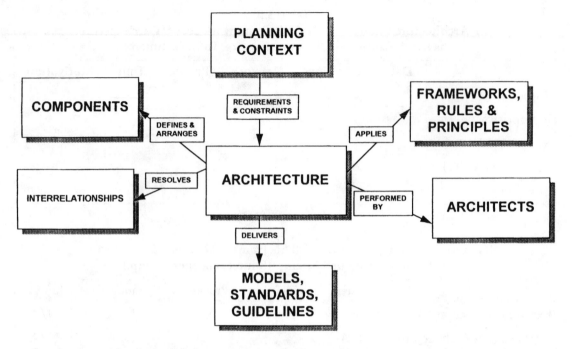

Figure 3.3   I/T Architecture Framework IV. Unlike the other architectural frameworks, these authors portrayed an I/T architecture in the structure of a data entity diagram. (Source: Paradigm Shift.)

not exist any satisfactory way to model them. Consider the alternative examples provided by different drawing communities:

- *Industry Consulting and Market Research Community (Thoughtware Leaders)*
  This group is composed of both market research firms and leading I/T consultants. Figures 3.5 and 3.6 show representative drawings from this community. These proponents can't agree on the number of elemental models, let alone how to present them.

- *Vendors*
  This group consists of I/T vendors who are selling an I/T architecture. Figures 3.7 and 3.8 illustrate the popular DEC NAS architecture and the withering IBM SAA architecture. One cannot help but notice the gross difference in presentation.

- *Architects*
  Architects are individuals within an I/T organization whose responsibility is to define and manage the I/T architecture. Figures 3.9 and

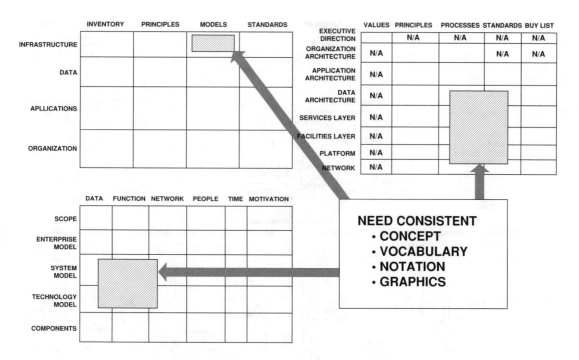

Figure 3.4 **Processing Architecture. The shaded areas approximate the definitional areas for the processing architecture.**

3.10 and Table 3.7 are collected examples from architects. It is interesting to note the high functional level of Figure 3.9, the layered perspective of Figure 3.10, and the "architecture as roles and components" perspective of Table 3.7.

● *Developers*
Developers are those individuals charged with developing specific business applications. They actually have to get something done. Figures 3.11 to 3.14 are collected examples of developer-created architecture diagrams. Note the absence of any similarity between them.

You can easily find other examples by just attending an industry seminar, talking to your vendors, asking your own architects or developers, or reading the I/T industry press.

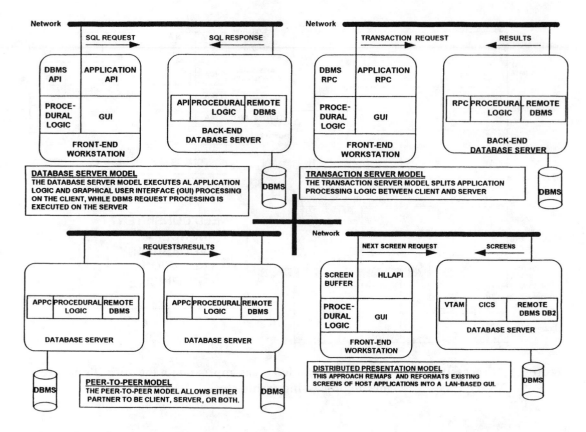

Figure 3.5   Four Faces of Client/Server. This modeling technique shows four models of
client/server computing. (Source: Coopers & Lybrand.)

The Problem with Architecture

Even a cursory view of the architecture drawing methods that have been
presented yields the following critical analysis:

- There is no meaningful notation.

- There is no consistent notation.

- It is not clear what each drawing is trying to communicate and at
what level.

- What does each drawing *mean?* If you gave any one of the drawings
to 12 people, what is the probability of getting two consistent inter-
pretations?

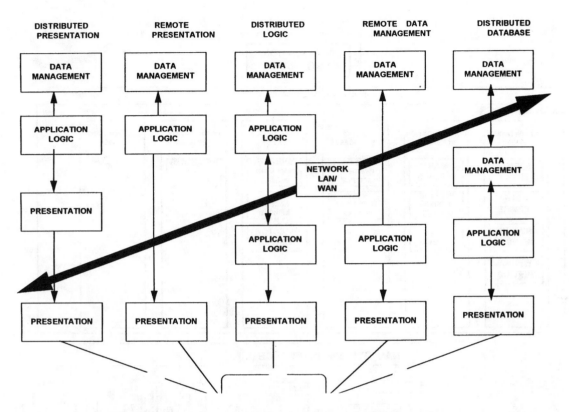

Figure 3.6   Models of Client/Server Computing. This modeling technique illustrates five
models of client/server computing. (Source: Gartner Group.)

- They do not share or state a solid underlying concept of what they are trying to communicate.
- Who is the audience for these drawings?
- Could all of the players in the development arena guide their work by these drawings?
- Can you tell whether the drawings are consistent or correct?
- They focus on applications architecture to the exclusion of the equally important issue of the operations architecture.
- They do not communicate the dynamics of a reach, range, and maneuverable architecture—that is, interoperability, scalability, portability, heterogeneity, and adaptability. They do not animate the way in which the architecture behaves.

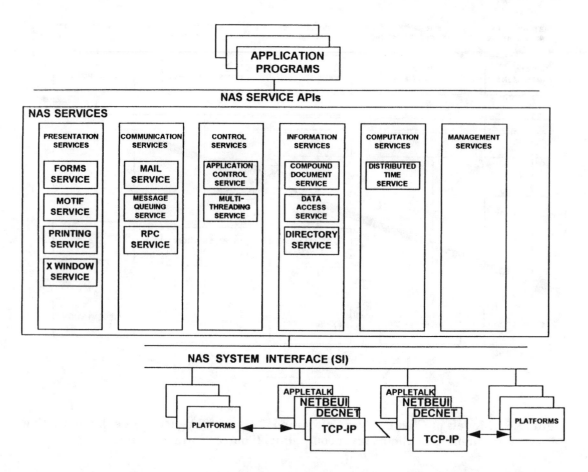

Figure 3.7   DEC NAS Architecture. DEC presents its I/T architecture as sets of APIs and services. (Source: DEC.)

In summary, while they serve the purpose of good bluffs, a masquerade of knowledge, they do not meet the requirements for formal engineering communication through rigorous diagramming methods.

Summary

The critical problem confronting the I/T architect is the absence of any methodology to manage the drawing of network computing architectures (the framework subareas defined in Figure 3.4). Without such a capability, the I/T community engages in a game of bluffing, where everybody nods

LANGUAGES
PROCEDURES LANGUAGE
PROGRAMMING LANGUAGE
APPLICATION GENERATOR
SERVICES
DATABASE QUERY
DIALOG PRESENTATION
COMMUNI-CATIONS
COMMON PROGRAMMING INTERFACE
APPLICATIONS
LANGUAGES
APPL. GENERATORS
QUERY REPORT WRITER
TRANSACTION MNGT
COMM. ACCESS MNGT
DATABASE MNGT
DATA CENTER SYSTEMS MNGT
NETWORK SYSTEMS MNGT
DATA/ STORAGE MNGT
DIALOG MANAGER
INTERACTIVE
JOB ENTRY
SECURITY
SYSTEM CONTROL
S/370 AS/400 PS/2
MOUSE
KEYBOARD
COLOR & EMPHASIS
SCROLLING
DATA ENTRY
SELECTION
MESSAGES
HELP
CUA
CCS
OBJECT CONTENT ARCHITECTURES
DATA STREAMS
APP. SERVICES
SESSION MNGT
NETWORK
DATA LINK CONTROL

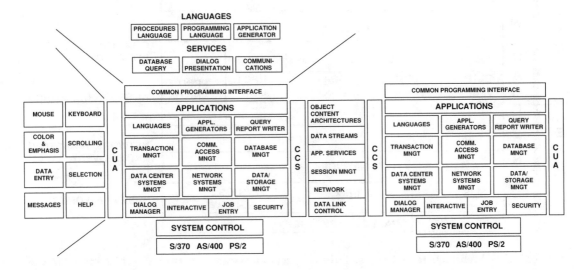

Figure 3.8 IBM SAA Architecture. IBM presents SAA as a layer model. (Source: IBM.)

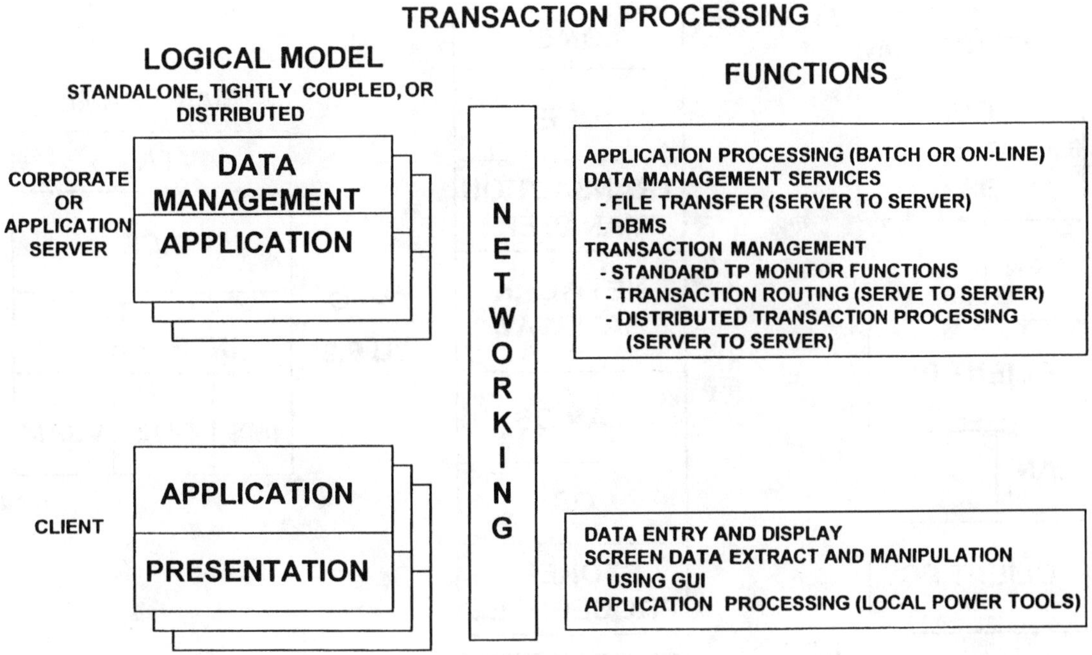

TRANSACTION PROCESSING
LOGICAL MODEL
STANDALONE, TIGHTLY COUPLED, OR DISTRIBUTED
FUNCTIONS
CORPORATE OR APPLICATION SERVER
DATA MANAGEMENT
APPLICATION
NETWORKING
APPLICATION PROCESSING (BATCH OR ON-LINE)
DATA MANAGEMENT SERVICES
- FILE TRANSFER (SERVER TO SERVER)
- DBMS
TRANSACTION MANAGEMENT
- STANDARD TP MONITOR FUNCTIONS
- TRANSACTION ROUTING (SERVE TO SERVER)
- DISTRIBUTED TRANSACTION PROCESSING (SERVER TO SERVER)
CLIENT
APPLICATION
PRESENTATION
DATA ENTRY AND DISPLAY
SCREEN DATA EXTRACT AND MANIPULATION USING GUI
APPLICATION PROCESSING (LOCAL POWER TOOLS)

Figure 3.9 Architecture as Function. This architect views architecture from a functional perspective.

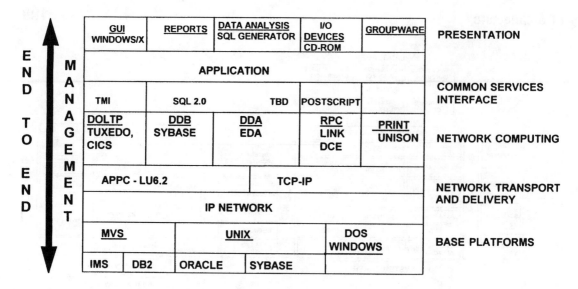

Figure 3.10 Architecture as Layers. This architect views architecture as a layering problem.

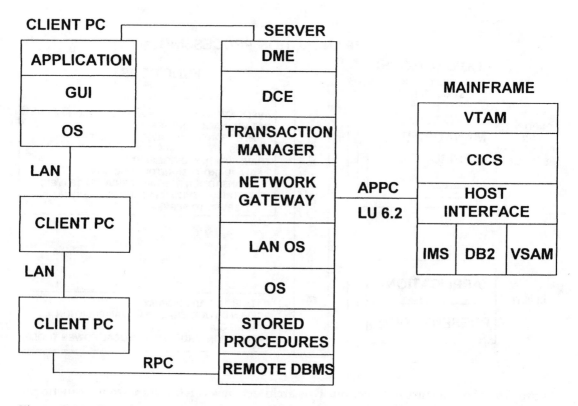

Figure 3.11 Developer Architecture Drawing I. This is an example of a developer's view of a three-tier architecture.

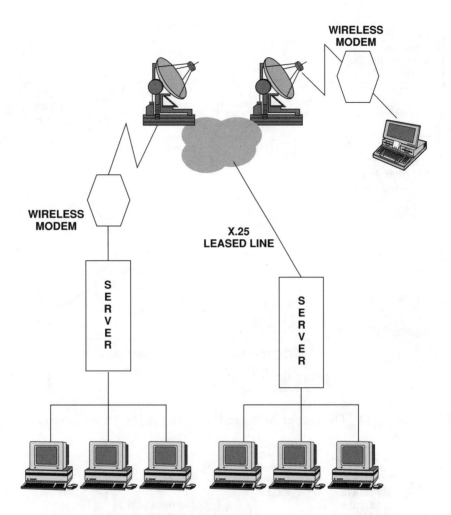

Figure 3.12   Developer Architecture Drawing II. This example
extends the drawing methodology to include wide-area wireless
communication.

in token agreement to some meaningless pseudo-diagramming technique.
If you doubt this, perform a controlled experiment and give the same diagram to a group of people, ask them to interpret it individually, and compare their incompatible answers.

This situation is intolerable. No respectable engineering discipline
would implement anything as sophisticated as client/server computing
without the corequisite availability of a formal drawing method. There
must be a standardized way to understand, communicate, and share

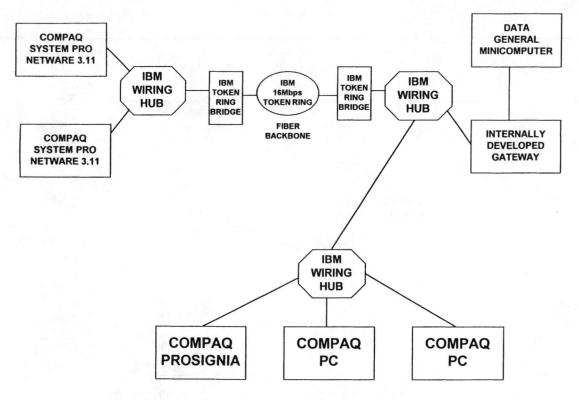

Figure 3.13   Developer Architecture Drawing III. This drawing is from a hospital.

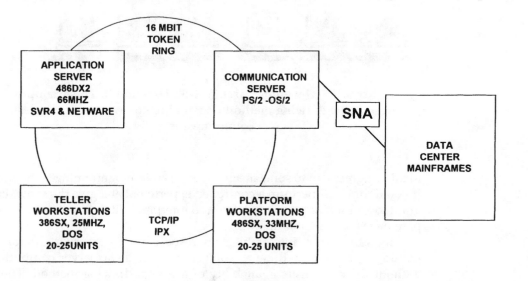

Figure 3.14   Developer Architecture Drawing IV. This drawing is from a bank.

Table 3.7

Diagramming Methodology. This architect envisioned architecture as simply filling in functional roles by computing geography.

End-User Computing Environment			Local Area Network			Workgroup Server			Wide Area Network			Regional Application Server				Mainframe Data Center Server			
HW	OS	Middle-ware	OS	Protocol	HW	OS	Middle-ware	DBMS	Network Layer	Protocol	HW	OS	Network Interface	Middle-ware	DBMS	OS	Network Interface	Middle-ware	DBMS

113

physical processing architectures that balances the needs for simplicity and specificity. We will provide such a method in the next section.

3.3 DIAGRAMMING I/T ARCHITECTURES

The purpose of this section is to provide a formal vocabulary, graphical notation, and textual notation for drawing network computing architectures. The definition of a technique is complicated by the pressing need to balance simplicity and specificity. The proposed technique does this, and may be adopted at the user's discretion to provide more or less detail according to the individual's goals and objectives.

The core problem with modeling reach, range, and maneuverability architectures is similar to the traditional manufacturing product structure or bill of materials problem. Starting with primitives or components, an architecture grows into subassemblies, assemblies, superassemblies, and so forth. With this growth comes the traditional problem of configuration management. What is required in an architectural drawing, then, is to understand what the primitive components are, how those components are assembled into bigger parts, and how those bigger parts are related to still other larger parts.

The proposed methodology will be presented as a set of *notions*. A notion is an explanatory idea. Each notion will be individually explained and integrated with prior notions to set the stage for developing still further notions. In some cases, *asides* will be presented to provide some preparatory ideas to explaining a notion. *Summary notions* will be interjected periodically to summarize the ideas that have been developed.

While the primary benefit of the drawing technique is the ability to communicate client/server architectures unambiguously, it also serves as a step-by-step explanation of a client/server environment. While some readers may be tempted to skip this section, this section may alternatively be viewed as a primer on the elements that compose a client/server environment. It is therefore of equal benefit to those who simply wish to improve their understanding of the nature of client/server computing, regardless of whether they will ever have to create or maintain architectural drawings.

Methodology Overview

Figure 3.15 provides a simplified 20,000-foot overview of an architecture drawing. It may be understood as follows:

1. Configured platforms interoperate with each other. A configured platform is a processor with an operating system on which one or more program layers operate.

2. Program layers are executable programs that are written in one or more languages. If correct design practices are followed, a program layer does only one program function: presentation, processing, or data management.

3. Program layers interoperate with each other through service paths. A service path is a finite set of service calls that can communicate both physically and semantically with a service path on another configured platform.

4. An interoperability path is illustrated by a filled-in circle.

5. An interoperability path has certain attributes, such as the middleware framework used, the slowest speed of the path, whether it

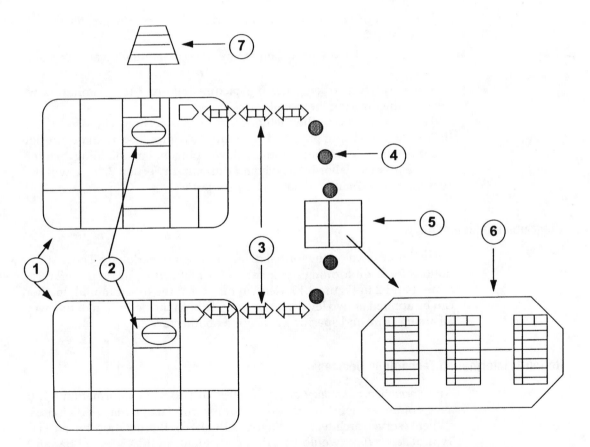

Figure 3.15   Drawing Overview. An architecture drawing shows the configured platforms, service paths, and networking that compose the network computing environment.

supports transactions, and a pointer to a definition of the internetworking used to communicate physically between service paths.

6. An internetworking diagram shows the networking options chosen for each network transversed to connect the service paths.

7. Important resources, such as databases, are identified and related to the program layers and configurations that manage them.

In reading the diagrams:

- Lower-case letters identify variables.
- A "#" indicates a variable number.
- { . . . } indicates a list of 0 to n variables where n is greater than or equal to 1.
- [. . .] indicates a list of 1 to n variables where n is greater than or equal to 2.
- Variables that are irrelevant in any particular situation are left blank.

You may wish to keep the big picture (Figure 3.15) in mind as we develop the drawing methodology.

The presentation of the methodology in this section will assume that the technique is being practiced without any computer-automated design aid. It will be evident that manually developing and maintaining architecture is extremely labor-intensive and difficult. In Section 3.4, we will discuss the requirements for automated support.

Diagramming Methodology

We will now develop the formal diagramming methodology. The first five notions focus on forming the notation for platforms and program layers, items 1 and 2 in Figure 3.15. Keep in mind that the diagramming method can be applied at two levels; it can provide both the definition of the overall architecture and specific application architectures.

Notion 1: Information Technology Devices

An *information technology device* (ITD) is any kind of information appliance, computer, network station, or dumb terminal that may participate in a client/server architecture. Figure 3.16 shows the notation for an ITD. Typical *device types* would be a dumb terminal, an IBM 3090, a PBX, an X terminal, an Apple PDA, an AT&T GIS 3550, or a Teradata DBC.

Notion 2: Platform

A *platform* is an ITD with an associated operating system (if applicable). The processing area of the platform is divided into a "Program Layer Area" and a "Service Area" (both to be explained in Notion 3). Figure 3.17 illustrates a platform.

Notion 3: Program Layers

Any I/T application should be understood as consisting of three basic *program layers* that can interface with each other. These layers are:

1. *Presentation layer (PN):* the layer that handles application logic with regard to collecting, preparing, and presenting data.
2. *Processing layer (PR, a.k.a. function layer):* the layer concerned with application business logic.
3. *Data layer (DT):* the layer concerned with data management (addition, deletion, selection, and modification of data records).

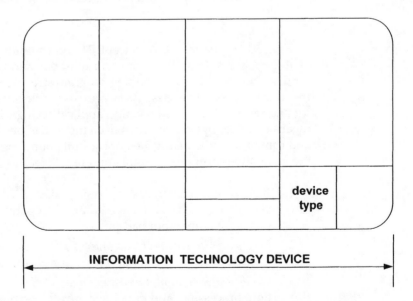

Figure 3.16   Information Technology Device. An ITD is any kind of device that can participate in the client/server environment.

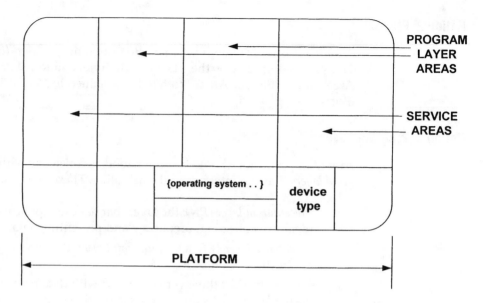

Figure 3.17   Platform. A platform is an ITD with an associated operating system (if applicable) and the partitioning of the computer processing area into program layer areas and service areas.

Figure 3.18 illustrates this concept. This partitioning is the basic structure of all software systems. It positions for reusability and defines opportunities for distribution. While partitioning program structures into these three segments is the best way to design software to enable interoperability, portability, and reconfiguration, in practice, application logic is often bundled. This means that the application codes from more than one layer are intertwined and cannot be separated. When one admits bundling to the layer concept, there are three additional possible program layers, as follows:

1. *Bundled presentation and processing layer (PNPR):* presentation and processing logic is intertwined and inseparable within a program; this is a common but bad practice.

2. *Bundled processing and data layer (PRDT):* processing and data logic is intertwined and inseparable within a program.

3. *Bundled presentation, processing, and data layer (PNPRDT):* presentation, processing, and data logic are all intertwined and inseparable within a program.

A bundled layer (i.e., PNPR) on a platform is not the same thing as two separate PN and PR layers on the same platform. The PNPR layer is one

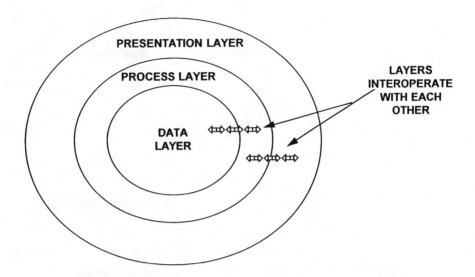

Figure 3.18   Program Layers. Programs consist of presentation, processing, and data layers.

intertwined glob of logic, while the PN and PR layers are individual programs that can be manipulated individually. This is an important distinction, because it vastly influences scaleability, portability, and reconfigurability.

While modern program practices rule against implementing bundled layers, it is necessary to include their structures in order to deal with mainframe legacy designs. It should also be understood that data logic services are normally provided by third-party DBMS products. Consequently, PNPRDT layers are extraordinarily rare, and PRDT layers are reserved for object-oriented databases that include methods. Applications normally interface to a DT layer through a vendor-provided application program interface (API). We will ignore PNPRDT layers from this point forward.

Notion 4: Configuration

A *configuration* is a platform on which 1 to *n* program layers are executing. A given program layer type may exist 1 to *n* times for 1 to *n* different applications. Figure 3.19 illustrates the notation for a program layer on a configuration. The variables are as follows:

- *Layer type:* identifies the type of layer (i.e. PN, PR, DT, PNPR, or PRDT).

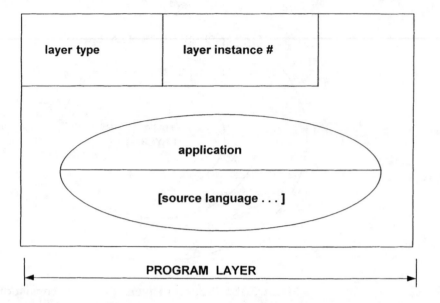

Figure 3.19   Program Layer Notation. Program layer notation identifies the type of layer, the instance number of the layer on the configuration, the name of the application, and the source languages that compose the application.

- *Layer instance #:* an integer that uniquely identifies this layer on this configuration (i.e., layer 7). It has no significance other than as a unique numeric identifier.
- *Application:* the name of the application running in this layer.
- *Source language:* a list of the source languages from which this application is built (i.e., C, COBOL, C++, BASIC, etc.).

Program layers from 1 to *n* execute on a configuration in the "Program Layer Area," as shown in Figure 3.20. While a configuration inherits variables from its defining platform, the following additional variables are also defined:

- *Configuration instances #:* indicates the number of instances of this configuration in the architecture.
- *Geography:* indicates where this configuration is geographically located.
- *Tier #:* indicates the architecture tier of this configuration. A typical four-tier architecture would be as follows:

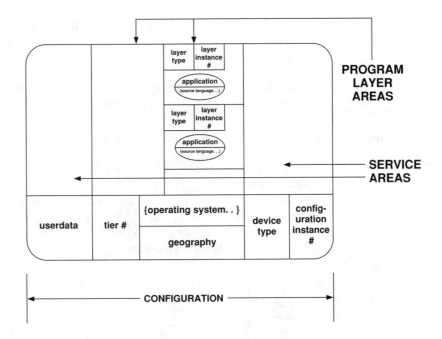

Figure 3.20   Configuration. A configuration consists of 1 to *n* program layers and configuration-dependent variables.

1. *Tier 1:* mobile (nomadic) information technology devices.
2. *Tier 2:* desktop information technology devices.
3. *Tier 3:* departmental, workgroup, or campus processing and data servers.
4. *Tier 4:* corporate processing and data servers.

- *Userdata:* to be populated with any data the user would like about the configuration (or its platform and ITD building blocks). Possibilities could include MIP rating, storage capacity, or mean time to failure and mean time to repair statistics.

A configuration diagram must exist for each information technology device within the architecture. Nonprogrammable information technology devices do not have any program layers.

Notion 5: Building Block Configurations

There are five *building block configurations* for any platform (i.e., a PN, PR, DT, PNPR, and PRDT set of program layers). Any other configuration can be built by joining the building block configurations as many times as necessary. Figure 3.21 illustrates this idea. This idea is important later because it means that from only this relatively small set of configurations per platform, one can create any and all configurations by creating as many joins as needed. One therefore only has to be concerned with designing interoperability around these basic configurations.

Summary Notion 1

We have now completed the notation scheme for building configurations (items 1 and 2 on Figure 3.15) and their constituent elements (information technology devices, platforms, and program layers). We will now turn our attention to developing the ideas surrounding service paths (item 3 on Figure 3.15). *Service paths* are the vehicle through which program layers on different configurations interoperate.

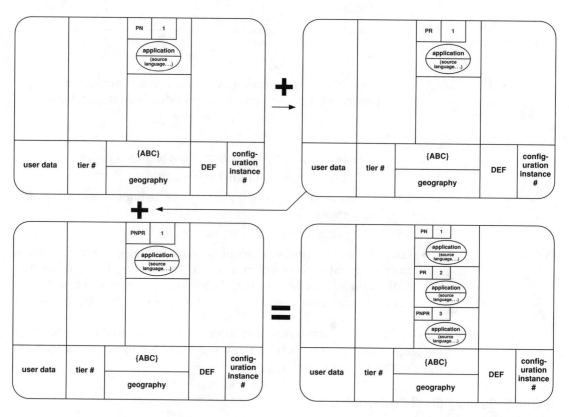

Figure 3.21   Configuration Joints. For a given platform, all configurations can be developed by joints involving the basic five program layers.

Aside 1

A fundamental software idea, especially prevalent in networking computing, is that application programs confine their interest to the business application. When they have need of major software functions, they invoke them through service requests. The service (transaction management, data access, messaging, electronic data interchange, etc.) is invoked through a standardized application program interface (API), or by knowledge of a protocol format. The service interface hides the inherent complexity of delivering the service to the requesting program layer, makes the program layer dependent only on the interface, and most important with network computing, hides all the interoperability issues. When a whole set of services is so bundled to deliver rich interoperability services to a program layer, the overall service is called *middleware*. Middleware must embrace two service paths and make them interoperable.

Notion 6: Services

A program layer avails itself of major software function by invoking services. A service request consists of four components, as follows (see Figure 3.22):

1. *Service type:* identifies a unique class of service. Table 3.8 provides a list of types of services.
2. *Service interface:* identifies the interface that is being invoked. For example, for a service type of transaction management (TM), possible interfaces could include:
   - CICS Embedded Language
   - IMS Call Interface
   - IDMS Embedded Language
   - Cooperation API
   - ATMI
   - Tuxedo API
3. *Service interface level:* an interface may be defined at one of three levels of transparency in the following order of increasing transparency:
   - *L1:* the networking protocol and location of the invoked program layer must be known.
   - *L2:* only the location of the invoked program layer must be known.
   - *L3:* neither protocol or location need be known. This is ideal for later reconfiguration of the architecture.

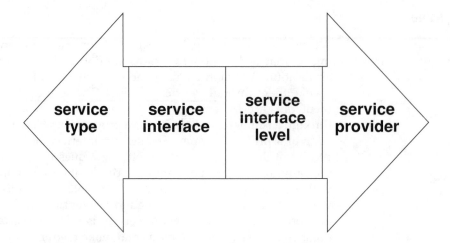

Figure 3.22   Service Structure. A service is defined by four attributes.

4. *Service provider:* identifies the software that provides the service interface. For example, the Cooperation API is provided by the Cooperation product from AT&T, and the ATMI interface is provided by Tuxedo.

Figure 3.23 show the data-entity relationship among the components that compose a service request. It may be understood as follows:

- A service type is manifested through multiple service interfaces. A service interface supports one service type.
- A service interface exists at one service interface level. A service interface level is shared by many service interfaces.
- A service interface is provided by a service provider. A service provider may provide multiple service interfaces.

The same service provider can support multiple service interfaces concurrently for the same service type. This situation is common when a service supports both a proprietary legacy API and a new standard API. This is the case with Tuxedo, which supports the old Tuxedo API and the standard ATMI interface. Figure 3.24 shows a modified version of Figure 3.22 to illustrate this situation. This notation is used only for economy of notation; the same result could be as readily achieved by having two services connect to the program layer area with the same service type but different service interfaces. In our examples, we will avoid this notation.

Table 3.8
Service Types. Program layers invoke services to access
needed functionality.

Service Types	Service
TM	Transaction Management Services
CI	Communication Services
RPC	Remote Procedure Call Services
DA	Data Access Services
OS	Operating System Services
TE	Terminal Emulation Services
OP	Output Services
UI	User Interface
TR	Transport Services
EDI	Electronic Data Interchange Services
MSG	Messaging Services
FT	File Transfer Services

Notion 7: Service Paths

A service may invoke from 0 to n other services recursively. This means that a service, in turn, may require utilization of another service. The service invoked directly by the program layer is called the *header service*. A concatenated string of services is called a *service path*. Figure 3.25 illustrates three examples. Figure 3.25a shows a *simple service path* (only one service call path). Figure 3.25b shows a *complex service path* (multiple service paths emanate from the header service). The thin vertical bar in Figure 3.25b should be read as an "or." The notation shown in Figure 3.25b is for economy of space, and could just as well be shown as two separate simple service paths.

In some cases, a service needs to invoke another service to perform a reference function (i.e., directory service, security service, etc.) before proceeding forward toward interoperability. We call this an "and" service path. This means that the invoking service invokes this service *and* returns to complete the simple or complex service path. As shown in Figure 3.25c, the "and" service path is denoted by a thick vertical line. The notions of simple service paths, complex service paths, and "and" service paths are recursive and may be intermixed as required.

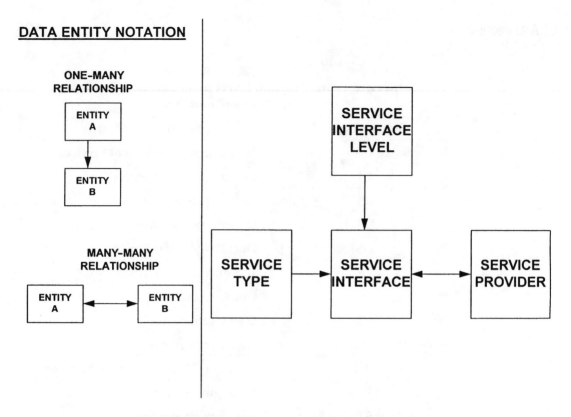

Figure 3.23 Service Component Relationship Structure. The attributes of a service exist in a complicated set of relationships to each other.

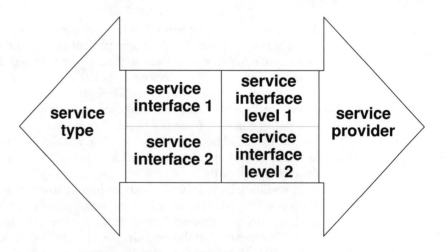

Figure 3.24 Modified Service Structure. The service structure illustrated in Figure 3.22 may be modified to support the case where a service provider provides two service interfaces for a service type.

Notion 8: Service Path Interoperability

A service path may or may not involve interoperability. A service path that doesn't require interoperability with other program layers (on the same or other configuration) is called an *insular service path*. They may be drawn if the service is of prime importance, but in general, they are not material to the subject at hand, and drawing clutter can be minimized by ignoring them. Recall that the essence of reach, range, and maneuverability is in scaleability, interoperability, portability, reconfigurability, and adaptability. None of these is manifested by insular service paths.

A service path that requires interoperability is called an *interoperability service path*. An interoperability service path requires a *service prefix* before

(A): A SIMPLE SERVICE PATH

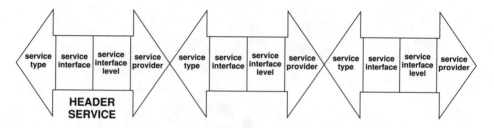

(B): A COMPLEX SERVICE PATH

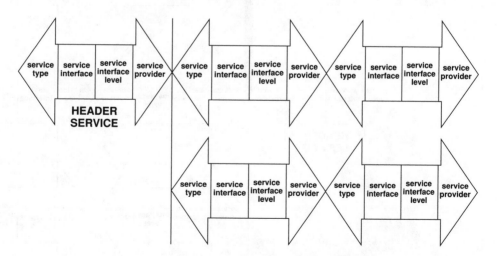

Figure 3.25   Service Paths. A service may recursively invoke other services to create a simple or complicated service path.

(C): AN AND SIMPLE SERVICE PATH

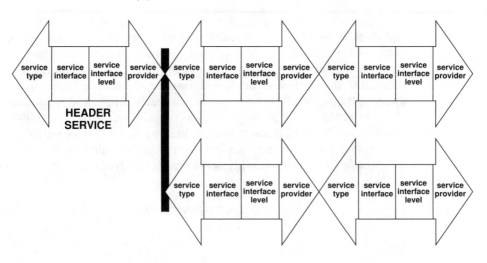

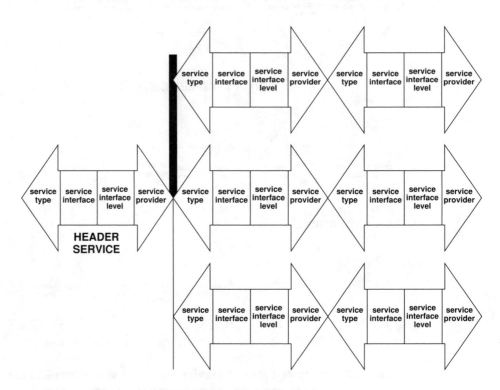

Figure 3.25   (*Continued*)

the header service. This is shown in Figure 3.26. This prefix is required whether the interoperability occurs between program layers on the same configuration or between program layers on different configurations.

The attributes of a service prefix are as follows:

- *Interoperability domain:* program layers may interoperate with each other only within defined execution domains. A domain defines an interoperable execution space. A program layer may interoperate within multiple domains concurrently. When two service paths interoperate, they must share a domain, or interoperability cannot take place.

- *Interoperability role:* a program layer invokes a service with an intended interoperability role. The permitted roles are:
  - *CL:* client
  - *SR:* server
  - *CLSR:* client or server
  - *PE:* peer
  - *SD:* sender (in a file transfer sense)
  - *RR:* receiver (in a file transfer sense)

For two service paths to interoperate, they must share a pair of permitted interoperability roles, as shown in Table 3.9. In invoking a service path, a program layer may have more than one choice of role consistent with the capabilities defined by the header service.

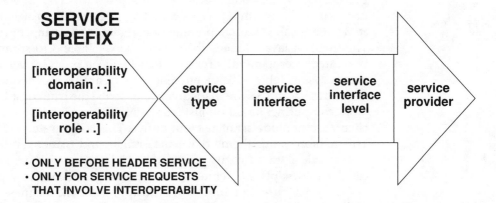

Figure 3.26   Service Prefix. Service paths that involve interoperability between program layers require a service prefix before the header service.

Notion 9: Associating Program Layers to Service Paths

Each service path is associated with its invoking program layer (Figure 3.27). The service prefix is placed next to the invoking program layer, and the service path extends into and through, if necessary, the service area.

Summary Notion 2

Figure 3.28 shows what two configurations with associated service paths would look like. This completes item 3 on Figure 3.15. We turn our attention to investigating how these service paths connect physically and semantically to permit interoperability.

Aside 2

An interoperability event is shown by a series of darkened circles between the end services of the two service paths. This is shown as item 4 in Figure 3.15. There are many issues that surround defining a permitted interoperability event, and they will be developed in following notions. The descriptors of the interoperability event are described using a *middleware box* (item 5 in Figure 3.15) and an *internetworking definition drawing* (item 6 in Figure 3.15).

Notion 10: Interoperability

Program layers may interoperate with each other only though service paths in certain permissible combinations. When a program layer interacts with another instance of the same type of program layer, it is a *distributed interoperability event,* and it is called distributed presentation, distributed processing, or distributed data. When a program layer interacts with an instance of a program layer of a different type, it is a *remote interoperability event*, and is called remote presentation, remote processing, or remote data. The invoked layer defines the remote "xxx." Table 3.10 summarizes the permitted interoperability relationships between program layers and their names. Using Table 3.10 as a reference, it is clear that the models presented in Figures 3.5 and 3.6 are inadequate to describe the true complexity of network computing. Based on just using PN, PR, and DT layers, there are 32 client/server models, not just four or five. This is illustrated in Figure 3.29.[3] This reinforces our theme that reach, range, and maneuverable architectures, while extraordinarily powerful and advantage-rich, are very complicated, and disciplined architecture engineering is needed to support them.

Figure 3.29 provides another way to appreciate the business maneuverability provided by a reach, range, and maneuverability architecture. An application, like water that molds itself to the shape of the container, can configure itself in any of the 32 ways. If you had 32 branch offices, each could run the same application, but on the specific architecture that was appropriate to each. It is from this versatility that the great advantage of network computing grows. Having chosen an architecture, as business circumstances evolve, the application can nimbly reconfigure itself to better serve the emerging needs. So a reach, range, and maneuverability architecture conveys business advantage by adapting itself to the business, rather than requiring the business to adapt itself to the architecture.

Summary Notion 3

The first three conditions of interoperability are as follows:

1. The two program layers are a valid pair of layers (Table 3.10).
2. The two program layers share a common interoperability domain (Notion 8).
3. The two program layers share a valid pair of interoperability roles (Table 3.9).

We will next explain the middleware box (Figure 3.15, item 5), which completes the interoperability description between the two program layers.

Notion 11: Middleware Box

The middleware box further describes the conditions of interoperability, as follows (see Figure 3.30):

Table 3.9
Interoperability Roles. Interoperability may occur only between service paths with permitted interoperability combinations.

	CL	SR	CLSR	PE	SD	RR
CL		X	X			
SR	X		X			
CLSR	X	X	X			
PE				X		
SD						X
RR					X	

- *Middleware:* defines the middleware framework that oversees the connection between the program layers. Table 3.11 describes the classes of middleware and specific frameworks for each class. The middleware framework testifies to the validity of the two service paths to work with each other.

- *Transaction support:* indicates whether this interoperability event supports transactions. A transaction is a unit of work that meets the ACID test. The acid test states that for a unit of work to be a transaction, it must meet each of the following conditions:

   1. *Atomicity:* either the entire unit of work is completed or none of it is done.

   2. *Consistency:* the object of the unit of work either moves from one consistent state to another consistent state or remains in the original state.

   3. *Insulation:* the unit of work executes as though it were the only unit of work executing.

   4. *Durability:* once the unit of work is completed, the consequences of the unit of work are, in fact, the new reality.

   Transaction support applies primarily, though not exclusively, to database updates ("Begin Work," "Commit Work," and "Abort" type commands), and the ability of the middleware to support transactions is fundamental to the design of on-line transaction processing systems, operation support systems, and business process automation systems. Transaction support is indicated by the phrase "T=Yes" or "T=No."

- *Networking speed range:* indicates the lowest and the highest speeds for the set of networks that transactions will transverse in this interoperability event. Unlike in traditional host-centered computing, where transactions generally transversed one wide area network, in network computing it is common for a transaction to transverse a set of networks (a local area network, a backbone network, one or more wide area networks, a backbone network, and finally another local area network). Each network may have different transmission speeds (see Figure 3.31), and speed is fundamental to application design.

   This cell is populated with the lowest and highest network speeds for the internetworking. The next cell, *internetworking diagram,* gives the name of a specific diagram that shows the internetworking used and the associated speed of each individual network. The network speed range is customarily expressed in Kbps or Mbps.

- *Internetworking diagram:* is the name of a separate diagram that shows the sequence of networks transversed in completing this interoperability event. Notion 12 will explain this diagram.

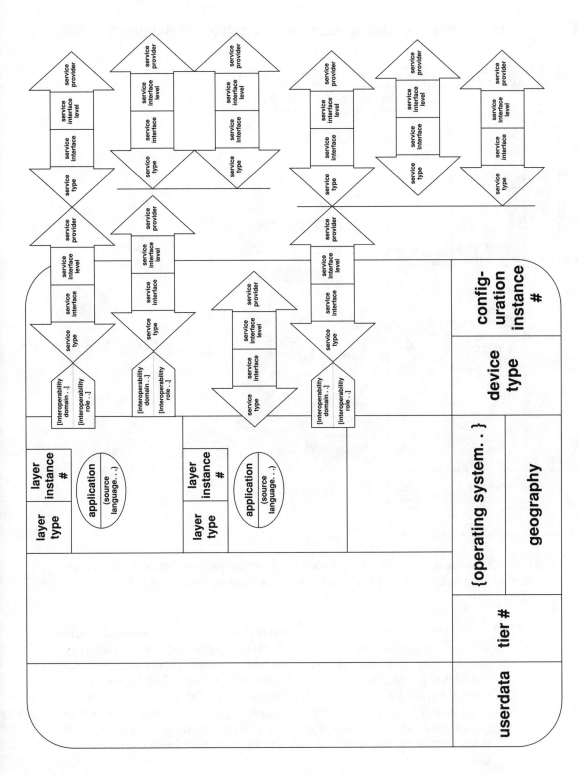

Figure 3.27   Associating Service Paths with Program Layers. The service prefix is placed next to the invoking program layer, and the service path extends into and through the service area.

133

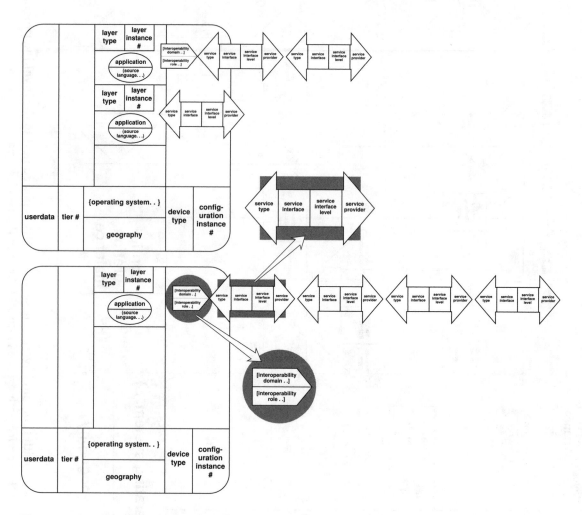

Figure 3.28   Configurations with Service Paths. The program layer on each configuration has an interoperability service path, but how do they interoperate?

The middleware box is the central information source about the rules for data exchange. Together with the service paths and the internetworking diagram, it is asserting that the two program layers can exchange data both physically and semantically. When multiple program layers from multiple configurations all interoperate and share the same middleware box definition, all the interoperability paths can junction at the single middleware box. This eliminates clutter, improves visualization of interoperability, and makes it easier to append additional configurations later.

Aside 3

A communication network is a collection of communication equipment and other media that, as an autonomous whole, permits data exchange between information technology devices. The OSI reference model (Table 3.12) is a layered set of generic functions that every network must fulfill. The lower levels, levels 1 to 4, define the network interface. The higher levels, levels 5 to 7, define the application interface. With the move to reach, range, and maneuverability architectures from host-centered architectures, the networking environment is being evolved from one of a single wide area network to one of internetworking, where a transaction must transverse multiple networks to get from one configuration to another (see Figure 3.32). Because networking is extremely complicated and we wish to balance simplicity of diagramming versus specificity, we will suggest a diagramming methodology to portray internetworking with the following two constraints:

- Any communication devices whose functions are primarily internetworking, routing, translation, signal amplification, or efficiency will

Table 3.10
Permitted Interoperability between Program Layers. This table
identifies permitted interoperability between program layers.

						PNPR		PRDT	
			PN	PR	DT	PN	PR	PR	DT
Invoking Program Layer		PN	DPN	RPR	N/A	DPN	RPR	RPR	N/A
		PR	RPN	DPR	RDT	RPN	DPR	DPR	RDT
		DT	N/A	RPR	DDT	N/A	RPR	RPR	DDT
	PNPR	PN	DPN	RPR	N/A	DPN	RPR	RPR	N/A
		PR	RPN	DPR	RDT	RPN	DPR	DPR	RDT
	PRDT	PR	RPN	DPR	RDT	RPN	DPR	DPR	RDT
		DT	N/A	RPR	DDT	N/A	RPR	RPR	DDT
Legend			DPN: Distributed Presentation DPR: Distributed Processing DDT: Distributed Data N/A: Not Applicable				RPN: Remote Presentation RPR: Remote Processing RDT: Remote Data		

ARCHITECTURE DESCRIPTION   ARCHITECTURE ILLUSTRATION

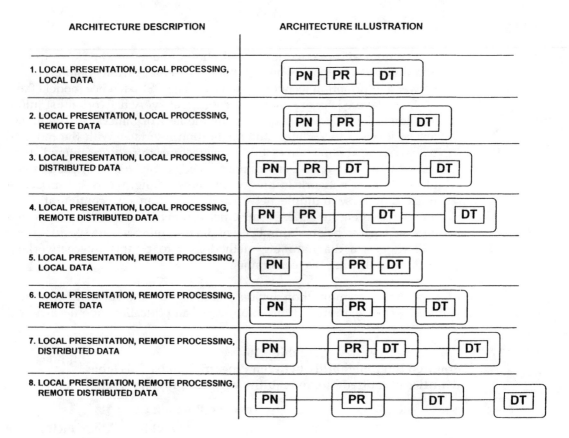

ARCHITECTURE DESCRIPTION
1. LOCAL PRESENTATION, LOCAL PROCESSING, LOCAL DATA
2. LOCAL PRESENTATION, LOCAL PROCESSING, REMOTE DATA
3. LOCAL PRESENTATION, LOCAL PROCESSING, DISTRIBUTED DATA
4. LOCAL PRESENTATION, LOCAL PROCESSING, REMOTE DISTRIBUTED DATA
5. LOCAL PRESENTATION, REMOTE PROCESSING, LOCAL DATA
6. LOCAL PRESENTATION, REMOTE PROCESSING, REMOTE DATA
7. LOCAL PRESENTATION, REMOTE PROCESSING, DISTRIBUTED DATA
8. LOCAL PRESENTATION, REMOTE PROCESSING, REMOTE DISTRIBUTED DATA

Figure 3.29   Client/Server Models. There are 32 basic client/server models, not 4 or 5 as previously indicated.

not be shown. Specifically, we will not illustrate routers, brouters, bridges, modems, codecs, hubs, concentrators, or front end processors (FEPS).

- We will be interested in understanding the sequence of networks transversed at the network interface level of the OSI model. Most important, we will be interested in level 3, the Network Layer, which defines the type of network being transversed. The specific networking protocols used will be mapped to the OSI model for diagramming purposes.

We wish to capture the sequence of networks transversed, the types of networks they are, and their speed.

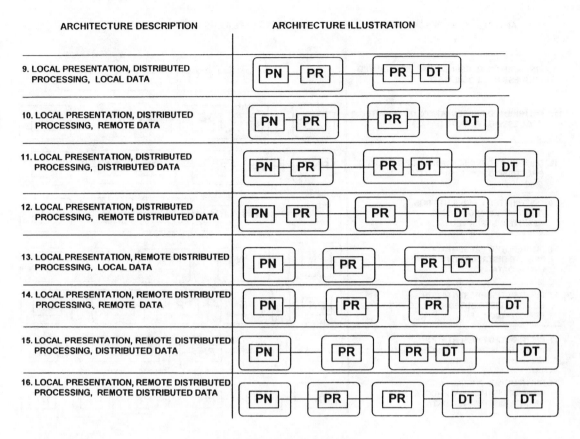

ARCHITECTURE DESCRIPTION   ARCHITECTURE ILLUSTRATION

9. LOCAL PRESENTATION, DISTRIBUTED
   PROCESSING, LOCAL DATA

10. LOCAL PRESENTATION, DISTRIBUTED
    PROCESSING, REMOTE DATA

11. LOCAL PRESENTATION, DISTRIBUTED
    PROCESSING, DISTRIBUTED DATA

12. LOCAL PRESENTATION, DISTRIBUTED
    PROCESSING, REMOTE DISTRIBUTED DATA

13. LOCAL PRESENTATION, REMOTE DISTRIBUTED
    PROCESSING, LOCAL DATA

14. LOCAL PRESENTATION, REMOTE DISTRIBUTED
    PROCESSING, REMOTE DATA

15. LOCAL PRESENTATION, REMOTE DISTRIBUTED
    PROCESSING, DISTRIBUTED DATA

16. LOCAL PRESENTATION, REMOTE DISTRIBUTED
    PROCESSING, REMOTE DISTRIBUTED DATA

Figure 3.29 (*Continued*)

Notion 12: Internetworking Diagram

It is desirable to portray the sequence of networks that the transaction will transverse (see the right side of Figure 3.32). This will be done as follows:

- A network diagram (Figure 3.33a) is used to describe any individual network. The variables are as follows:
  - *Network name:* the internal name given to the network. By this, we do not mean its generic name, but the appellation given to the network as its internal business identifier.
  - *Network speed:* the speed at which transactions transverse the network, in Mbps or Kbps.

ARCHITECTURE DESCRIPTION   ARCHITECTURE ILLUSTRATION

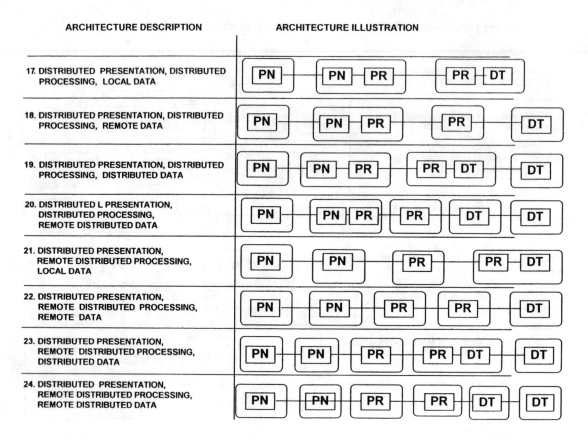

17. DISTRIBUTED PRESENTATION, DISTRIBUTED PROCESSING, LOCAL DATA

18. DISTRIBUTED PRESENTATION, DISTRIBUTED PROCESSING, REMOTE DATA

19. DISTRIBUTED PRESENTATION, DISTRIBUTED PROCESSING, DISTRIBUTED DATA

20. DISTRIBUTED L PRESENTATION, DISTRIBUTED PROCESSING, REMOTE DISTRIBUTED DATA

21. DISTRIBUTED PRESENTATION, REMOTE DISTRIBUTED PROCESSING, LOCAL DATA

22. DISTRIBUTED PRESENTATION, REMOTE DISTRIBUTED PROCESSING, REMOTE DATA

23. DISTRIBUTED PRESENTATION, REMOTE DISTRIBUTED PROCESSING, DISTRIBUTED DATA

24. DISTRIBUTED PRESENTATION, REMOTE DISTRIBUTED PROCESSING, REMOTE DISTRIBUTED DATA

Figure 3.29   (*Continued*)

- *User data:* any information the user would like to document about the network (e.g., LAN operating system, LAN topology, network reliability measures, etc.).
- *Transport layer:* the name of the transport solution (e.g., Netbios, IPS/SPX, or TCP).
- *Network layer:* the name of the network solution (e.g., IP, x.25, NCP, or FDDI).
- *Link layer:* the name of the link layer solution (e.g., 802.x or SDLC).
- *Physical layer:* the name of the physical layer solution (e.g., RS449, FDDI physical interface, or RS232).

This defines the characteristics of a network. The definition of the transport and network layers is particularly important (the link and

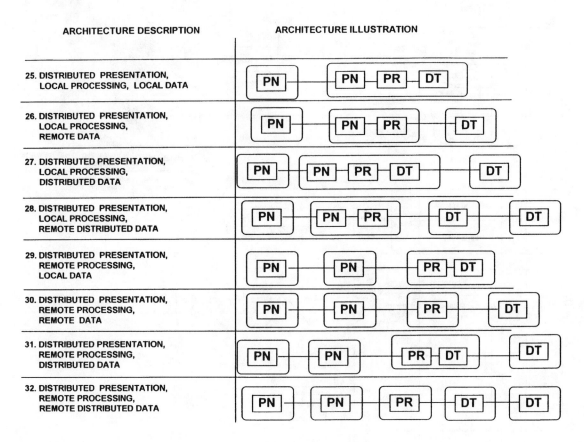

Figure 3.29   (*Continued*)

physical layers much less so), because they define the type of network (e.g., X.25 packet switching, SNA, ATM, etc.).

- An internetworking diagram (see Figure 3.33b) is simply an ordered set of network diagrams where a straight line is used to connect networks.

It is not uncommon for a network to encapsulate another network's protocols within it. It creates a virtual network, appearing to use one set of OSI layers while it is physically operating at a different level. We are interested in the appearance layers.

A few points about internetworking diagrams:

- If the internetworking diagram becomes clumsy to draw because of the large number of networks being transversed, draw only the

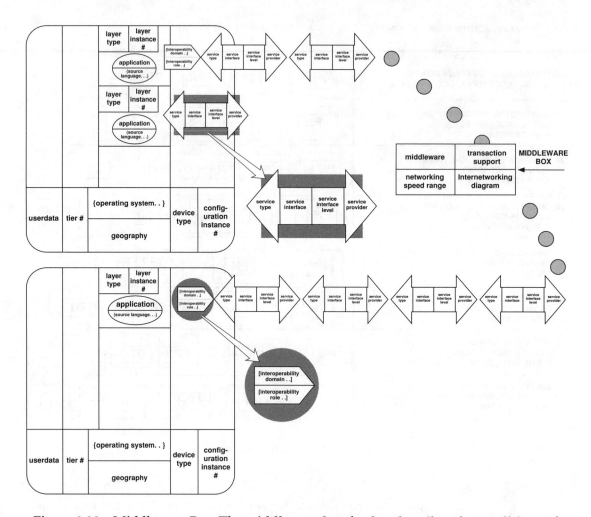

Figure 3.30   **Middleware Box. The middleware box further describes the conditions of the interoperability between the two program layers.**

end networks (the networks that interface with the service paths) and the slowest network and the fastest network in between. Use dotted points between the networks to indicate that networks are missing.

- If part of the internetworking is unknown (externally addressed electronic mail, electronic data exchange, etc.), draw as many of the networks as you know and end the drawing with dotted points to indicate that networks are missing.

Table 3.11
Middleware. There are multiple classes of middleware and for each
class there are multiple products.

Middleware Classification	Exemplary Frameworks
Distributed File Systems	RFS, NFS
Messaging	VIM, MAPI, CC:MAIL, AOCE, CMC, X.400 (MHS)
Distributed Function (Processing)	RPC, DCE (RPC), APPC, SOCKETS
Distributed Database	DRDA, OBDC, RDA, EDA/SQL, ODAPI, SQL-ACCESS
Distributed Transactions	X/Open-ATMI, Tuxedo, Transacrc, Top-End
Object Request Brokers	COBRA
Mainframe Message Switching	MSC, ISSC
Distributed Presentation	X Windows
Directory Services	X.500
Terminal Emulation	3270 Emulation, Async Terminal Emulation
File Transfer	FTAM
Network Management	CMIS, SNMP, Netview, DME
OSI Transport Level Interface	IPX/SPX, Netbios, UNIX TLI
Telephony	AT&T/Novell Telephony Interface
EDI	X.12
Intraprocessor Interoperability	DDE, OLE, UNIX IPC (messages, semaphores, shared memory, named pipes)

- For interoperability between program layers on the same configuration, the internetworking diagram reduces to a network diagram and places the interprocess communication option used (e.g., messages, shared memory, named pipes, etc.) in the network cell.

- The *internetworking diagram* is purposefully drawn as a separate diagram (this makes it a *part*). It may be pointed to by many different *middleware boxes* that use the same internetworking.

Notion 13: Service Path Length

As stated before, a service path is a set of services invoked by a program layer. Generally, service paths terminate with the diagramming of the OSI Layer 7 service (see Table 3.12). Typical Layer 7 services are file transfer, distributed transaction management, electronic mail, and remote or distributed data access. It is not uncommon for one Layer 7 service to invoke another Layer 7 service—for instance, a distributed transaction management service may invoke an RPC service. The absolute final level of a service path specification is to the interface to the Level 4 Transport Layer. Most service paths can be defined with the specification of no more than two or three services, and often only one, if the program layer is directly invoking the Level 7 Application Level interface.

Table 3.12
OSI Reference Model. The OSI model provides a reference through which
any network can be described.

	Layer Number	Layer Name	Layer Definition
Application Interface	7	Application	User level formats, interfaces, and procedures for application interfacing.
	6	Presentation	Management of entry, exchange, display, and control of data.
	5	Session	Session administration services, control of data exchange, and synchronization operations.
Network Interface	4	Transport	Transfer of data between sessions.
	3	Network	Form and route packets across networks.
	2	Link	Data flow initialization, control, termination, and recovery.
	1	Physical	Electrical and mechanical interfaces to communication media.

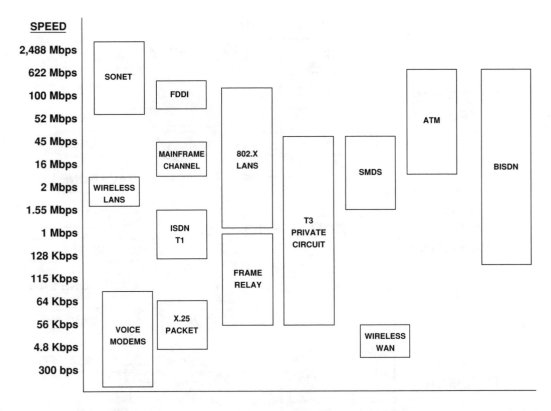

Figure 3.31 Network Speeds. As information is exchanged between configurations, the transactions may transverse multiple networks, all of which may transmit at strikingly different speeds.

Summary Notion 4

This completes the discussion of internetworking, item 6 on Figure 3.15. The conditions of interoperability are, then, as follows:

1. The two program layers are a valid pair of layers.
2. The two program layers share a common interoperability domain.
3. The two program layers share a valid pair of interoperability roles.
4. There exists a middleware box that validates the service paths.
5. There exists an internetworking diagram that supports both physical and semantic connectivity between the participating program layers.

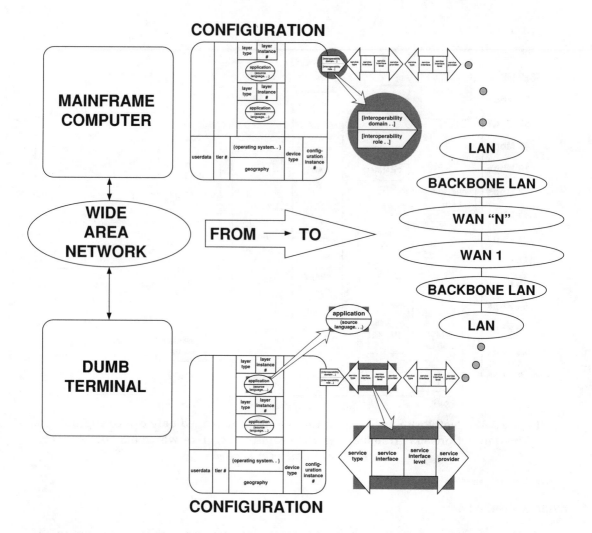

Figure 3.32   Internetworking. In the future, transactions will routinely transverse multiple networks.

The interoperability path starting on one configuration with a service prefix, continuing with a service path, a middleware box, and an internetworking diagram, and ending on another platform with a service path and a service prefix is called an *end-to-end service path*.

We will next discuss item 7, network resource, from Figure 3.15.

Notion 14: Network Resource

A network resource is any type of resource that you wish to emphasize in the drawing. The most prevalent type of resource is a database. By diagramming database servers, one can visually ascertain where data servers are positioned and what resource manager or database manager controls them. Figure 3.34a shows the notation for a resource. The variables are as follows:

- *Resource type:* the type of resource (e.g., database, color printer, etc.).
- *Resource name:* the business name of the resource (e.g., employee database).
- *Layer instance number:* the number of the program layer on the owning configuration that controls the resource (see Notion 4).
- *{commit group name . . . }:* the names of two-phase commit groups that this resource belongs to. This supports identifying which databases participate in two-phase commits.

Figure 3.34b shows an alternative notation specifically for a database resource.

Notion 15: Systems Operations

There are two architectures that operate and interact concurrently: the application architecture and the systems management architecture. We refer to systems management—those functions that administer, manage, and operate the computing environment—as *operations, administration, and management (OA&M)*. Table 3.13 summarizes the typical OA&M functions at the platform and application levels. A business application is not usable if is not operable; equal attention must be paid to the design of the production operations architecture that provides network computing-oriented OA&M services.

Figure 3.35 restates Figure 3.17, showing the program layer areas and the service areas, but makes the important additional statement that the right program layer and service areas are exclusively reserved for the application architecture, while the left program layer area and service areas are exclusively reserved for illustrating the OA&M architecture. You may have noticed that in all the examples since Figure 3.17, the program layers and service paths have been shown on the right. This was not an accident; they were application program layers and service paths. The bifurcation of the program layers and the service areas into strict application and OA&M segments makes the function of layers and service paths immediately discernible, and also permits the easier creation of separate

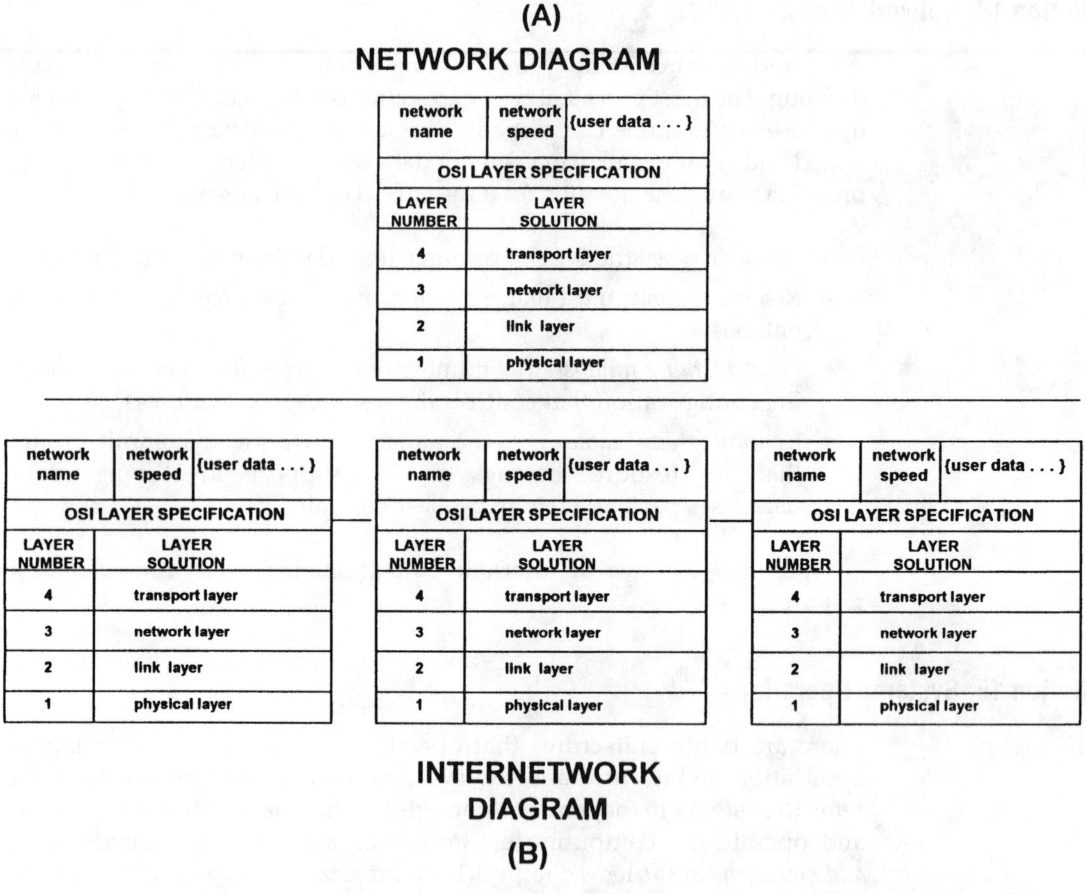

(A)
NETWORK DIAGRAM

network name	network speed	{user data . . . }
OSI LAYER SPECIFICATION		
LAYER NUMBER	LAYER SOLUTION	
4	transport layer	
3	network layer	
2	link layer	
1	physical layer	

network name	network speed	{user data . . . }
OSI LAYER SPECIFICATION		
LAYER NUMBER	LAYER SOLUTION	
4	transport layer	
3	network layer	
2	link layer	
1	physical layer	

network name	network speed	{user data . . . }
OSI LAYER SPECIFICATION		
LAYER NUMBER	LAYER SOLUTION	
4	transport layer	
3	network layer	
2	link layer	
1	physical layer	

network name	network speed	{user data . . . }
OSI LAYER SPECIFICATION		
LAYER NUMBER	LAYER SOLUTION	
4	transport layer	
3	network layer	
2	link layer	
1	physical layer	

INTERNETWORK DIAGRAM

(B)

Figure 3.33   Internetworking Diagram. An internetworking diagram is a sequence of network diagrams that shows the ordered paths of networks transversed between communicating program layers.

architecture diagrams as desired. It is important to recognize that since OA&M support is needed to run the business applications, and since the business applications have a quest to achieve ever greater reach, range, and maneuverability, it is important that the OA&M services also strive for perfect reach, range, and maneuverability so that they can adapt in effortless harmony with the business applications.

Figure 3.36 shows an architecture drawing that includes OA&M services. OA&M program layers and application layers may or may not interoperate, based on the definition of roles, domains, service paths, and middleware. Generally, the program layers that perform OA&M services

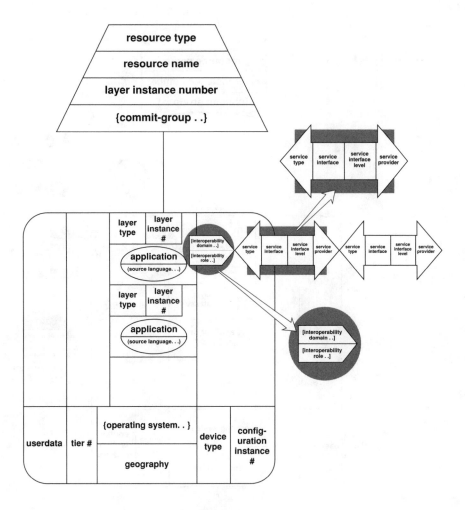

(a): Any Resource

Figure 3.34   **Network Resource. Databases are the most common type
of diagrammed network resource.**

are referred to as monitoring agents or element monitors. They are illustrated using the exact same notation as application program layers, except of course that they are positioned on the left to distinguish their function. It is sometimes advantageous to extend the contents of the "application" variable within the program layer to identify the type of OA&M function performed (per Table 3.13) and the managed entity (i.e., the entire configuration, a specific program layer, or a specific service).

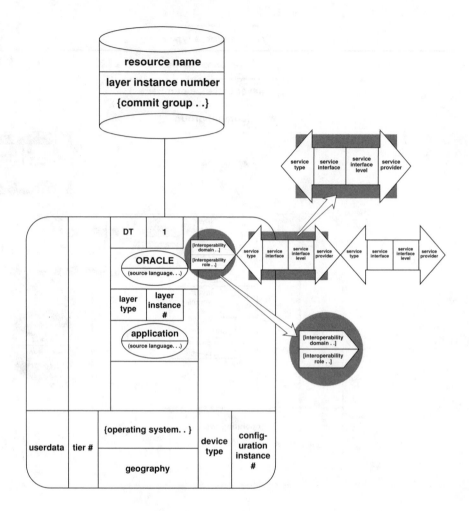

(b): Database Resource

Figure 3.34   (*Continued*)

OA&M services may join with shared middleware boxes and reuse the same internetworking diagrams. When one studies an architecture diagram, one can immediately comprehend how both the application and the OA&M support services operate. The first without the second is useless; the second without the first is purposeless; you must have both. Most alternative diagramming techniques make no provision for the integrated portrayal of OA&M services.

Table 3.13
OA&M Functions. Industrial-grade operations, administration, and management of the
network computing environment are mandatory and must be architected.

OA&M Level	Function	Examples
Application	Software Release Management	Distribution, Installation, Testing, Change Control, Backout, Intersite Coordination
	Monitoring	Component Connectivity, Message Movement, File Transfer Completion
	Performance Management	Proactive Prevention, Trend Analysis, Tuning, Bottleneck Resolution, Trending
	Change Management	Application Movement, Topology Management, Directory Maintenance
	Backup/Restore	Full/Incremental Backup and Restore, Media Management, Off-Site Archival Storage
	Database Administration	Space Management, Permissions, Restart, Sizing
	Security Administration	User-Id & Password Administration, Incident Tracking
	Help Desk	User Query Resolution
	Job Management	Batch Job Startup, Scheduling, Monitoring, Output Distribution
Platform	Configuration Management	Provisioning, System Software Distribution, Installation, Directory Management Name Management, Change Management
	Fault Management	Help Desk, Trouble Identification & Tracking, Tiered Support, Problem Isolation & Resolution
	Performance Management	Measurement, Tracking, Turning
	Security Management	Access Permissions, Violation Monitoring, Permission Levels
	Accounting	Billing Identifiers, Billing, Asset Utilization

(Source: Bernard H. Boar, *The Art of Strategic Planning for Information Technology*, John Wiley & Sons, 1993).

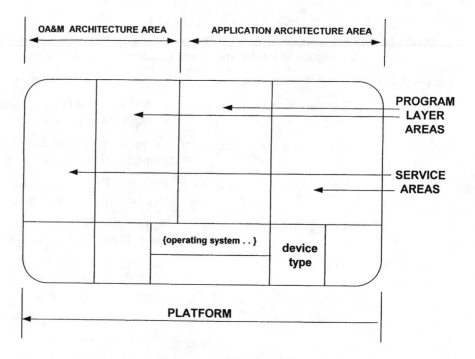

Figure 3.35   OA&M Program and Service Areas. OA&M functions are shown solely on the left program layer and service areas.

OA&M services are typically managed through one or more control centers. Individual application configurations have agents or element monitors executing on them that communicate back to the managing control center. The control center is not an attribute of the application architecture, but a reusable architecture that connects to multiple application architectures. One would handle this as follows:

1. Draw an architecture diagram reflecting the OA&M configurations, program layers, service paths, middleware boxes, and internetworking diagrams for the control center. In a control center configuration, the OA&M program layers that are managing remote agents must appear on the right-hand side of the program layers areas. On the control center configurations, the OA&M managers are the business application. The OA&M agents for the control center configurations appear on the left-hand side of the control center configurations.

2. The diagrams end at middleware boxes and have incomplete internetworking diagrams.

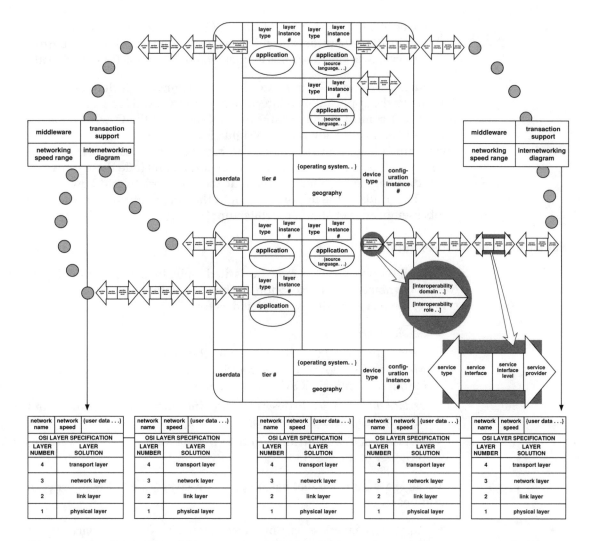

Figure 3.36   OA&M Architecture. An OA&M architecture uses the exact same notations as the application architecture, except that it originates from the left program and service areas on each configuration.

3.   Attach a *label connector* to the middleware box. You have now built a reusable architecture drawing reflecting the OA&M services from the control center perspective.

4.   Draw the application architecture diagram.

5.   Draw the OA&M services on the application architecture diagram and terminate them in an identical middleware box with the same

label connector as in step 3, above. Overlay the two drawings at that point (they share the same middleware box definition) and join the two internetworking diagrams to understand the complete network path.

Figures 3.37 and 3.38 illustrate this label connector technique. Figure 3.37 shows the application architecture perspective, and Figure 3.38 shows the OA&M control center perspective. (Notice that the OA&M manager program layers are shown on the right side.) As one builds up reusable architectures (e.g., control centers, database servers, process servers, EDI gateways, electronic mail gateways, etc.), one can include these drawings in all drawings by connecting them at the appropriate middleware box point. This leads to the important insight that an architecture is often just a subassembly of yet another architecture.[4]

Notion 16: User Interface Services

User interface services may be issued only by PN program layers (dumb terminals are an exception). When diagramming a user interface service, the service entity is completed as follows:

- *Service type:* UI
- *Service interface:* a code to denote the interface (e.g., MGUI for Microsoft Windows, CHAR for character terminal, SYNC for synchronous terminal, SCAN for scanner, etc.).
- *Service interface level:* describes the interface (i.e., keyboard and screen, GUI, virtual reality goggles, etc.).
- *Service provider:* null for dumb terminals; otherwise, the software provider of the interface.

Because a dumb terminal has no program layers, the following special conditions apply:

- A program layerless user interface emanates from the service area of the dumb terminal service area.
- The interoperability path from the controlling configuration terminates at the service area; there is no service path on the dumb terminal. There would normally be no middleware specification in the middleware box.

It is important to note that when an intelligent device emulates a dumb terminal, the above does not apply. The following cases are illustrated:

(*a*) A PN layer interface—Figure 3.39

(*b*) A dumb terminal interface—Figure 3.40

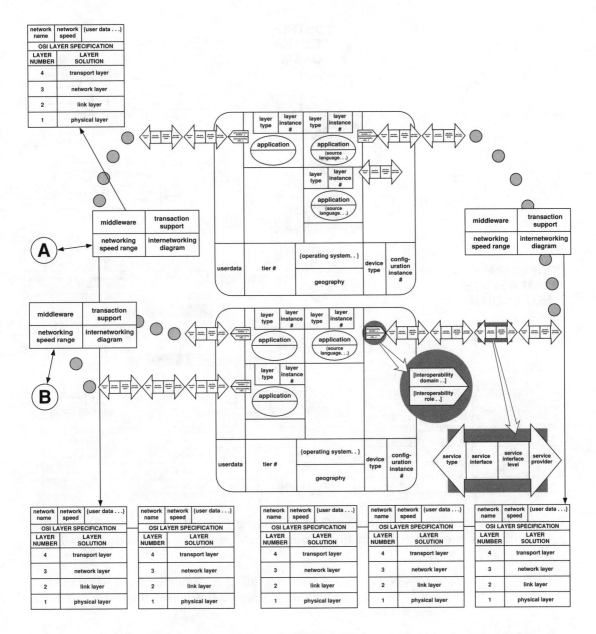

Figure 3.37 Connecting Architecture: Application Diagram. A control center architecture is connected to an application OA&M agents by a connection label.

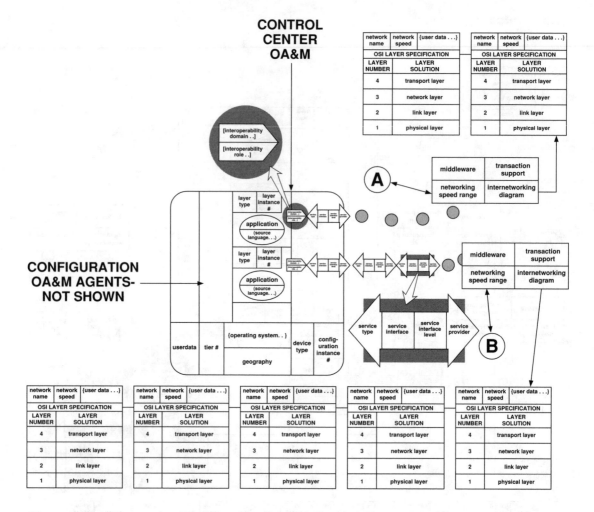

Figure 3.38   Connecting Architecture: OA&M Control Center Diagram. A control center architecture is connected to an application OA&M agents by a connection label.

(c) A PN layer interface emulating a dumb terminal—Figure 3.41. (Notice the difference in diagramming this versus the above dumb terminal interface.)

Stick figures are sometimes placed at the end of user interfaces to clearly show the points where people interact with the system.

Notion 17: Source or Sink

A source or a sink is an unknown configuration with which the architecture interoperates. When we say "unknown," we mean that we do not

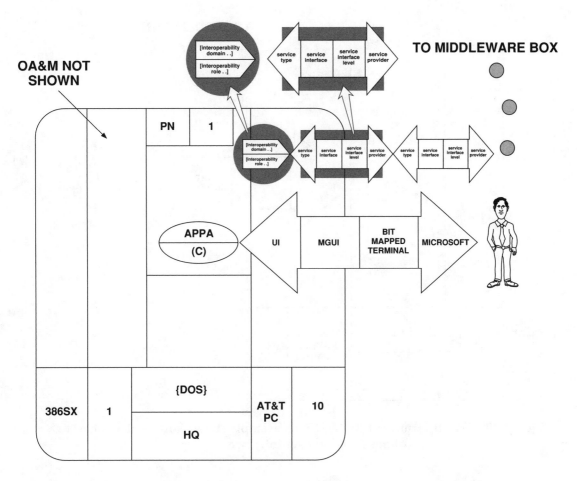

Figure 3.39   PN User Interface. This example shows how a user interface is diagrammed for an intelligent ITD.

necessarily know the configuration, some of the internetworking, or the service path executed on the source or sink. A source is a configuration that sends transactions to our architecture; a sink is a configuration to which our architecture sends transactions; and a source/sink is a configuration that sends and receives transactions. The most typical situations involving sources and sinks are electronic mail, interoperability with suppliers or customers, and electronic data exchange.

Figure 3.42 shows how a source, sink, or source/sink is diagrammed. The information technology device is identified as a source, sink, or source/sink. It is then diagrammed the same way as a dumb terminal, except the internetworking diagram is necessarily incomplete. (We don't know the networking beyond some gateway point.) It is assumed that

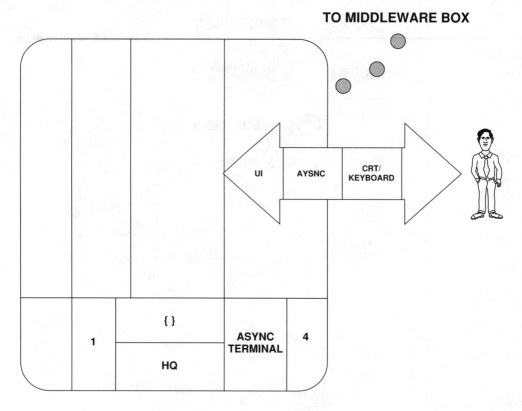

TO MIDDLEWARE BOX

Figure 3.40   Dumb Terminal Interface. This example shows how to diagram a
dumb terminal user interface.

what makes the interoperability work is agreement on the networking at the gateway point and the middleware definition.

Sources, sinks, and source/sinks represent a desirable evolution for architecture. As standards mature, ITDs, platforms, and configurations will lose architectural importance. Architecture then focuses on identifying the header services through which services are invoked and the guiding middleware framework. This vastly simplifies the effort of designing and managing the I/T architecture.

Notion 18: Intraconfiguration Interoperability

Program layers on the same configuration interoperate the same way as program layers across configurations. Figure 3.43 illustrates the diagramming of the interoperability between two program layers on the same configuration. The only exceptions to this rule are as follows:

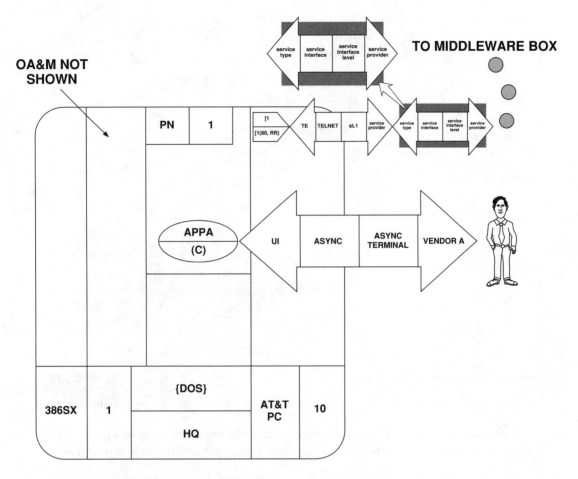

**Figure 3.41   Terminal Emulation. This example shows how to diagram an intelligent
device that is emulating a dumb terminal.**

- There is only one network drawn in the internetworking diagram—
  this represents the interprocess communication method selected.
- Most of the data elements on the network diagram are meaningless,
  except for the network layer definition, which should be completed
  with the name of the interprocess communication vehicle used (i.e.,
  pipes, messages, etc.).

If you look back at Figure 3.29, you will observe that interoperability
between program layers on the same configuration is quite common.

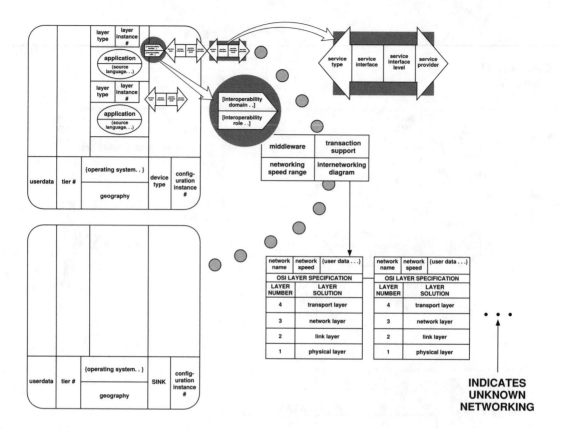

Figure 3.42 Sources and Sinks. Sources and sinks are configurations outside our domain of control or detail knowledge with which the architecture interoperates.

Notion 19: Drawing Attributes

There are a number of defining attributes of network computing that must be manifested in a selected drawing methodology. We will now review 12 characteristics of network computing for inclusion, and amend the drawing technique to illustrate them where required.

A. Interoperability

Definition: Interoperability is the ability of the drawing technique to illustrate the flow and exchange of information between information technology devices.

Analysis: This is obviously richly illustrated by the methodology through service paths, interoperability paths, middleware boxes, and internetworking diagrams.

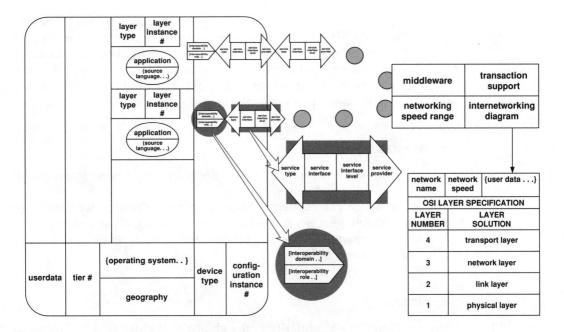

Figure 3.43   Intraconfiguration Interoperability. Interoperability between program layers on the same configuration is diagrammed using the same notation as interconfiguration interoperability.

B. Operability

Definition: Operability is the ability of the drawing technique to communicate the OA&M architecture.

Analysis: OA&M is given equal attention in the diagramming technique, and uses the exact same notation and graphics to be illustrated.

C. Heterogeneity

Definition: Heterogeneity is the ability to mix and match products from multiple vendors.

Analysis: The diagramming technique is nonrestrictive in its ability to represent any and all vendors. When appropriate, provision is made for identifying the specific vendor of a product. The drawing technique is vendor-neutral.

D. Legacy Inclusion

Definition: Legacy inclusion is the ability of the drawing technique to model legacy architectures and integrate with them with the client/server computing architecture.

Analysis: Traditional closed host-centered architectures, such as IBM MVS/VM, or minicomputer proprietary architectures, such as VAX/VMS, are diagrammed using the same notation. Due to dated programming practices, there are usually many clustered PNPR program layers. The ability to scale, port, and reconfigure is minimal, due to the non-openness of the environments.

E. Adaptability

Definition: Adaptability is the ability of the drawing technique to be amended to illustrate changes.

Analysis: The elements that compose the drawing technique are completely generic. Any new component, operating system, information technology device, source language, or service interface is easily incorporated.

F. Modularity

Definition: Modularity is the ability of the drawing technique to communicate the parts from which the architecture is constructed.

Analysis: The drawing technique is built from numerous parts—information technology devices, platforms, configurations, services, service paths, middleware boxes, and so on. As presented so far, however, there is no specific parts list. Table 3.14 provides a list of "parts tables" that should be included with an architecture.

G. Reach

Definition: Reach is the ability of the drawing technique to communicate the accessibility to network services from both wired and wireless information technology devices, regardless of the geography (local, same building, same city, same state, same country, same world) of the device.

Analysis: The drawing technique supports showing interoperability from both wired and wireless technologies. Configuration attributes include *geography*, which identifies the locale of the device; this could be *mobile*. Personal Digital Assistants, notebook computers, and palmtops are all considered information technology devices. Their reach can be diagrammed through the appropriate drawing of service paths, interoperability paths, middleware box, and internetworking diagram.

Table 3.14
Parts Tables. Twelve tables are required to list the parts
from which the architecture is built.

Table Name	Table Contents
1. Information Technology Devices	List of all information technology devices
2. Operating Systems	List of all operating systems
3. Platforms	List of all information technology devices plus operating system pairs
4. Source Languages	List of all source languages
5. Service Interfaces	List of all service interfaces
6. Service Providers	List of all service providers with associated interfaces
7. Services	List of each service (service type, service interface, service inter-faced level, service provider)
8. Middleware	List of all middleware frame-works
9. Network Names	List of all networks
10. OSI Layers	List, by layer type, of all OSI layers
11. Resources	List of all resources
12. Commit Groups	List of all commit groups

H. Range

Definition: Range is the ability of the drawing technique to communicate what services, resources, and data are available to a requester, and the means of access.

Analysis: Services, both processing and data, are portrayed as program layers with associated interoperability paths. High-value resources, including the ability to highlight commit groups, are identified separately on the diagrams.

I. Maneuverability

Definition: Maneuverability is the capacity of the drawing technique to communicate the architecture's dexterity to reshape, reform, or otherwise alter its structure to meet changing business conditions. Maneuverability is itself a function of three notions:

- *Scaleability:* the ability to move program layers, in total, with associated service paths and interoperability at the *binary* (*load, execution*) level from one platform to another and maintain all interoperability.
- *Portability:* the ability to perform scaleability at the *source code* level.
- *Reconfigurability:* the ability to selectively (at the program layer level) choose a layer, reconfigure its relationships with associated layers, port the layer to a different platform, and maintain all interoperability.

Each notion builds on the others and imbues the architecture with an increasingly chameleonlike character. It is assumed in the following analysis that the service interface level of the header service (see Notion 6) supports invoked service transparency. If it does not, programming changes will be required.

Analysis: The attributes of maneuverability build on each other and will be presented in ascending order of metamorphosis power:

(i) Scaleability: Scaleability is the ability to move program layers at the *binary* (*load, execution*) level, in total, from one platform to another, maintaining all interoperability. When scaling, the internetworking between platforms may change. End-to-end service paths are subject to change, but the header services and the middleware framework must remain constant. This makes the scaling transparent to the application. Scaling is normally done to acquire improved price or performance, or to react to a change (positive or negative) in resource requirements such as MIPs, memory, or storage.

To illustrate scaleability, it is necessary to amend the architecture diagram with an *End-to-End Service Path Table*. An End-to-End Service Path Table shows all possible paths between configurations. Table 3.15 illustrates the structure of the table. Holding the header services and middleware constant (from the original interoperability), it is necessary to select one or more new end-to-end service paths for the new platform pair. One can then redraw the architecture diagram, replacing the original end-to-end service paths with the new end-to-end service paths. Scaling may be done only if a substitute path may be established for each original end-to-end service path.

Table 3.15
End-to-End Service Path Table. This table shows all the end-to-end service paths supported within the architecture.

End-To-End Service Path Table

End-To-End Service Path

Configuration		Service Path		Middleware	Internetworking				Service Path		Configuration	
Platform	Program Layer	Header Service	Remainder Service Path		OSI LAYERS	Network 1	Network 2	Network "N"	Remainder Service Path	Header Service	Program Layer	Platform
					Transport							
					Network							
					Link							
					Physical							
					Transport							
					Network							
					Link							
					Physical							
					Transport							
					Network							
					Link							
					Physical							

(ii) Portability: Portability is the ability to perform scaleability at the *source code* level. You must be able to do all that is required to perform a scale, but before that, you must be able to move the source code to the target platform and remake (compile and link) the application. This necessitates the availability of a Port Group Table, which identifies a group of platforms across which portability is feasible, and the existence, for each source language, of a minimum set of make/build/compile tools. This table asserts that for the Port Group for a given language, there exists a mapping of tools that permits each source program to be remade on the target platform. To port between platforms, there must be a Port Table for each program layer source language. Table 3.16 illustrates a Port Group Table. Once you have ported the source code, you now have a binary (load/executable) module on the target platform, and the port must be capable of being scaled. So porting may be understood as promoting the application to the point where it can be scaled; it is source-level scaling.

(iii) Reconfigurability: Reconfigurability is the ability to choose a layer selectively (at the program layer level), reconfigure its relationships with associated layers, port the layer to a different platform, and maintain all interoperability. Reconfigurability is the acme of maneuverability, because it lets one completely reshape an application. Using Figure 3.29 as a reference, Figure 3.44 shows some possi-

Table 3.16
Port Group Table. The Port Group Table shows the mapping of make, build, or compile tools between platforms.

Port Group Table Name:_____ Source Language:_____			
	Platform 1	Platform 2	Platform "N"
Tool Type	**Tool**	**Tool**	**Tool**
Compiler			
Linker			
Call Library			
Precompiler			
Make			
Editor			
Librarian			
Etc.			

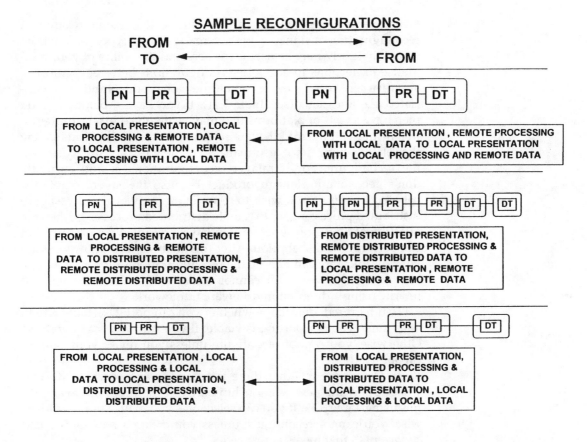

Figure 3.44 Reconfigurability. Reconfigurability permits one to change the relationships between program layers while maintaining complete interoperability.

ble reconfigurations. In doing a reconfiguration, one must establish revised interoperability between the reconfigured program layers, perform a selected port (if required), and reestablish interoperability with other communicating program layers. Reconfigurations often have a domino effect: moving one layer results in a series of changes of relationship that has to be managed. A specific reconfiguration is called a reconfiguration instance.

Reconfiguration requires performing a three-step analysis:

Step 1: Reconfiguration Instance Analysis

(1). Establish whether your middleware can transparently handle the changes in intraprogram layer relationships and interprogram layer relationships that are directly due to the change desired. A reconfiguration instance typically revises both types of relationships. Table 3.17 may be used to understand the ability of your middleware selections to support reconfigurations between platforms. You fill a cell with the names of middleware products and their associated classifications (see Table 3.11). If you have n platforms, you then have n^2 sets of platforms that may be involved in a reconfiguration instance. If the middleware selection that is currently managing the relationship cannot also manage the new relationship, you cannot reconfigure. For intralayer reconfigurations, if you currently don't need a middleware product because the layer is not distributed (that is, if you wish to reconfigure from local processing to distributed processing, or to remote distributed processing), then the question of interest is whether you have a middleware product that can perform the distribution. After this analysis, you know whether your middleware can handle the reconfiguration. If it can, you may continue. Otherwise, you cannot reconfigure unless you wish to rewrite using a different middleware framework.

(2). If required, determine whether you can port. Use Table 3.16 to determine whether porting is viable. If you can, you may continue. Otherwise, you cannot reconfigure unless you revise your porting capability.

(3). Determine whether there is an end-to-end service path that will support the new relationship between the program layers. Do this using Table 3.17. If you can select one, you may continue. Otherwise, you cannot reconfigure unless you create a new end-to-end service path that meets your need.

Step 2: Same Configuration Interoperability Analysis

(4). It may be the case that there were interoperating program layers on the same configuration of the program layer that was reconfigured. Logically, this situation is the same as if the original layer had been scaled. One then must use Table 3.17 to determine whether a new end-to-end service path can be established for each interoperating program layer. If you can select one, then you may continue. Otherwise, you cannot reconfigure unless you create a new end-to-end service path that meets this need.

Step 3: Different Configuration Interoperability Analysis

(5). It may be the case that program layers elsewhere than the host configuration for the reconfigured layer interoperated with the reconfigured layer. For these layers, perform the procedure in step 2. As is the case with step 2, it may also be necessary to establish brand-

Table 3.17
Reconfiguration Middleware Table. This table affirms the ability of a middleware product to support a type of inter- or intraprogram layer relationship.

Middleware Reconfiguration Table							
Reconfiguration		Platform Pairs					
Type	Instance	P1 & P2	P1 & P1	P2 & P2	P1 & P3	P2 & P3	Etc.
Intraprogram Layers	Local Presentation to Distributed Presentation						
	Distributed Presentation to Local Presentation						
	Local Processing to Remote Distributed Processing						
	Remote Distributed Processing to Local Processing						
	Local Processing to Distributed Processing						
	Distributed Processing to Local Processing						
	Local Data to Remote Distributed Data						
	Remote Distributed Data to Local Data						
	Local Data to Distributed Data						
	Distributed Data to Local Data						
Interprogram Layers	Local Presentation with Local Processing to Local Presentation with Remote Processing						
	Local Presentation with Remote Processing to Local Presentation with Local Processing						
	Local Processing with Local Data to Local Processing with Remote Data						
	Local Processing with Remote Data to Local Processing with Local Data						

new end-to-end service paths to support interoperability to both layers of a layer that became distributed.

Reconfiguring is an iterative process. An act of reconfiguration causes a domino effect, and often, many reconfigurations are done concurrently. One needs to play with the architectural components to come up with the new optimum architecture.

J. Openness

Definition: Openness is the capacity of the drawing technique to communicate the use of standards that enable fluid interoperability.

Analysis: Communicating openness requires the addition of a standards table to the methodology. The standards table should itemize the governing standard for each service interface, OSI layer, and middleware framework. If it was not obvious before, it should be crystal clear now, following the discussion on maneuverability (scaleability, portability, and reconfigurability), that adherence to standards is fundamental to the successful management of a reach, range, and maneuverable architecture. Unless one adheres to standards, the combinations and permutations of end-to-end service paths grow exponentially.

Allegiance to standards is the only means to enable orderly control of the number of permutations. Without standards, the architecture, like a virulent cancer, will endlessly mutate until it becomes an unmanageable clutter of incompatible and noninteroperable components. With standards, not only can the combinations and permutations be minimized, but component substitution becomes possible without disrupting the environment. Decisions regarding middleware, service interfaces, and OSI layers must be standards-based. Particularly important standards are POSIX, XPG, COSE, X Windows, TCP-IP, X.400, X.500, CORBA, DCE, and SQL. If a pundit tells you to ignore standards and proceed with proprietary solutions, her advice is spurious.

Notion 20: Narratives

It is sometimes advantageous or necessary to annotate the drawings. This is done by putting a *narrative number* of the form "N#" (where "#" is an integer) next to the specific item that you wish to elaborate on and then writing the narrative on a separate sheet. The "N#" is put in a circle on the drawing. The form of the narrative sheet is on the following page.

A typical use of a narrative is to give a precise specification (e.g., chip speed, memory, disk space, etc.) for a personal computer platform.

Mulciber Narrative
N#: _____
Architecture Drawing Name: _____
Architecture Page #: _____
Architecture Object Type: _____
Object Keys: _____
Date: _____
Version: _____
Prepared By: _____
Narrative:

Notion 21: Summary: What Is an Architecture Drawing?

We have now concluded our explanation of the architecture diagramming technique. A drawing consists of the following components:

1. An architecture drawing that shows the configurations, service paths, middleware boxes, resources, and interoperability paths (Figure 3.15 without item 7, the internetworking diagram).

2. Internetworking drawings that show the various networks traversed by end-to-end service paths (Figure 3.33b).
3. Parts Tables (Table 3.14).
4. End-to-End Service Path Table (Table 3.15).
5. Port Table (Table 3.16).
6. Middleware Reconfiguration Table (Table 3.17).
7. Standards Table.
8. Narratives.

The entire set of architectural elements is called a Mulciber Drawing, item 1 is called a Mulciber Architecture Diagram (MAD), and item 2 is called a Mulciber Internetworking Diagram (MID), all in remembrance of the fallen angel Mulciber. It should serve as a constant reminder of the Hell you will create if you do not construct your environment properly.

It is often advantageous to label MADs and MIDs with an identification label in the bottom right-hand corner, as follows.

Architecture Drawing Name:
Page Number:
Version:
Date:
Prepared By:

Notion 22: Types of Architectures

The following are classifications of architectural drawings:

- *Conceptual architectural drawing:* an architectural drawing that attempts to convey a general but ambiguous notion of the intent of an architecture. The reach, range, and maneuverability architectural drawing is the highest-level conceptual drawing. Many other instances of conceptual drawings were presented in Section 3.2; the technique used is at the discretion of the creator.
- *Logical architectural drawing:* a Mulciber drawing that identifies codes and relationships but does not identify specific solution products.
- *Grand schema architecture:* a Mulciber drawing that shows all the physical possibilities of your architecture.

- *Reference architectures:* views or slices of a grand schema architecture that represent frequently used subsets as specific solutions to certain types of business problems.
- *Value-added reference architectures:* reference architectures that have been amended with a full set of application OA&M (Table 3.13). This makes the reference architecture a high-productivity solution, because once the application is plopped down on it, the OA&M at both the system level and the application level is all ready to go.

The above sequence can, of course, be repeated at the application level.

Summary

Figure 3.45 superimposes the Mulciber drawing on one of the architectural frameworks. Remember that drawings may be done at two levels: a global level that shows all possibilities, and an application level that

	INVENTORY	PRINCIPLES	MODELS	STANDARDS
INFRASTRUCTURE	• PARTS TABLE		• MAD • MID	• STANDARDS TABLE • PORT TABLE • MIDDLEWARE RECONFIGURATION TABLE • END-TO-END SERVICE PATH TABLE
DATA	• MAD		• MAD	
APPLICATIONS	• PARTS TABLE		• MAD • MID	• STANDARDS TABLE • PORT TABLE • MIDDLEWARE RECONFIGURATION TABLE • END-TO-END SERVICE PATH TABLE
ORGANIZATION				

Figure 3.45   Mulciber Drawing Imposed on Architectural Framework. The Mulciber drawing provides the necessary information to complete many of the framework cells.

shows an application's choices. Since a drawing is composed of parts, there is predictable spillage of drawing elements into other than the originally targeted cells. Appendix A provides a glossary of Mulciber drawing terms, and Appendix B provides a starter set of Mulciber templates.

Conclusion

This section has attempted to focus your attention on the importance of a formal diagramming methodology to support the engineering of a reach, range, and maneuverable I/T architecture for the business. John Zachman of IBM said, "Decentralization of I/T without structure (i.e., without architecture) is CHAOS . . . anarchy! You can disintegrate (that is disintegrate) the business as quickly as you can sprinkle a few machines around."[5] Zachman's observation is undeniably correct, and many corporations are discovering, the hard way, the wisdom of his insight.

As is true with all engineering disciplines, complicated structures demand formal diagramming techniques to permit intelligible modeling. The methodology proposed in this chapter, its extensions and implications, provides a giant leap forward from the mishmash of amateurish techniques currently in use. The exemplary diagramming techniques that were presented are adequate for conceptualization and casual conversations, but are useless for serious architectural engineering. Like all innovations, however, this methodology is born deformed. Used as a reference and not as a straitjacket, it can help each organization build a specific notation customized to its requirements. Through such a refinement process, the innovation grows to become rich and robust. While some may initially criticize the technique as being too complicated, such criticisms are meaningless in themselves. A model bears the burden of mirroring reality. If one is to suggest that a modeling technique is too complicated, then one must step forward with an alternative technique that provides equal or greater knowledge about reality, but in a simpler manner. Simple but meaningless diagrams may be food for simple minds, but will not help you build advantage. Test all drawing techniques against Notion 19 criteria, and you will be readily able to distinguish sham techniques from modeling methods of substance. You are not in the data communications business, you are not in the voice communications business, you are not in the mainframe processing business, you are not in the PC retail store business, you are not in the network computing business or the data storage business; you are in a business that transcends them all: you are in the information movement and management business. Your architectural drawing technique must reflect the character of information movement and management.

The exodus from the mainframe environment to the promise of network computing offers unparalleled promise, but at a price. The price is the necessity of moving the I/T organization from an artisan culture to an engineering culture. The reach, range, and maneuverability environment is a classical bill of materials (product structure) environment, and that exceedingly complex world of who interfaces with whom and who connects to whom can be managed only through formal engineering discipline. Sir Francis Bacon said, "For the most part, man is architect of his own fate."[6] We have therefore architected a nomenclature to help us manage our fate. It is not enough, however, to know what is right; the knowledge must be applied. Understanding without action yields no benefit. It is your responsibility to design your I/T architecture. You are not a victim of circumstances beyond your control; you bear the burden of creating your own good fortune or misfortune by your actions.

3.4 DIAGRAMMING EXTENSIONS

The purpose of this section is to provide some extensions to the basic diagramming technique that was introduced in the previous section. It should be obvious (and it will be the first extension) that architecture requires automated support. It is simply too tedious, labor-intensive, and error-prone to maintain the drawings by hand. Consequently, almost all of the suggestions that follow assume that you either buy or build a computer-aided design (CAD) tool to support your architecture design and maintenance efforts.

Extension 1: Architecture CAD Tool

An architecture CAD tool consists of a workstation with access to a database that maintains the architectural rules and structure. The software enforces the diagramming rules and choices made by the architecture team. Figure 3.46 is a sketch of what a partial schema to support Mulciber diagrams would look like. Much of the schema is concerned with maintaining the rules of the architecture, as opposed to each physical manifestation of the architecture.

Access rights and privileges have to be divided between two types of architects, master architects and application architects. Master architects decide on the overall set of rules and possibilities. They define the boundaries and interoperability of the architecture. Application architects then build specific architectures at the business application level from a selected subset of the master architecture.

There are two levels of architectural enforcement that can be imagined for such a tool:

1. *Level 1: Rigorous Enforcement:* master architect defines all the rules. Application architects can create only architectures that comply

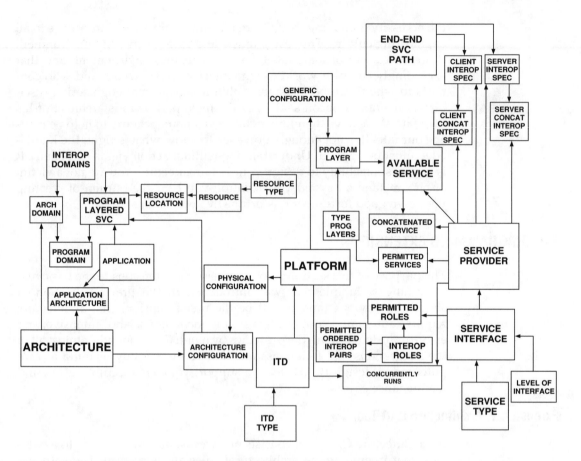

Figure 3.46   MAD Schema. This data entity drawing shows part of the database schema required to automate the generation of Mulciber drawings.

with the rules; no deviations are possible. If application architects want something special, they have to have the master architect alter the master architecture to permit it.

2. *Level 2: Intelligent Drawing Tool Only:* application architects may draw any architecture they wish. The tool is intelligent, in that it understands the drawing rules but does not enforce established standards.

With automated support, architectures can be maintained concurrently in three time dimensions at both the infrastructure and application levels:

*   *Current:* drawings of the architectures that are in place now.

*   *Work in progress:* drawings of the development work in progress that will lead to the next release. This is your tactical architecture plan.

- *Vision:* drawings of the long-term ambitions of the architecture. This is your strategic architecture plan.

With automated support, levels of drawings can be easily presented. For casual conversations, the Mulciber diagrams can be presented at a higher level. For more serious design, further decomposition diagrams can be developed. With automation and an agreed-to lowest level of conventions, different summary levels of drawings targeted for different audiences can easily be generated.

One of the greatest benefits of automated drawing support, besides the labor savings and quality improvement, is documentation. All the drawings, tables, and any desired where-used analysis can be easily supplied. The database is also incredibly beneficial in doing what-if impact analysis when changes are suggested in architectural components. New product debates can be fact-based, as opposed to the normal political and religious nature of product selection.

Extension 2: Requirement Specifications

A structured model of application business requirements can be maintained. This model identifies clusters of requirements by requirement type. The requirements can then be associated with architectures, platforms, configurations, middleware, and so on. In this way, there can be direct linkage and alignment of the architectural selections to specific business needs. From a business requirements perspective, one can look at the architecture and its subcomponents and identify which elements are best suited as requirement satisfiers.

Extension 3: Application Taxonomy

Am application taxonomy (Table 3.18) can be maintained and related to both architectures and the architectural elements that are best suited to those applications. This demonstrates the alignment of I/T architecture to business application categories. Application size can be a function of total number of users, maximum number of concurrent users, and size of database.

Extension 4: Software Taxonomy

The domain of software interest of the architecture can be extended to include all software elements by platform. A software taxonomy (exemplary partial taxonomy, Table 3.19) can be used to catalog all software products that are supported. This aids in meeting the inventory requirements of the architecture frameworks.

Table 3.18

Application Taxonomy. Application types can be related to specific architectures or components to show how the architectural selections solve business problems.

| | Business Practices | | | | | | | | | |
| | Run the Business | | | | Analyze the Business | | | Share Business Information | | |
Size	On-Line Transaction Processing	Operational Support Systems	Business Process Automation	Light Record Keeping	Modeling	Information Retrieval	Ad Hoc Decision Support	E-Mail	Conferencing	Groupware
Small										
Medium										
Large										

Table 3.19

Software Taxonomy. Architecture inventory requirements can be met by amending the architecture to include a software taxonomy.

| | Database Management | | | | | Data Management | Utility Tools | | | |
Platform	Inverted	Hierarchical	Network	Relational	Object	Backup/ Restore	Log Analyzers	Load/ Unload	Index/Pointer Checkers	Space Analyzers
P1										
P2										
P3										
P4										
Pn										

Extension 5: Migration Aids

Most of the applications that were built in the host-centered environment are not maneuverable. So while one cannot easily scale, port, or reconfigure them, it is possible to ease their redevelopment with the aid of migration tools. One can therefore amend the architecture to include mappings of migration aids, to assist developers in moving applications from one incompatible architecture to another.

Extension 6: Measurements

An architecture database contains all the elements that compose the architectures and the relationships between those components. It is straightforward, then, to automatically generate measurement reports that show the trends in number of elements, number and types of relationships, reusability, platforms, configurations, and so on. It will become quite clear from such reports whether your architecture is holding together or moving toward a state of entropy.

Extension 7: Accessibility

An architecture database should be made accessible to all members of the information community. It is in the interest of architecture cohesion to give all members of the community (architects, designers, analysts, developers, etc.) access to architecture information. This accessibility should be extended to your vendors, as well. After all, they have to sell their products into your architecture, which is extremely difficult to do if they don't know what it is. A stealth architecture is of little value.

Extension 8: Customer Satisfaction

In almost all surveys of user satisfaction with information systems, three items that predictably appear are reliability, capacity, and performance. Given that you have modeled the architectures in your database, it is a small hurdle to add additional data elements to model reliability, capacity, and performance, as well. A reliability subsystem can run off the architecture database to predict reliability for architectures. Actual reliability measurements can then be compared. In the same vein, alternative architectures can be priced at differing reliability points.

Since the architecture understands the notions of scaling, porting, and reconfigurations, it is reasonable for an artificial intelligence subsystem to import capacity statistics from architectures and propose changes to capacity planners. If you view end-to-end service paths as the corporate information highway system, then transactions are the cars and trucks of the system.

Given that you have already captured the characteristics of the highway system, if you are supplied additional information about the character of the transactions, transaction performance modeling is practicable. Solution modeling then permits order-of-magnitude improvements in customer satisfaction by being able to propose alternative price or performance solutions at varying reliability, capacity, performance, and maneuverability points. Customer satisfaction can be proactively attacked: you always meet reliability commitments, you always meet performance obligations, and you preempt capacity problems.

Extension 9: Scaleability Metrics

Scaling is done for a purpose: to improve throughput, price and performance, availability, and so on. The End-to-End Service Path Table (Table 3.15) may be extended to include additional columns for each end-to-end service path to document key metrics for the path. Typical metrics are cost/transaction, transactions/second, mean time to repair, mean time to failure, and cost per user. In this way, one can judge the trade-offs to be achieved by performing a scaling activity.

Summary

Once a database is implemented that defines the I/T architecture, what you do with it is constrained only by your imagination. Architecture is the heart of I/T; it therefore is not surprising that having collected architecture information, you can exploit it in any and all directions. Take the OA&M functions that were introduced in Table 3.14—using the architectural OA&M drawings as a reference, you can develop the complete processes to support those functions.

There is an untapped wealth of opportunity for the I/T organization to improve its business alignment through the medium of architecture. These extensions are only the beginning of what a creative staff will be able to do once the database is in place. It is worth the commitment.

3.5 IMPLICATIONS

The purpose of this section is to list some of the "therefores" of architecture. Having made the reach, range, and maneuverability decision, and understanding it at the depth that you do, what are the implications? What should stand out to the attentive observer of architecture?

The following are the primary implications that astute I/T management should appreciate as architecture derivatives:

- *Automate:* architecture cannot be done manually. It demands computer-aided design assistance based on a drawing model. A car manufacturer is not expected to keep track of all the components and drawings of a car in Esther's, Steve's, Marie's, Matt's, and Vicki's heads, and neither can your architects.

- *Artisan to Engineer:* architecture requires your staff to behave as engineers and not as artisans. Architecture design and development is a problem analogous to a bill-of-materials engineering problem, not a Picasso painting. Engineers, not artisans, address configuration management problems.

- *The Era of the Architect:* the role of architect becomes the most important technical role in the I/T organizations. Architects must have a renaissance appreciation of technology and be able to function both at the heights of abstraction and the depths of details.

- *Standards:* reach, range, and maneuverability (scaleability, portability, and reconfigurability) are functions of adherence to standards. Learn about standards, participate in standards organizations, and implement standards-based products.

- *Vendors:* vendors should understand that they sell to your architecture. You must form alliances with your key vendors to deliver to you ready-to-integrate components and horizontal support alliances. Vendors who will not sell to your architecture or participate in support alliances shouldn't be your vendors. Conversations with vendors regarding enhanced and new products all take place in the context of how the new product will fit into or enhance your architecture.

- *Primacy of Middleware:* the winner is middleware. Middleware is the most important architectural decision, because it ties your platforms together. The ultimate end of architecture would be to simply specify the middleware frameworks and the header service APIs. One then could have completely open interoperability by treating everyone as a source or sink.

- *Skill Set:* I/T staff have traditionally been an inch wide and a mile deep in their technical knowledge. Since network architectures are horizontal architectures, emphasis will have to be placed on developing more well-rounded individuals. Staff members who can conceptualize horizontally will be of premium value to the business.

- *End-to-End Solutions:* the I/T organization no longer sells parts; it sell complete solutions. When a customer needs a system, the I/T organization responds with a complete business application on a complete end-to-end architecture with complete end-to-end OA&M.

- *Variety Vs. Standards:* the constant tension between the desire by users for endless variety and choice and the needs for standardization and discipline to enable reach, range, and maneuverability must be resolved. The best way to settle this dilemma is by standardizing the service paths from clients, and by permitting users to choose the information appliance of their choice as long as it will adhere to the service paths. In this way, variety can be maintained at the point of use by treating the user information devices as sources and sinks, but enterprise interoperability can also be assured.

- *Reeducation:* there will be extensive need for reeducation in the I/T community. While much of this reeducation will focus on network computing, it also needs to focus on what engineering is and what it means to be a competitor.

- *Architecture Process:* architecture is a process, not an event. I/T processes have to be developed to evolve, communicate, and enforce the architecture. Process design centers around the notion of an Architecture Review Board that is responsible for overall architecture administration. This includes change approval, project architecture reviews, deviation approvals, and architecture information dissemination and communication to the greater I/T community.

- *Implementation Approach:* the order of attack for creating an architecture where there is none is as follows:

  1. Do an inventory of your I/T assets—platforms, configurations, software, communications networks, and so on.

  2. From the inventory, create a Mulciber drawing that reflects the actual architectures in use. This drawing blueprints, for better or worse, the existing architecture. Do not be surprised to discover that you have islands of computing, fortresses of computing, poor reach, worse range, and negligible maneuverability. Many existing architectures are best described as incoherent. This is the problem.

  3. Create a logical Mulciber drawing of what you wish to have. A logical Mulciber drawing shows the types of platforms, configurations, services, and communications without identifying specific products. It provides a generic picture of configurations, services, and interoperability. You may also wish to draw a logical diagram for the existing architecture.

  4. Create a Mulciber drawing that shows the entire new architecture. This can encompass a grand schema of the architecture.

5. Take slices or views of the grand schema. The views should represent high-reuse reference drawings that are specific solutions for common problems like an office architecture, a high-end transaction processing solution, or a departmental decision support solution. All application architectures should be understood as a view of this grand architecture.

In this way, you understand where you are, what the logical architecture is to be, the grand solution, and more manageable subsolutions that are focused on specific customer problems. Table 3.20 shows how these notions of logical architectures, grand schema architecture, and view architectures can be joined with the previous section's notion of a current architecture, work-in-progress architecture, and future architecture to illustrate the classes of architecture drawings you may wish to develop, When you walk down the columns in Table 3.20, you achieve architectural coherence. When you walk across the rows in Table 3.20, you define the gaps between what is and what is to be and discover the necessary strategic architecture programs to be initiated.

Architecture involves big changes, and "they" will quickly test you to discover whether your commitment is deep or hollow. You should consider this carefully; what you undertake is not trivial. If you do not have the stomach to commit to it, it is more efficient not to do it. Pretenses are time-consuming, expensive, and wasteful. It is much more efficient to go directly to a state of architecture anarchy without an architectural pretense layover. Since they will quickly find you out, you must have commitment to match the deep and far-reaching nature of your strategy. Expediency, the normal practice of I/T management, is the death rattle of architecture.

Table 3.20
Architecture Dimensions. An architecture group must decide which types of architectures it will maintain in which time domains.

Architecture Types	Architecture Time Domains		
	Current	Work in Progress	Vision
Logical			
Grand Schema			
Reference Architectures (Views of Grand Schema)			

Architecture commitment requires a utilitarian view of computing. Utilitarianism means that the needs of the many take precedence over the needs of the few. Every project will be able to justify why it will be more advantageous for it to be granted an exception. What they won't discuss is what that variance does to your reach, range, and maneuverability. The true arithmetic of architecture variances is that net variance benefit equals individual project gain less business reach, range, and maneuverability loss.

It is not the case that optimizing the pieces results in optimizing the whole. To the contrary, architectural cohesion results in no one being perfectly optimized but the whole being optimized. This is inherent in the commitment to an architecture. If optimizing the parts is your objective, architecture efforts will fail. What you must desire first and foremost is universal reach, range, and maneuverability.

In the I/T community, there is an enormous interest in architecture that includes learning, planning, designing, and sharing. The only aspect of architecture that is not achieving resounding success is compliance. This is to be expected. Compliance demands collective behavior, and collective behavior demands compulsion. If you are to be serious about architecture, then your governance rules must include penalties for noncompliance. The I/T community is populated with artisans and individualists who share a profound dislike for any and all standards. If you wish to achieve a reach, range, and maneuverability environment, you will have to demonstrate strong commitment and enforce compliance.

3.6 SUMMARY

It is the normal practice, in a summary section, to restate all the primary ideas of the chapter. However, architecture is of such strategic importance that we will confine this summary to reemphasizing the rationale that makes I/T architecture the most important component of I/T reengineering. Sun Tzu said,

> A victorious strategy is not repeated, the configuration of responses to the enemy are inexhaustible. . . . Water configures its flow in accord with the terrain; the army controls its victory in accord with the enemy. Thus, *the army does not maintain any constant strategic configuration of power; water has no constant shape.* The end of an army's form is formlessness. One who is able to change and transform in accord with the enemy and wrest victory is termed genius.[7]

What is required, then, is the ability to continuously reshape and alter oneself, to be in a dynamic state of metamorphosis, to be like water and be able to take any application shape or configuration appropriate for each and every circumstance.

This is the reason that a reach, range, and maneuverability architecture is of such fundamental business importance. When your architecture achieves a higher state of reach, range, and maneuverability, it becomes a contortionist, able to adapt itself perfectly to the needs of each user. Advantage does not flow from the business applications that operate on top of the architecture, but from the architecture, which conveys its chameleonlike character to each application. The business then can create a constantly moving target for the competition, can surgically adapt itself to each business opportunity and excite its customers, and can provide just the correct solution for each business opportunity. An application in a fixed architecture can, at best, provide temporary advantage. An outstanding application on a reach, range, and maneuverability architecture can convey sustainable competitive advantage. How will another match that which is formless? How does another benchmark against you when your chameleon character makes you unknowable? The configurations of business initiatives and business defenses are then inexhaustible.

When the basis of strategic I/T power permits endless permutations of solutions for the business, what customer need cannot be met? What new technology cannot be assimilated? What business opportunity cannot be grasped? Against what does your competitor attack? Against what does your competition defend? What competitor gap cannot be assaulted? What failing cannot be corrected? When the basis of strategic I/T power is formlessness, what advantage is not obtainable?

When your architecture climbs the ladder to the rung of reach, range, and maneuverability, it achieves the state of a pivot position. A pivot position places an asset or resource at a carefully chosen crossroad that allows the asset to spring in any direction dictated by business needs. When an architecture can respond dynamically to fluid business requirements, how much less an expense to be ruthlessly slashed and how much more a prized partner to be exploited as the means of implementing business policy and initiatives. Is this not exactly the change in fortune we seek for I/T? So when one achieves a perfect reach, range, and maneuverability architecture, one's architecture is like water and has no fixed form; the architecture can reshape itself on command to meet any and all challenges. When you achieve a reach, range, and maneuverability architecture, you have won the war of movement, because your architecture is movement. When you achieve a reach, range, and maneuverability architecture, you accomplish a state of perfect strategic alignment with the business. I have witnessed many presentations on architecture. Typically, the compulsory first overhead states the same worn set of objectives as all other presentations given to the executive management. It states that the goals of architecture are to improve leverage, increase economies of scale, improve information exchange, and facilitate data accessibility. The concepts that can be used to command the marketplace are reduced to lumpen mediocrity. Architecture is not just another component of I/T. It is the path to a deep and far-reaching vision of I/T that enables the business to prevail through finesse rather than through confrontation. The architecture presents to each application a dowry of shared reach, range, and maneuverability. Rather than each application having to discover, build, and sustain these attributes independently, they are all inherited for free from the architecture. In this manner, peerless leverage is realized for and through the I/T assets.

This notion of I/T architecture, its importance and its consequence, is, without reservation, the most important idea in this book. If you have time to deliberate on only one idea and power to initiate only one strategic move, that strategic move is architecture. While the other actions that are proposed later in this book are material to alignment, architecture is the golden tip of the I/T reengineering arrow. There is nothing you can do that will be more critical to future I/T success and business alignment than architecture. Do not be hesitant, do not be distracted, do not be confused, and do not be shortsighted. Start the journey to reach, range, and maneuverability now!

Postscript

Of all the major professional sports played in North America—baseball, football, ice hockey, and basketball—only ice hockey has the feature that players change on the fly. In all of the other sports, player substitution may occur only during a play stoppage. In ice hockey, however, players have to be able to leave and enter the ice without losing the tempo or rhythm of the game. It is very demanding. If you don't change on the fly well, you are left with tired players on the ice, the loss of momentum, or worse, a penalty for having too many players on the ice. Changing on the fly is a unique and difficult feature of the game. It requires endless practice.

Business is certainly more like ice hockey than other sports in this characteristic. Business must also always be able to change on the fly. There are no game stoppages during which to make orderly substitutions. Customer service, product delivery, marketing, and so on—all must deliver value while changing on the fly. As in hockey, those businesses that are superior at changing on the fly have a distinct advantage, because they can maintain the marketplace offense or defense and change without missing a beat. A business can no longer, however, change on the fly without concurrently altering its information systems. This is another view of why a reach, range, and maneuverability architecture is so critical: because it enables a business to change on the fly.

NOTES

1. Sun Tzu, *The Art of War.*
2. The reader should refer to material provided by the framework author for the specific definitions of each architectural item.
3. In Figure 3.29, "local" means nondistributed, and is relative to a moving currency. The current platform for local placement is set relative to prior layer remote and distribution choices. If we say "local presentation and local processing," then the processing layer is on the first platform and is nondistributed. If we say "distributed presentation and local processing," then the processing layer is on the second platform. If we say "distributed presentation, remote processing, and local data," then the data layer is on the third platform.
4. If you make architectural drawings very modular, you can use this technique to connect them. This supports using architectures as subarchitectures of each other, interfacing architectures, and relating your architectures to customer and supplier architectures.
5. J. Zachman, "A Framework for Information Systems Architecture," *IBM Systems Journal.*
6. Sir Francis Bacon, *The Essays.*
7. Sun Tzu, *The Art of War.* Italics added.

4

I/T Planning and Forecasting

The purpose of this chapter is to provide an analysis of how to reengineer I/T forecasting and planning methods to dramatically improve the assimilation and integration of new information technologies into the business. Historically, most I/T organizations, in sympathy with their monopoly mainframe status and mindset, engaged in shortsighted technology planning. The consequence of this has been that many internal I/T organizations missed two great shifts in computing. First they missed the PC wave, and they are only now beginning to catch up to outsourcers with the client/server wave. Technology planning basically equated to incremental evolution of the technological status quo.

A new attitude needs to be adopted, one that directly links technology acquisitions to business advantage. As the pace of new technology introductions accelerates, the I/T organization has to increase its rate of technological assimilation, while avoiding technological anarchy. Technology planning starts with what the I/T organization has always done worst: long-term technology scanning and prospecting with explicit linkage to business advantage. The reengineered technology planning and forecasting approach starts with business process requirements and asks how a new technology might solve those needs, rather than locating a new technology that looks nifty and then asking where can it be applied. The structure of this chapter is as follows:

- *4.1. The Business Logic of I/T Planning and Forecasting*
  This section explains what is meant by aligning technology planning and forecasting with the business.

- *4.2. Model-Based I/T Forecasting*
  This section provides a framework for performing aligned I/T technology planning and forecasting through the use of business and technology models.

- *4.3. Summary*
  This section summarizes the primary ideas of this chapter.

Sun Tzu said, "It is easy to take over from those who do not plan ahead."[1] Many of the sources of customer dissatisfaction itemized in Figure 1.12 have their genesis in poor technology planning and even worse business linkage. If the internal I/T organization does not meet the compelling business need for aligned, continuous, rapid, and orderly technology transfusions, the customers will find outsourcers who will.

4.1 THE BUSINESS LOGIC OF I/T PLANNING AND FORECASTING

The purpose of this section is to explain what is meant by linking technology planning to the business. As we learned in Section 1.3, where we analyzed what "strategic alignment" means, there is a wide breach between the literal translation of a phrase and insightful dissection of it. We will now do a crisp analysis of what "aligning I/T planning with the business" means. This will prepare us for the following section, where we will develop a new process that magnifies that alignment.

Strategic Directions and Strategy Themes

As illustrated in Figure 1.2, the business strategy process should provide directives and assumptions to define the playing field for I/T strategy formulation. The directions that the business wants to take will often be presented in executive speeches, strategy summary documents, discussions with the media and financial community, various forms of business literature, and internal executive correspondence.

The following are extracts of business direction from public AT&T documents that attempt to capture the strategic direction of the business:

- Business mission: leverage assets and competencies
  - Bring people together
  - Give them easy access to each other and information, any time, anywhere
- Focus on markets where we can serve needs of customers and shareowners
- Best-in-class (quality) products and services
- Technological superiority
- Partnerships, alliances, and new ventures
- Market leadership
- Exceed customer expectations
- Stimulate network demand

- Speed in delivery
- Efficiency in delivery
- Compete on value added
- Strategic direction: the world's networking leader
  - Global network
    - Worldwide hold/grow share in existing and new markets
    - Enhanced intelligent network features
    - Extend network: global, wireless, broadband
    - Expand services: personalized, all information forms
  - Products and systems
    - In global markets, supply full line of best-in-class products, including voice, visual, messaging, computing, data
    - Link products to global network
    - Increase share of world's network infrastructure: wireless, CATV/entertainment, private networks
  - Integrated solutions
    - Help customers define and address information needs
    - Integrate offerings: advice, networks, equipment, software, services, financing
    - Design, build, and manage customized networks: virtual, turnkey, outsource, public, private, hybrid
- Globalization
- Interoperability within and with others
- Decentralization for local adaptability
- Customization to fit the individual
- Acceleration for rapid response to increasing complexity
- Internal economy designed for competitive fervor
- Adaptability by moving programming closer to point of use
- Survivability for continuity of services
- Security for safeguarding the integrity of information
- Data as corporate resource
- Cross-organizational systems and reused systems
- Software productivity
- Operating cost reductions
- Information management as basis of competitive superiority
- Integrated information system solutions

- Radically improve business processes
- Emphasis on use of AT&T products and services
- Common standards
- Use I/T for superior responsiveness to customer needs, enhance the value of AT&T products, and enhance employee quality and productivity
- Adopt distributed processing model
- Alignment of goals, alignment of product offerings, alignment of technology, and alignment of resources
- Align information systems with corporate strategy
- No credit for hard work—only results count
- The name of the game is speed
- Eliminate redundancy, promote reuse, and dramatically reduce development cost
- Cross-functional systems
- Standardized data architecture
- Basis of competitive superiority
  - Business processes
  - Time to market
  - Quality
  - Showcasing AT&T products and services
- Efficient, flexible design and building of reliable, reusable software systems
  - Software architecture
  - Development process
  - Data management
  - User interface
- Compete on ability to deliver products with large software content quickly, inexpensively, and with quality
- Compete on ability to deliver products differentiated by their software technology
- Use software to help deliver customized solutions
- Standard and open systems for global markets
- Required: software architecture and builder skills core competency

If we consolidate this information using the Quilt of Advantage metaphor (Figure 1.17), all of these directions from ten sources can be reduced to the following:

AT&T will win in the marketplace through quality, market leadership, alliances, speed, speed, and more speed, value added, integration, customization, maneuverability, cost advantage, productivity, leverage and reuse, alignment, showcasing of products and services, software-rich solutions, and globalization.

We now understand the business direction in concise, operational terms. The process of translating executive statements into concise business directions is called *strategic theming*.

Key Business Processes and Capabilities

You win in the marketplace by applying your selected strategic themes to your business capabilities—that is, your key processes that deliver value to the customer (see Section 2.4 on business reengineering). Figure 4.1 illustrates the notion of infusing your key business processes with your

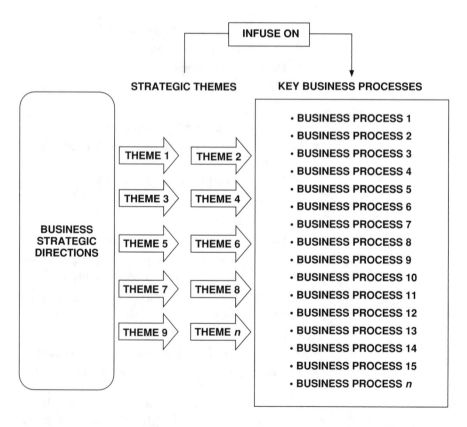

Figure 4.1   Business Process Alignment. The key capabilities of the business must be infused with the business strategic themes.

strategic themes. Typical business processes are product development, provisioning, customer billing, and inquiry or service delivery. This aligns your daily operations and business planning with your strategy. But where does I/T fit in?

Enabling/Realization Technologies

You win in the marketplace by applying strategic themes to key business processes through information technology. As shown in Table 2.4, emerging technologies can be classified by their primary appeal. As shown in Figure 4.2, you select strategic theme-rich technologies and use them to enable the key processes. In this way, you align technology planning with the business, because both your selected key processes and your chosen emergent technologies have their genesis in the same strategic themes that originated from a single business strategy,

Summary

This section has explained what is meant by business–I/T planning alignment. Alignment occurs when the advantages inherent in a technology match the strategic themes that the business wishes to impose on its business processes. When you spawn your technology prospecting activities with the strategic themes, you can assure yourself of picking technologies that deliver business advantage. If you pick technologies starting from a technology-centric perspective, alignment is a gamble. Since there is no reason to gamble, it is prudent to understand your business strategic themes, understand the key business processes of the business, and explore for technologies that will invest those processes with the strategic themes.

4.2 MODEL-BASED I/T PLANNING AND FORECASTING

The purpose of this section is to improve the alignment between information technology planning and forecasting and the business through a model-based approach. The basic notion is that the quality of the planning effort is best managed through the use of a set of customer models, technology models, and product or service models. Through management of these models, timely decisions can be made as to what technologies will best meet current and anticipated customer needs. I/T planning or forecasting is driven by three parameters:

1. *Time horizon:* the time frame covered by the plan or forecast.
2. *Breadth:* the domain of technologies covered by the plan or forecast.
3. *Depth:* the level of detail covered by the plan or forecast.

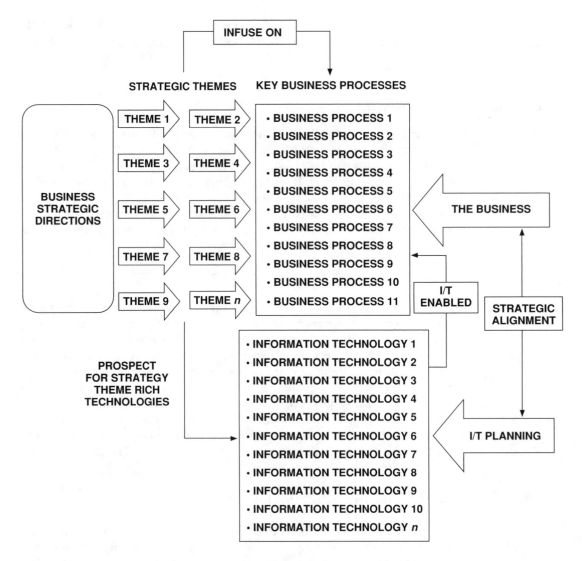

Figure 4.2   Business–I/T Planning Alignment. Emergent I/T technologies align with the business because they both share the same lineage.

As shown in Figure 4.3, there are generally four distinct forecasts or plans that feed each other; the descriptions of each type are itemized in Table 4.1. As one approaches the present, one moves from forecasts to plans. Forecasts are measured guesses about the future. Plans are commitments to actions. The remainder of this section will focus primarily on long-term technology scanning, which is the most strategic element of the planning succession.

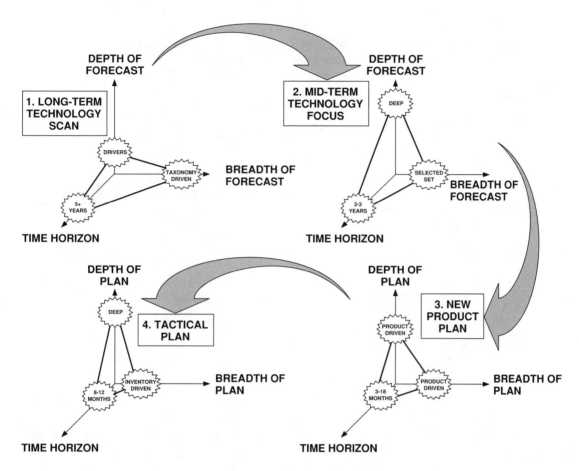

Figure 4.3   I/T Planning/Forecasting Dimensions. I/T planning and forecasting is a function of three dimensions.

Long-Term Technology Scanning

Long-term technology scanning is concerned with taking a broad view of the industry, technology, and customer needs. The objectives to be achieved are as follows:

1. Engage in a foresighted and farsighted scan of I/T.
2. Develop a thorough understanding of technology and industry currents.
3. Anticipate discontinuities for the dual purpose of taking advantage of them and not being taken advantage of by them.

Table 4.1
Forecasts and Plans. Most I/T technology planning is consumed by plans, forecasts, and an architecture plan.

Plan or Forecast (P) or (F)	Time Horizon	Depth	Breadth	Purpose
Long-Term Technology Scan (F)	5+ Years	Major Drivers	Taxonomy-Driven	1. Foresighted and farsighted scan of I/T. 2. Understand technology currents. 3. Anticipate discontinuities. 4. Draw conclusions on significant trends. 5. Select best prospects.
Mid-Term Technology Focus (F)	2–3 Years	In-Depth Evaluation + Lab Models	Selected Set with Most Promise	1. Reduce emergent technology set to most promising. 2. In-depth investigation of best prospects. 3. When, where, and how forecast. 4. Full business advantage analysis.
New Product Plan (P)	3–18 Months	Complete Product Plan	Product-Driven	1. Develop specific new and enhanced product plans. 2. Ensure alignment of products with business needs.
Tactical Plan (P)	0–18 Months	Complete Plan for Inventory	Inventory-Driven	1. Plan covering changes to entire I/T inventory over tactical horizon.

4. Draw conclusions on significant trends that require strategic actions.

5. Select best prospects for an in-depth analysis (mid-term technology focus of best prospects).

Figure 4.4 provides a high-level picture of the process. The process is as follows:

1. *Data sourcing:* external sources (vendors, industry news, market research houses, seminars, academics, consultants, and internal analysis) provide a wealth of raw information about I/T trends and directions. "Raw" does not mean that it is not structured or insightful, but that it is not structured or insightful to your specific needs.

2. *I/T taxonomy:* a classification system provides a structured framework through which to collect and group the raw information. A piece of information may relate to multiple classification elements. Figure 4.5 shows an example of classification structure for the information services industry. You need to develop a classification

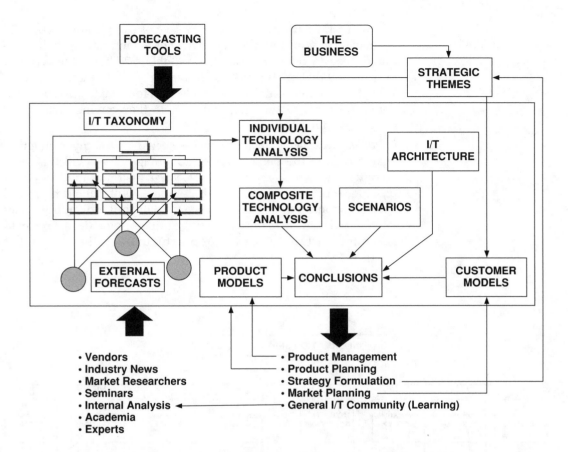

Figure 4.4 Long-Term Technology Scan. The process turns raw data about the industry, technology, your customers, and your products into forecasts and conclusions requiring strategic attention.

system that exceeds your customary domains of interest. It must be spacious—you don't want to be caught blindsided again—and it needs to be easily adaptable for the addition of new subclasses and elements. Remember, you are not searching for confirmation of your beliefs, you are searching for opportunities and discontinuities that may very well render your beliefs obsolete. Figure 4.6 shows an archetypical superstructure, Figure 4.7 shows the substructure for the Storage class, and Figure 4.8 shows the subsubstructure for the decomposition of tape storage from Figure 4.7. The classification system must, by design, be endlessly extensible and decomposable. As you receive information from your data collection network, with the fresh perspective of classification, you will be amazed at your initial myopic view of the industry and the continual need to refine the taxonomy. Table 4.2 shows the types of information that are typically collected for each taxonomy element. Table 4.3 illustrates sample data collection for item 8 (applications), item 9 (barriers to success), and item 16 (key buying factors) for imaging and multimedia.

3. *Individual technology analysis:* each selected taxonomy element is analyzed from the perspective of advantage. How will this technology blend with our architecture, what customer models will it provide solutions for, what product models will it meld into? The analysis should not just restate the raw data, but look at it with an internal twist. What is the competitive impact, what does it mean to our infrastructure, and what opportunities or threats does it impose?

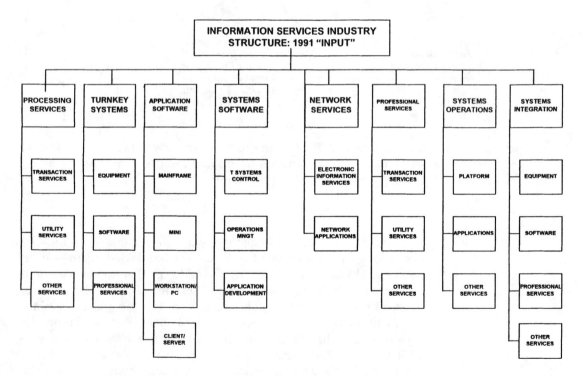

Figure 4.5   Information Services Industry Taxonomy. This is an example of a complete industry segment taxonomy used by the market research firm Input. (Source: Input.)

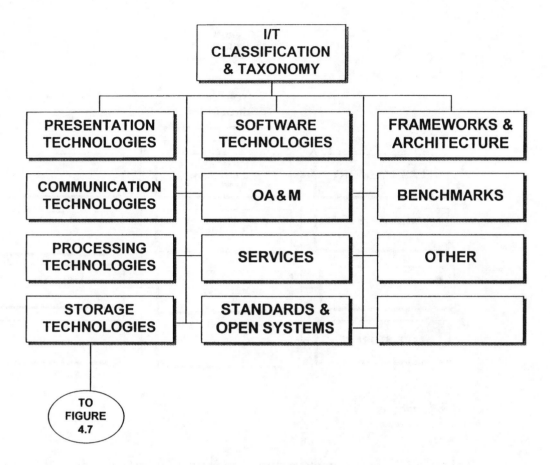

Figure 4.6   I/T Taxonomy. This framework may be used as the starting point for developing the highest level of the I/T taxonomy.

A "guesstimate" of both the likelihood of adoption of a technology and the time frame of that adoption can be developed by analyzing the data you have gathered from three perspectives:

a. *Customer attractiveness:* how attractive is the technology to the potential customer?

b. *Supplier value proposition:* how will the suppliers package and support the technology to make it attractive?

c. *Vendor defense:* how will existing suppliers defend the status quo technology to delay or prevent substitution?

From an analysis of these three forces, the adoption potential of a promising technology can be discerned.

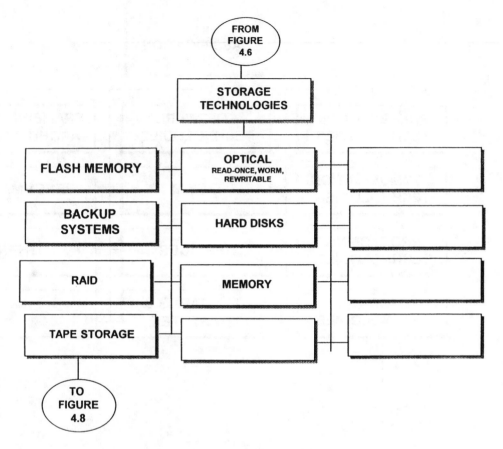

Figure 4.7   Storage Substructure. The Storage Technologies subject from Figure 4.6 can be broken down into this structure.

4. *Composite technology analysis:* promising individual technologies are now viewed in terms of solution groups. The same questions as above are asked.

5. *Product models:* provide models of the clusters of I/T that are being or will be used, and show how those clusters solve customer needs defined in customer models. (These will be discussed fully later.)

6. *Customer models:* provide models of customer requirements. (These will be discussed fully later.)

7. *Scenario generation:* by use of a variety of forecasting tools (S curves, timeline monitoring, price and performance curves, life cycle

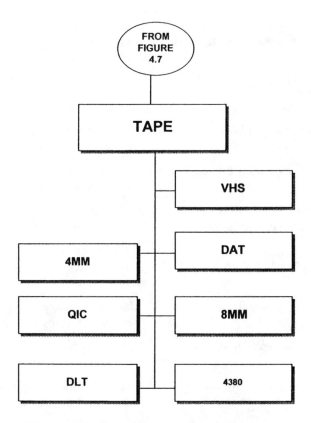

**Figure 4.8 Tape Storage Subsubstructure.
This structure further refines the Tape Storage element from Figure 4.7.**

curves, Delphi technique, etc.), develop a set of scenarios of possible industry futures. A good scenario provides a statement of the scenario, the rationale for the scenario, dates and probability, and the opportunities or threats posed to the organization by the scenario.

8. *Conclusions:* identifications of the major trends and possible impact on the business. Components of a conclusion might include:

   • *Mega-trends:* major industry drivers that are shaping I/T products and services over the forecasting horizon.

   • *Prospects:* selected technologies that appear deserving of further in-depth analysis based on the initial assay.

   • *Actions statements:* statements of specific anticipated changes, their impact on the business, and possible preemptive response.

Table 4.2
Taxonomy Data Collected. The following are the typical types of information collected about a taxonomy element.

Data Type	Description
1. Advantage	The strategic advantages of this technology.
2. Technology Unit Forecasts	3–10-year forecasts (and histories) of projected sales for the technology in units.
3. Technology Dollar Forecasts	3–10-year forecasts (and histories) of projected sales for the technology in dollars.
4. Technology Price and Performance Trends	3–10-year forecasts (and histories) of projected price and performance trends in a technology-appropriate dimension.
5. Vendor Market Shares	3–10-year forecasts (and histories) of projected vendor market shares.
6. Market Segmentation	Alternative ways to segment or fragment the markets for this technology.
7. Critical Success Factors	Competencies and capabilities that are critical to success with this technology.
8. Applications and Advantage	Typical business applications that would use the technology and the advantage accrued.
9. Barriers to success	The primary barriers to successful utilization of this technology.
10. Configurations	Alternative configurations with associated pluses or minuses.
11. Add-On Services	Identification of what additional products and service opportunities can piggyback on this technology.
12. Substitution	Identification of what technologies this technology will displace and how the incumbent technology will defend itself.
13. Technical Specifications	Specific technical specifications that define the technology.
14. Feature and Functionality	The features and functions of this technology.
15. Dependence	Other technologies, events, or infrastructure capabilities this technology is dependent on.
16. Key Buying Criteria	The factors that drive purchase decisions by the customer.

Table 4.3
Taxonomy Data Examples. The following illustrates the type of information collected
for imaging and multimedia, as per Table 4.2.

Information Technology—Imaging		Information Technology—Multimedia	
Applications (Item 8 from Table 4.2)	Key Buying Factors (Item 16 from Table 4.2)	Barriers to Success (Item 9 from Table 4.2)	Key Buying Factors (Item 16 from Table 4.2)
1. Image archival	1. Service and support	1. Cost	1. Cost
2. Customer service	2. Training	2. Staff expertise	2. Reliability
3. Engineering drawings	3. Ease of use	3. Training	3. Scaleability
4. Knowledge worker support	4. Standards adherence	4. User resistance	4. Vendor credibility
5. Transaction processing	5. Performance	5. Confidence in technology	5. Service and support
6. Geographic information processing	6. Value and price	6. Proven case studies	6. Third-party applications
7. Electronic file cabinet	7. Works with third party DBMS and development tools		7. Platform and networking support
	8. Platform availability		

To be effective, the conclusions must generally be succinct and graphic, identify probabilities, be dated, and distinguish opportunities and threats. The data from the individual and composite analysis and from the scenario generation is available as evidentiary backup; more in-depth information is available for interested individuals and community education.

9. *Distribution:* share the information widely with the impacted community. A particularly important but often overlooked audience is the general I/T community. All benefit by being kept aware of the currents of the industry in which they earn their livelihood.

The heart of this process will be reviewed in more detail later under the heading of "alignment."

Justification

There are three ways, above and beyond the mundane need for planning, to justify this type of foresighted and farsighted approach to I/T planning:

organizational learning, market leadership, and (of course) I/T–business alignment. Each will be discussed separately.

1. Organizational Learning

Improvement requires a commitment to learning. A learning organization is an organization skilled at creating, acquiring, and transferring knowledge. It must be able to modify its behaviors to reflect the new knowledge and endlessly repeat the learning, acquisition, and transfer cycle.

I/T organizations have historically suffered from frozen mental models—rigid and unquestioned mental maps of how the I/T world works. The rallying cry for some host-centered computing zealots persists even today: "As it has been, it will be; as it will be, it has been." Many I/T people prefer "I/T as one would"; they more readily believe what they would rather be true as opposed to what is true.

As technology change accelerates, the rate of technology adoption hastens and the mean time to obsolescence of I/T skills halves. It will be mandatory to accept new knowledge openly, disregard dated conventional wisdom, and engage in rapid and shared change. By being a perpetual student of I/T, one prepares oneself to adapt gracefully. Being a good learner spills over into other areas of work and life, as well, and simplifies one's ability to cope with change in general.

As shown in Figure 4.9, the learning challenge is to make the need for change obvious as soon as possible so that strategic performance can be maximized. As one moves from anticipatory change to reactive change to crisis change, the strategic options available dwindle markedly. The struggle to preserve the status quo at any cost paradoxically works against the zealot's own interest. Continuous learning creates fertile ground for fluid acceptance, and dramatically shifts the receptivity of the organization to change to the left (see Figure 4.9).

This human trait of resistance to change has been a major subject of management consulting in the last few years. Many of the major consulting houses have "change practices" that focus specifically on managing change. One of the most popular and influential books of the last few years, *The Fifth Discipline* by Peter Senge, focuses on the dual problems of change and frozen mental models.

This issue is actually quite old, and was insightfully discussed by Francis Bacon in his *Novum Organum* (1620). Bacon developed the *doctrine of the idols* to explain how persistent false ideas and methods handicap scientific progress. The idols that prevent admittance of the new and different, according to Bacon, are the following:

- *Idols of the tribe:* idols that are founded in human nature and satisfy emotional needs at the price of reason and progress. Examples of

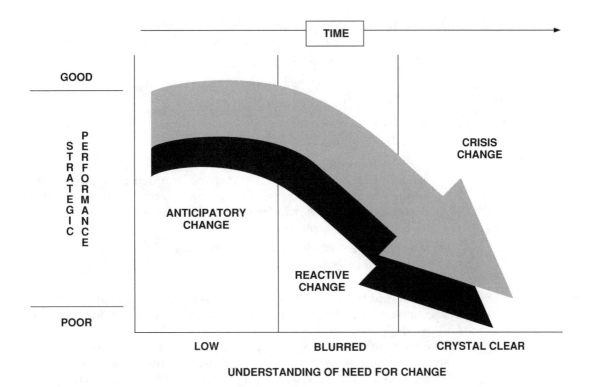

Figure 4.9 The Learning Challenge. The challenge of a learning organization is to move the crystal-clear state to the extreme left and thereby maximize strategic performance. (Source: *The Art of Strategic Planning for Information Technology*, Bernard Boar, John Wiley & Sons, 1993)

these idols are the tendency to cleave to what is already believed in spite of contradictory evidence, the tendency to pay great attention to evidence that confirms one's beliefs but disregard or ignore evidence that disconfirms it, and the desire for comfortingly superficial explanations of threatening or complicated phenomena.

- *Idols of the cave:* idols that originate in an individual's education or habits. An example of this is drawing incorrect inferences because one is not trained in the formal rules of logic.

- *Idols of the marketplace:* idols that originate in the ambiguity of the language. A perfect example of this is the phrase "death of the mainframe." Does it mean:

  1. The end of all presentation, processing, and data services occurring on a processor?

2. The end of proprietary chip-sets and operating systems at a certain price or performance level?

3. The end of the corporate data center?

4. The end of proprietary operating systems (e.g., MVS and VM)?

5. The end of a price class of processors?

6. None of the above?

7. All of the above?

A "mainframe" might be an MVS processor functioning as a server, or an NCR 3600 processor using symmetrical multiple processing with Intel microprocessors and offering more computing power than any IBM mainframe ever did. These ambiguities are the idols of the marketplace.

● *Idols of the theatre:* idols that originate in blind allegiance to dogma; faith-based beliefs.

It is extraordinarily difficult, if not impossible, to engage in a continuous technology transfer program when your organization is populated by idol worshippers.

The more subtle and sophisticated understanding of technology forecasting and planning is that it provides a means of indirection. If the acme of strategy is to win without fighting, then the acme of indirection is to prevent or preempt resistance to change before it even occurs. By using the results of your technology planning and forecasting process as part of a creditable information dissemination and exchange program, you slowly and quietly alter the staff's perceptions of technology—perceptions of where technology is going and of the staff's evolving role and opportunities. The surprise of change is removed, and the newer technologies become a natural result of the repeated information exchanges. Understood this way, technology forecasting and planning moves way beyond its mundane charter and takes on significant strategic significance. How much easier to introduce the abundance of new technologies that await us if there is no resistance to be overcome. Sun Tzu said, "Those who are good at getting rid of trouble are those who take care of it before it arises."[2] Use information technology planning and forecasting not only to fulfill its direct purpose, but as a delicate means of indirection to alter the organization's receptivity to change. Understand I/T forecasting and planning as a grand finesse approach of indirection to overcome resistance by destroying its seeds. Understand and apply forecasting and planning as a killer of obstacles. Use learning to cleanse from the organization the sin of idolatry, the abomination of worshipping specific information technologies. There is no salvation to be found in database management systems, transaction monitors, remote procedure calls, graphical user interfaces, procedural languages, communication protocols, or any other information technology elevated to the status of demigod. If the staff has an emotional or spiritual need to idolize something, it is best that they adore the customer, whose satisfaction is the sole source of permanent prosperity.[3] In this way, from a single action, you concurrently anticipate the future, plan for it, and remove barriers to it.

2. Market Leadership

Some strategy theorists define strategy as the ability to change more quickly than the marketplace. There are four basic company strategies:

1. *Follow customers:* the suppliers are always behind the customers. They wait until a customer asks. Unless they enjoy a monopolistic influence in the marketplace, their market gradually erodes, as customers abandon them for suppliers who can immediately meet their needs.

2. *Lead customers temporarily where they don't want to go:* the supplier leads the customer to a dead end, or to a position ultimately detrimental to the customer but beneficial (at least in the short run) to the supplier. Customers eventually respond by repudiating the supplier.

3. *Lead customers where they want to go:* the supplier leads the customer to where it is in the customer's best interests to go. The supplier is ahead of the market and creates it. The supplier must have a deep understanding of the customer's needs and how technology changes can better meet those needs.

4. *Meet customers:* the supplier delivers products and services to the market in harmony with market demand. The supplier is in perfect synchronization with the market. The supplier must have a perfect understanding of the customer's needs and how technology changes can better meet those needs.

Figure 4.10 illustrates these alternative market leadership approaches. Being a customer follower is viable only for an I/T organization that will remain a monopolist, but that organization will certainly not achieve customer satisfaction. Leading customers temporarily where they don't want to go leads to market failure—witness the problems of DEC, IBM, and Wang over the last few years. The only two that are viable for an I/T organization seeking to deliver value and achieve alignment are leading or meeting customers, and both require outstanding technology planning and forecasting.

The second justification for forecasting and planning is the need to be able to lead or meet the marketplace. The I/T organization must move from a position of market entry follower to one of prudent pioneer. If you follow the marketplace, your customers will desert you. If you lead customers where you want to go, they will eventually forsake you. If you are to meet them or lead them, you must be ahead of the technology curve and thoroughly command their needs. That can be accomplished only through excellence in information technology forecasting and planning.

3. Alignment

As illustrated in Figure 4.2, I/T planning–business alignment requires the selection and introduction of information technologies that enable busi-

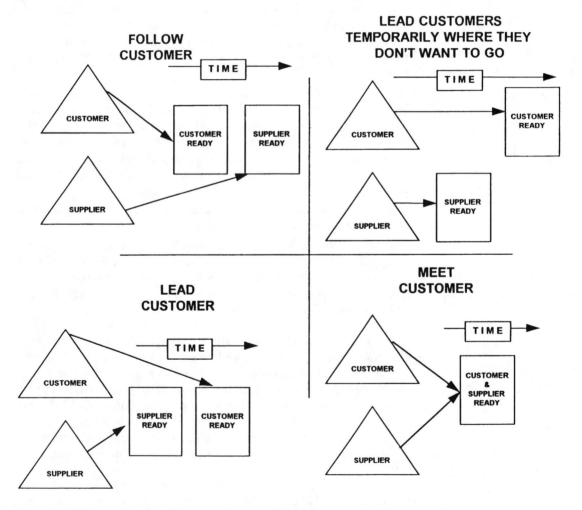

Figure 4.10   Market Leadership. Which market model do you follow?

ness processes to achieve the strategic theme objectives set for them by the business planning process. This can be accomplished by using a model-based approach to planning based on customer models, product models, and technology models, as follows:

- Figure 4.11 shows the relationship between strategic themes and I/T products and services. The flow of the matrix models is as follows:

  1. Strategic themes are mapped to specific business units or their subentities. We now understand what are to be the strategic drivers for those entities.

  2. Business units or subentities have key processes, value chains, or capabilities (we will hereafter refer to all three of these as processes) upon which they wish to infuse the strategic themes. These processes are the most fundamental to the business entity's success. We now understand what processes we must focus on.

  3. Processes have from 1 to n functional requirements. The collection of requirements for a process is called a function cluster. We now understand the driving requirements for a process.

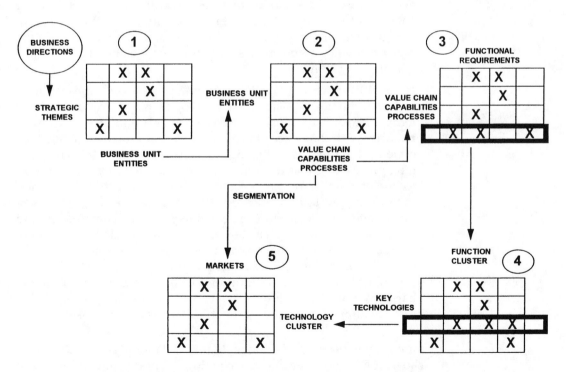

Figure 4.11   Planning Models I. This illustration models the translation of strategic themes into I/T products and services.

4. Function clusters assemble a set of key technologies that can meet the requirements of the function cluster. A group of technologies that meets the needs of a function cluster is called a technology cluster. We now understand what clusters of information technologies assembled in what combinations satisfy functional requirements.

5. The processes from step 2 above are segmented into markets and matrixed with the technology clusters. The intersection of a technology cluster with a market segment defines a product or service. We now understand what products we need to meet the needs of what market segments.

Matrices 1, 2, and 3 provide a customer model. Matrix 4 provides part of a technology model, and Matrix 5 provides a product model. Starting with a strategic theme, you can trace the realization of that theme by tracing through the matrices. An I/T product or service is then understood to be a cluster of technologies composed of individual key technologies. Together, these key technologies meet the requirements of a function cluster, which in turn meets the needs of a customer who is attempting to infuse a set of strategic themes on her processes. This model requires a continual flow of new or enhanced information technologies to create ever better key technologies (see matrix 4), and to better enable the creation of ever richer technology clusters to satisfy function clusters. This is where I/T planning comes in.

• Figure 4.12 shows how the I/T planning process feeds the evolution of key technologies. The key technologies may be understood in terms of their individual life cycle position (introduction, growth, maturity, or decline—see Matrix 4a) and in terms of the combined life cycle position for the technology clusters (see Matrix 4b). The planning process analyzes emerging technologies in terms of the current technology model, the architecture model, and the strategic themes. In this way, new technologies are selected. These new technologies fit into or alter the architecture, meet strategic theme requirements, and create richer technology clusters to meet functional cluster requirements. Matrices 4, 4a, and 4b constitute a technology model.

The I/T planning process realizes alignment with the business by providing a coherent and continuous feed of technologies that are in harmony with the architecture and the strategic themes, and that directly improve the value of the solution technology clusters.

From this perspective, it is evident that I/T planning is an endless race of who can introduce enabling technologies more quickly and with greater precision so that the business has access to the most robust I/T products and services.

Summary

This section has provided a methodology to perform I/T planning and forecasting that ensures alignment of new I/T selections with the needs of the business. Most I/T planning functions suffer from three gaps:

1. There is no systematic forecasting of long-term I/T trends or systematic analysis of the implications.
2. There is no breadth of forecasting; people look for what they want to see.
3. Technology planning is not in explicit alignment with the business.

The approach presented herein rectifies these shortcomings.

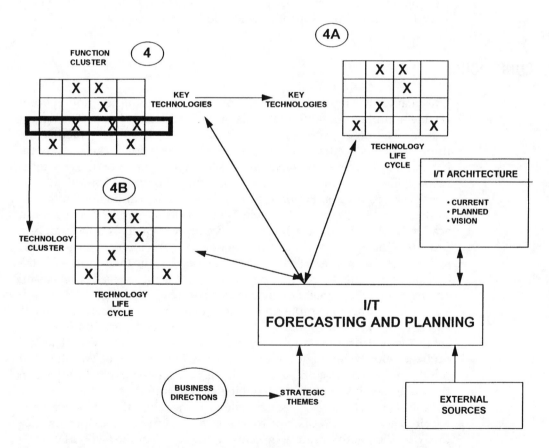

Figure 4.12   Planning Models II. The technology models ensure a continuous infusion of superior technologies to enable ever improved technology clusters.

Aside

If you are serious about performing world-class technology planning, then you require a detailed engineering methodology to project technology clusters and associated attributes such as price/performance, reliability, and performance. The best book available for this is *Technology Projection Modeling of Future Computer Systems* by Al Cutaia (Prentice-Hall, 1990). The book provides a robust methodology for assembling clusters and making informed projections about their future attributes. While following a method, as prescribed in Cutaia's book, is important to alignment and market leadership, it is absolutely invaluable when it comes to organizational learning. The creditability that following such a method imparts to the planning staff makes it much easier to educate the I/T community and chip away at its biases. It promotes the level of the debate from emotion-based opinion to engineering-based forecasting. Unfreezing organizational mental maps is not an easy undertaking, and being armed with superior data and methodology is a key to success.

4.3 CONCLUSION

This chapter has argued for the importance of aligning technology forecasting and planning with the needs of the business. While some suggest that forecasting is a hopeless exercise because no one can predict the future with any accuracy, when it comes to information technology, nothing could be farther from the truth. As shown in Figure 4.13, the true technology life cycle includes pure research, laboratory feasibility, and operating prototypes. Figure 4.14 provides a practical demonstration of the Figure 4.13 technology life cycle. Whether the research is being done in academia or in industrial research laboratories, journals and symposia provide a sharing of findings and patents filed, and a forum for informed speculation. There is ample time to react if one has the long-term scanners on and is willing to acknowledge the unpleasant as well as pleasant omens. Even when a technology enters the introduction stage of the product life cycle, there is ample time to adapt, because of infrastructure constraints, market education, and the time required for diffusion and achieving a critical mass to bring prices to mass market levels. The real problem with technology forecasting is not the absence of warning, but the absence of will to coldly assess what is coming and judge its impact on the embedded investment of technologies and human resources.

Although technology forecasting inherits the reputation of its infamous cousin, economic forecasting, they are very different. Economists routinely predict, with uncanny inaccuracy, the future of the GNP, CPI, inflation rates, unemployment rates, treasury bill rates, prime interest rates, and exchange rates. However, economic forecasting is built on economic models driven by variables that, in truth, no one really understands. Their relationships, situational dominance, and relative weights are all guessed at but poorly understood. Completely unexpected and unanticipated events (poor weather, wars, economic cartels, political upheavals, etc.) further make economic forecasts highly suspect. Technology forecasting, particularly I/T technology forecasting, is built on the technology life cycle that provides warnings for those who are attentive. The economic future is driven by poorly understood variables and fortune, while the technology future is driven by a well-understood and necessary set of technology development stages.

What technology that is being introduced now was not speculated on three to five years ago in the industry press, by market researchers, by vendors, or by pundits? Do you believe that there will be a new technology introduced next year or the year after that is not currently being speculated about? Because I/T is an engineering-based discipline, technologies do not arise spontaneously and are not distributed to customers overnight. There is plenty of warning if you are looking at the technology radar screen without blinders on. Anomalies that appear on the screen that contradict or discredit your beliefs should not be disregarded to pro-

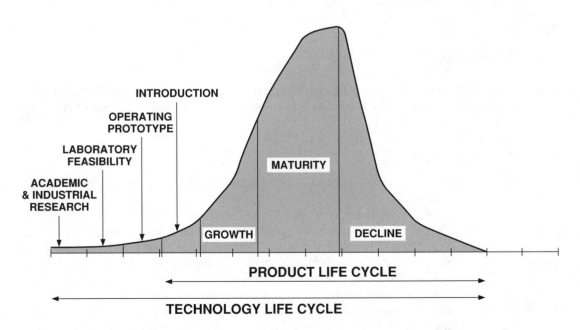

Figure 4.13   Technology Life Cycle. The complete technology life cycle includes research, laboratory feasibility, and operating prototypes.

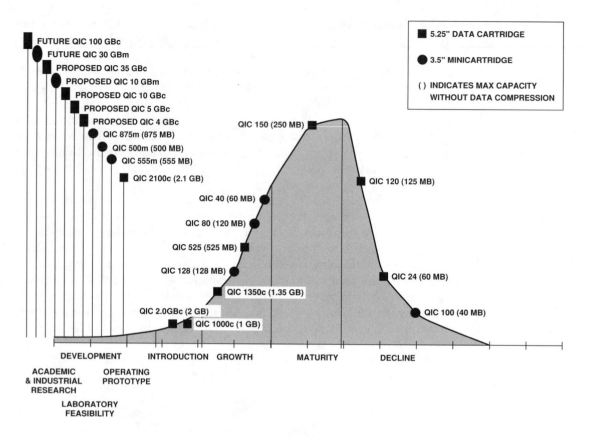

Figure 4.14   QIC Technology Life Cycle. The technology life cycle for quarter-inch cartridge tape illustrates how future developments can be foreseen. (Source: 3M.)

vide emotional comfort, but urgently studied to forestall financial discomfort.

While industry magazines publish headlines that scream "Techno Chaos" to attract readership, nothing could be farther from the truth. The superficial I/T industry chaos is, in truth, quite orderly. What is chaotic, if there be chaos at all, is our deficiency of placing structure on the analysis.

There is, however, a downside to technology planning. As shown in Figure 4.15, in Dante's *Inferno*, soothsayers, forecasters, and other futurists are sentenced to the eighth circle of Hell. This is because the future is to be known only to God. The implications of this on your forecasting and planning efforts I leave to you as an exercise.

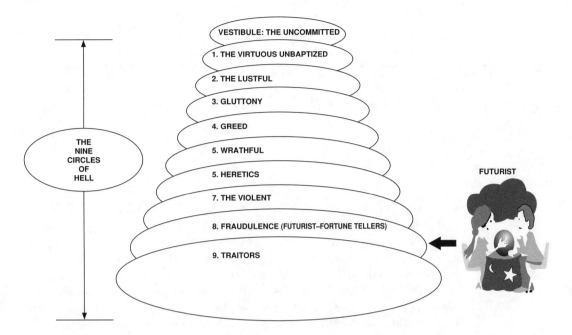

**Figure 4.15   The Divine Comedy: The Inferno. In Dante's *Inferno*, futurists are con-
demned to the eighth circle of Hell.**

NOTES

1. Sun Tzu, *The Art of War.*
2. Sun Tzu, *The Art of War.*
3. Worshipping the customer is a pretty good alternative. In Neitzsche's
Thus Spoke Zarathustra, Zarathustra suggests that if the people have a need
to worship something, they should worship donkeys. I think that customers are a better alternative than donkeys—or than DBMS, RPCs, GUIs,
and so forth.

5

The Economy

The purpose of this chapter is to analyze how the dual economic systems that govern the I/T organization's product and service exchange activities have to be reengineered. As shown in Figure 5.1, an I/T organization participates in two separate but highly interrelated economic systems: the *business economic system* that determines the rules of exchange between the I/T organization and its business customers, and the *internal economic system* that governs the exchange of services within the I/T organization. Though often neglected in strategy books and articles, the explicit design of the economic system is critical to promoting desired behaviors and motivating aligned decision making.

Any and all economic systems have to solve three basic and eternal problems:

- What will be produced, how much, and when?
- Who will provide the products and services, using what resources and technologies?
- For whom will the products and services be provided, who will receive what, and in what proportion?

The way these questions are answered results in a continuum of economic systems from highly efficient to grossly dysfunctional.

The rules for economic exchange are subject to design, like any other business process. In most I/T organizations, however, the economies have not so much been designed as they have resulted from "economic creep," the slow and incoherent adoption of economic rules outside of any integrating philosophy or framework. It is our contention that most I/T organizations today operate in economic systems that represent an unholy alliance between the worst of centralized communism and medieval feudalism. This results in gross distortions of economic behavior that prevent the efficient and effective delivery of I/T services to their customers. Perfect alignment between the business and the I/T organization cannot be

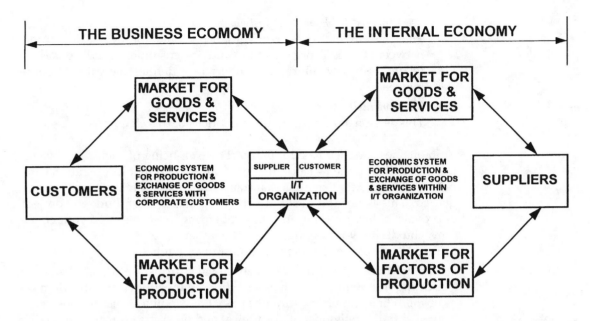

Figure 5.1   Dual Economies. The I/T organization participates in two economic systems concurrently: one that governs exchanges with the business unit customers, and another that governs the exchanges of goods and services within the I/T organization.

achieved when the economic systems motivate contrariant behaviors. The economies that govern I/T exchange must be reengineered to motivate collaborative behaviors and vigorously encourage decision making in harmony with business objectives.

The remainder of this chapter analyzes I/T economy design as follows:

- *5.1. Economic Models*
  This section provides abstract models of how both a fully centralized and a completely decentralized economic system work, and how economic systems may be evaluated for success.

- *5.2. Current I/T Organization Economic Systems*
  This section analyzes how many I/T organizations currently engage in the exchange of goods and services, and reaches some conclusions on the efficacy of those approaches.

- *5.3. How Should the Economic Systems Work*
  Using organizational economics, the study of transaction costs, as an analytical framework, this section analyzes how the rules of exchange for goods and services between the I/T organization and its customers should be arranged.

- *5.4. Proposed I/T Economic Systems*
  This system proposes a governance model for overseeing trade between the I/T organization and its customers, and considers related issues of migration. Governance defines the rules of commerce.

- *5.5. Conclusion*
  This section summarizes the main ideas of this chapter.

In business, money has dominion. The well-being of each person is so intricately tied to the functioning economic system that its operation cannot be ignored. Many actions that management takes are routinely disregarded. This is not the case with the rules that govern budgets, project approvals, billing for time, and project bidding. As you design your economy, you design your organizational behaviors.

Engels, one of the founders of communism, said:

> The economic structure of society always furnishes the real basis, starting from which we can alone work out the ultimate explanation of the whole superstructure of judicial and political institutions as well as of the religious, philosophical and other ideas of a given historical period. . . . the final causes of all social changes and political revolutions are to be sought not in men's brains, not in men's insights into eternal truth and justice but in changes in the methods of production and exchange.[1]

From this, it immediately follows that the incongruities between how business should operate and how the business does operate must be resolved in the economic system.

While many of the ideas of Engels and his comrades have deservedly fallen on bad times, it would be a fallacy to dismiss all of his ideas automatically. On this particular item, the centrality of economics to explaining behavior, I believe that Engels is right on target. So if we wish to achieve a more perfect state of alignment, we must change the methods of exchange to promote it. Otherwise, all our actions, however well intentioned, will be in vain, because we will have ignored the "final cause of all social change."

5.1 ECONOMY MODELS

The purpose of this section is to provide two polar and abstract models of economic systems. This will serve to establish a common set of notions about economic systems that we can exploit to analyze how I/T organizational economies currently work. We will then conclude this section by developing a set of criteria that can be used to judge the "goodness" of an economic system. We will later be able to use these criteria to judge both current economic systems and the proposed reengineered systems.

Completely Centralized Economy

In a completely centralized economy, all decisions are based on the judgment of the centralized *planners*. The system may be viewed as one of *planner sovereignty*, where the planners, based on some specified set of social or political values, make any and all resource allocation and deallocation decisions. All production and distribution responds to the planner's judgments. A macro-level description of this economic system is as follows:

- Decisions regarding consumption, investment, resource allocation, and production are made by a central authority.
- The central authority collects resource requests and issues deliberated orders to all economic agencies.
- Orders for production include all factors of production (labor content, technologies, capital investment, etc.).
- The central authority decides the rules of distribution for consumption.
- Consumers accept their allocation of products and services without any say in quality, terms and conditions, styling, and so on.

The success of such a system is intimately associated with the global wisdom of the planners, the information they have access to, and a consensus of community values.

Completely Decentralized Economy

In a completely decentralized economy, decisions are based on the marketplace dynamics between free and independent producers and self-interested consumers. The system may be viewed as one of *consumer sovereignty*, where producers attempt to anticipate consumer value preferences, and consumers select products and services that they deem satisfactory. Resource allocation and deallocation decisions are based on the profit motive for the producer and the value or cost motive for the consumer. All production and distribution responds to the shifting purchase decisions of consumers. A macro-level description of this economic system is as follows:

- Producers must anticipate what goods and services consumers will want, at what value points and in what quantities.

- Each producer must choose the mix of factors of production that will make its products most attractive to a discriminating consumer.
- Consumers must make trade-offs in meeting personal preferences before making a purchase decision.
- The problems of aligning customer demands with producer manufacturing are solved by a price and value system.
- Advertising is used to inform the consumer of the values associated with products.
- Based on consumer demand, production is adjusted to an equilibrium point where production equals consumption.

The success of such a system is intimately associated with prices, competition, and advertising (to make consumers aware of availability of products and services). The government in this environment plays the role of referee, defining property rights and remedies for breach of contract, but makes no economic decisions.

Criteria to Evaluate an Economic System

Since both of the extreme economic models presented share the same basic goals, though achievement is to be attained by radically different means, they and all the other variations are subject to common evaluation criteria. The performance of an economic system can be judged (with chosen weighting of factors) as follows:

- *Static Efficiency:* the raw productivity of the economic system to convert resources to products and services.
- *Dynamic Efficiency:* the growth in productivity of the economic system over time to convert resources to products and services.
- *Level of Output:* the total amount of goods and services produced.
- *Rate of Growth of Output:* the growth of output.
- *Customer Satisfaction:* the extent to which products and services meet consumer preferences.
- *Composition of Output:* the degree to which a variety of outputs are created to meet different market needs.
- *Adaptability to Change:* the ability of the economic system to adapt to changes in factors of production and consumer preferences.
- *Equity:* the degree to which prices provide a fair balance between producer costs and risk and consumer assessment of value.

Using this list, one can assess the power of an economic system to fulfill its mission.

Summary

A business, like a country, must choose an economic system to govern its internal exchanges of goods and services between organizational entities. At the extremes, the business can choose a completely centrally planned economy or a completely decentralized economy. In practice, most business economies use some interim variation. The actual economic system, though extraordinarily influential in determining business efficiency and effectiveness, is often an accident of asynchronous decisions. Regardless of the method chosen, the economic system is subject to evaluation through nine evaluation criteria. We will use these models and the evaluation criteria in the following sections to evaluate the performance of current I/T organization trading arrangements, and to determine how they should be altered to dramatically improve their performance.

5.2 CURRENT I/T ECONOMIC SYSTEMS

The purpose of this section is to assess the state of both economic systems that govern the I/T organization's trading practices. Are they robust economic systems that promote alignment and success for the business, or are they ossifying economies that are maladaptive and preempt success? Does the business economic system induce alignment, or does it prevent it? Does the internal economic system promote continuous transfer of new and improved technologies, or does it reward the old? Do the economic systems warrant applause, or do they demand to be reengineered?

The Business Economy

The position of the business economy can be assessed by translating the abstract economies that were introduced in the prior section into a set of practical questions. By answering the following questions, one can ascertain where the economic system rests on the continuum from completely centralized to completely decentralized.

1. *Allocation System:* how is market demand governed? Does a central planning council decide what will be maintained and developed, or do user organizations, individually and in consortiums, dictate their wishes by purchasing control of their own I/T dollars?

2. *Market System:* Are the user organizations free to choose any supplier, or must they use the internal I/T organization? Is the internal I/T organization free to choose not to supply desired services? Is the I/T organization free to sell its services to external customers? To what degree is the choice of technologies that may be used regulated?

3. *Resource (Budgeting) System:* Do the user organizations have control over their own I/T budgets, or does a central planning board allocate I/T expense as overhead (a corporate tax)? Does the I/T organization get its own budget, or does it receive revenue from its products and services, or *chargeback,* from which it funds itself? Is the I/T organization free to grow and contract, based on demand for its services, or is the I/T budget used as a way to throttle I/T expenses?

4. *Supplier System:* How does the I/T organization interact with its customers? Is it a sole supplier that takes orders, or does it operate using the market processes of a competitive business (sales organization, distribution channels, contracts, warrantees, etc.)?

The answers to these questions provide a picture of how the business economy works. Given that there are as many mutations of business economic systems as there are businesses, it is impossible to answer these questions for one and all. Each I/T organization must answer them for itself. Nevertheless, a composite answer for many archetype I/T organizations is as follows:

Q1. How does the allocation system work?

A1. A central planning committee composed of user representatives, development representatives, operations representatives, project management, and systems support meets and determines what projects will be funded and what resources will be devoted to application maintenance. User organizations negotiate as peers, not as customers, how their requirements will be met. Allocation is reduced to a political process, where influence is the prime ingredient used to shape decision making.

Q2. How does the market system work?

A2. The customer organization must use the internal supplier who enjoys a monopoly position. The I/T organization unilaterally determines what technologies will be used and in what quantities. By invoking the death phrase "not ready for industrial-grade use," the I/T organization may stop any technology from being used. Cursory measurement systems may be used to measure I/T performance, but they tend to focus on pure technology measurements as opposed to true customer satisfaction issues.

Q3. How does the budgeting system work?

A3. I/T costs are spread over user organization budgets as an overhead expense.[2] The amount spread is a function of the political allocation process. The I/T organization receives a budget at the beginning of the year, rather than earning revenue from its sales of services to its customers. In some cases, chargebacks are used to relate actual resource usage to specific customers. These chargebacks are usually unintelligible to the customers, because they are formulated in I/T units (CPU hours, DASD days, tape mounts, etc.) instead of customer units (accounts maintained, transactions processed, etc.). While service agreements may be in place, there are no economic penalties imposed on the I/T organization for failing to meet contracted service levels or due dates. The I/T budget is usually frozen and used as a means to throttle I/T demand.

Q4. How does the supplier system work?

A4. The I/T organization works in the manner of a monopolist. It determines the terms and conditions of exchange and expects the customers to be I/T-friendly. While most I/T organizations provide analysts, they do not provide business solution consulting services.

Typical business economies seem to be heavily biased toward the centralized planning model.

The Internal Economy

The internal economic system used to govern exchanges between I/T functional units is best described not by the notions of centralized or decentralized economies, but by the notion of medieval feudalism. Internal I/T organizations tend to be governed by vertical smokestack organizations (defined by a technology), which rule over their domain and have complete control of their budgets. Employees' loyalties are to their vertical managers, and the well-being of a community is directly proportional to the organizational leader's political ability to maintain the status of her technology. This system is analogous to feudalism, which dominated Europe from 900 to 1500 A.D. Feudalism was characterized by small districts, each ruled by a single nobleman. The nobility granted land to the tenants, who in return pledged fealty to their masters. Serfs worked the land while the master engaged in commerce with neighboring royalty. The master provided protection to his vassals and serfs by forestalling outside aggression and any reforms that challenged the feudal social, political, and economic order.

So while the business economy tends toward centralized planning, the internal economy tends to be a well-packaged 20th-century version of medieval Europe. What are the consequences of this remarkable alliance of 1930s communism with 1250 A.D. feudalism? Does this phenomenal combination yield a successful economic system or an economic tragedy?

Economic System Evaluation

Coupling a business centralized planning economy with an internal economy modeled on feudalism results in gross distortions and deformities of economic behavior, which have the effect of making the overall I/T organization ineffective, inefficient, and maladaptive. Specifically, the following distortions are introduced as a consequence of this preposterous economic union:

- Fulfillment of user needs is a result of politics by executives, rather than the wants of businesspeople close to the external customer.

- Priorities are decided by an impersonal bureaucracy, rather than by the people with the need.

- The I/T budget creates an artificial cap on demand. This results either in covert use of technology or user frustration with I/T.

- While the line organizations are under constant competitive pressures, the I/T organization is shielded from the unpleasantness of the marketplace. They share neither a sense of urgency nor the need for hustle.

- The I/T organization is focused on serving its supervisor rather than on serving your customer.

- User organizations cannot dynamically shift demands based on changing marketplace realities.

- I/T organizations have little motivation to innovate. New technologies are introduced on an I/T schedule, not on a schedule of business needs.

- The charging of I/T services to overhead or in indecipherable I/T units makes understanding costs impossible.

- There is no nimbleness in the process to support small, quick, advantageous projects.

- Not subject to competition or benchmarking, the internal I/T organization declares itself world-class but nobody really knows the truth of this claim. Users engage in subterfuge to hide expenses and hire external providers, resulting in growing distrust between I/T provider and customer.

We would like to make it clear that these results are a consequence not of the inherent nature of the game players, but of the system. You cannot avoid complying with the economic system. You can scream about quality, teamwork, cooperation, customer satisfaction, and so on until you are blue in the face, but if you really want to have them, you must first alter the economic system so that it stops creating deformities of economic behavior and starts forcing alignment of producer actions with customer needs. People will unfailingly do what the economic system tells them to do, not what fleeting verbal exhortations suggest.

Conclusion

The answers to the eight criteria for evaluating an economic system (static efficiency, dynamic efficiency, level of output, rate of growth of output, customer satisfaction, composition of output, adaptability to change, and equity) are found in Figures 1.12 through 1.14. Customers are grossly dissatisfied with all aspects of the results of the current economic systems. The dual economies have to be reengineered. We must say good-bye to bureaucratic central planning and feudalism, but how?

5.3 BASIS FOR IMPROVED I/T ECONOMIC SYSTEMS

The purpose of this section is to provide an analysis of how the economic relationship between the I/T organization and its clients should be framed. A reflex reaction to the economic calamity described in the prior section is either to outsource I/T (see Section 2.3) or move to a completely free market system where the internal I/T organization is just another equal supplier of I/T services. To develop a more thoughtful response, it is necessary to address two additional questions:

1. Should I/T services be internally or externally sourced, and if so,
2. How should the internal I/T economy be redesigned to infuse free market motivations and entrepreneurial behaviors?

The discipline of Organizational Economics can provide assistance in answering these questions.

Organizational Economics

Organizational Economics (OE) provides formal frameworks to assist in the analysis and design of organizational economic systems.[3] OE is built on the study of transaction cost analysis, which analyzes costs associated with customer/supplier exchanges. OE transaction cost models provide insights into judging whether internal exchanges (an internal business hierarchy) or external exchanges (the impersonal marketplace) will lead to cost minimization.

OE is constructed on three insightful and instructive axioms:

Axiom I: Organizations are governance mechanisms for supporting exchange.

Axiom II: The types of organizational arrangements needed to support any particular exchange and the associated costs will depend on the inherent characteristics of the exchange.

Axiom III: The types of organizational arrangements to govern any particular exchange will depend on the cost effectiveness of those arrangements, as compared with alternative arrangements.

Transaction cost analysis focuses on selecting the mechanisms required to mediate exchange equitably and efficiently. Transaction costs rationale is used to ascertain the optimum form of governance. The most desirable economic relationship is a function of selecting the mechanisms that minimize the total costs of negotiating, monitoring, adapting, and enforcing the flow of goods and services between the parties.

The basic choice to be made is whether to source outside or within the boundaries of the enterprise. In the first case, free marketplace mechanisms are depended upon to facilitate equitable exchanges; in the latter case, hierarchical organizational rules are used to ensure equity. The relative costs of market verse hierarchy have to be traded off to make a prudent decision.

Goal/Performance Framework

Transaction cost analysis provides two analytical frameworks to assist in making the choice. Figure 5.2 shows a goal/performance graph. The axes of the graph are the drivers of transaction costs, and may be understood as follows:

- *Performance ambiguity:* arises when any dimension of the exchange makes it difficult for either party to evaluate the performance of the other. The inability to measure performance or value is often the result of the intangible nature of a service. Higher ambiguity leads to escalated costs of negotiating, monitoring, and enforcing exchanges.
- *Goal incongruence:* arises when either party has the incentive to promote its interests (opportunism) at the expense of the other, because the expected return will exceed the return for cooperation. Drivers of self-serving behaviors are information advantage, relative power, and frequency of exchanges. When congruence of goals is possible, an extended relational governance adds value to the exchange.

Based on these transaction cost drivers, four possible choices for transaction governance are possible (see Figure 5.2):

I. *Impersonal Market (Goal Incongruence + Low Performance Ambiguity)*
Customers have little difficulty in monitoring the services they receive, and both parties can act opportunistically. Transaction costs are minimized through the impersonal marketplace.

II. *Relational Market (Goal Congruence + Low Performance Ambiguity)*
Customers have little difficulty in monitoring services, but due to goal congruence, collaboration through an extended relationship is most advantageous.

GOAL INCONGRUENCE

IMPERSONAL
MARKET
I

IMPERSONAL
HIERARCHY
III

LOW
PERFORMANCE
AMBIGUITY

HIGH
PERFORMANCE
AMBIGUITY

RELATIONAL
MARKET
II

RELATIONAL
HIERARCHY
IV

GOAL CONGRUENCE

Figure 5.2   Performance Ambiguity Vs. Goal Incongruence Graph. Performance ambiguity and goal incongruence drive transaction costs. Source: D. Bowen and G. Jones, "Transaction Cost Analysis of Service Organization-Customer Exchange," *Academy of Management Review* 11:2 (1986).

III. *Impersonal Hierarchy (Goal Incongruence + High Performance Ambiguity)* High level of transaction costs makes an internal impersonal hierarchy the least costly solution.

IV. *Relational Hierarchy (Goal Congruence + High Performance Ambiguity)* Performance ambiguity coupled with goal congruence leads to internal relational hierarchy as the superior governance mechanism.

If we superimpose the exchange situation for the I/T organization and its business unit customers on Figure 5.2, we believe that a first-cut analysis would lead to the positioning shown in Figure 5.3a. However, when you amend your analysis to add the critical importance of I/T to the creation of advantage, the intangibility of assessing and measuring I/T value, and the need for continual adaptability to respond to both business dynamics and technology dynamics, the best choice is a relational hierar-chy (see Figure 5.3b).

In summary, we believe that the use of the goal/performance transaction cost analysis tool leads to the conclusion that a relational hierarchy is the preferred governance mechanism for delivering I/T services to internal business unit customers. Careful design of the governance mechanism and the internal economy will be required to promote the best competitive market behaviors within the relational hierarchy framework.

An Aside

The goal/performance framework explains very simply but elegantly why so many internal I/T organizations failed at providing in-house PC stores. Since there was low performance ambiguity, the marketplace, impersonal or relational (Figure 5.2), was the preferable governance structure.

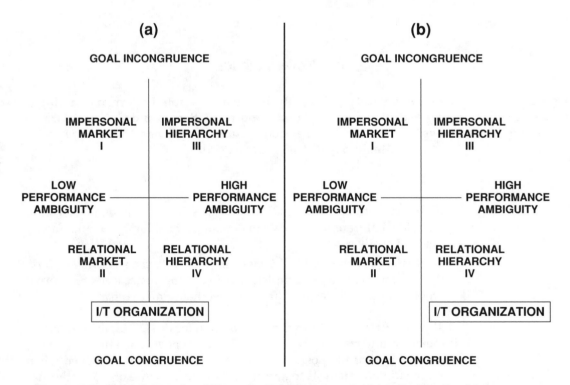

Figure 5.3   Superimposing I/T on the Performance Ambiguity Vs. Goal Incongruence Graph. I/T services are best delivered through a relational hierarchy.

Investment Character/Frequency Framework

A second tool provided by transaction cost analysis, illustrated in Figure 5.4, is based on the transaction cost drivers of "investment characteristics" and "frequency." The transaction cost drivers may be understood as follows:

- *Frequency:* the episodic or recurrent nature of the exchanges.
- *Investment characteristics:* classify the nature of the goods or services being exchanged:
  - Idiosyncratic: highly specialized goods or services.
  - Nonspecific: broadly marketable goods or services.
  - Mixed: a combination of the above.

As shown in Figure 5.4, the framework prescribes four governance mechanisms to manage exchange, as follows:

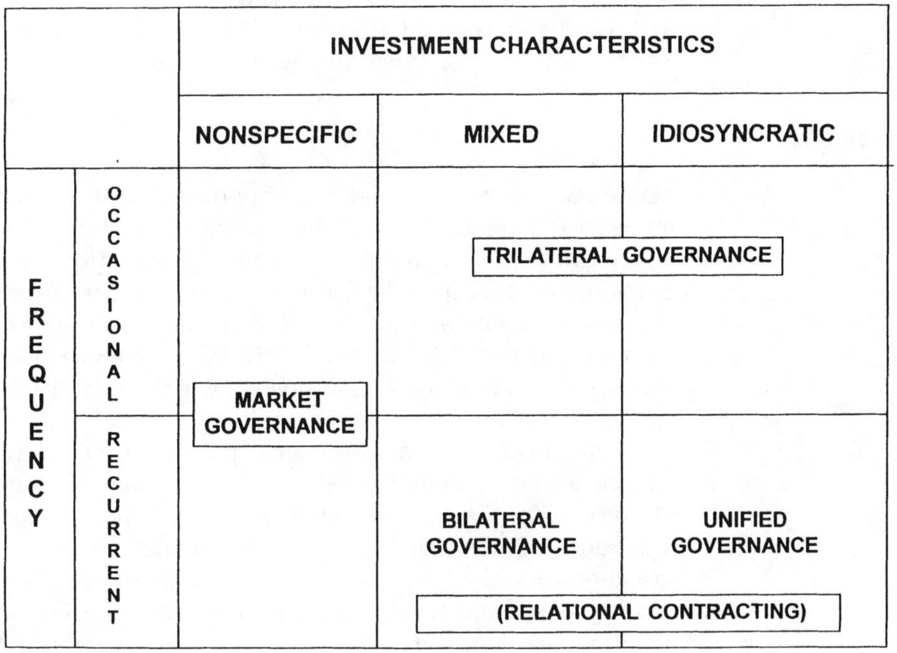

Figure 5.4   Investment Characteristics Vs. Frequency Graph. Investment characteristics and frequency of exchange are the drivers of transaction costs. Source: O. Williamson, "Transaction Cost Economics: The Governance of Contractual Relations," *Journal of Law and Economics.*

1. *Market Governance:* free market mechanism.

2. *Trilateral Governance:* free market mechanism tempered by explicit settlement rules to handle potential problems due to idiosyncrasy of products/services.

3. *Bilateral Governance:* joint government with extended relationship to deal with the inevitable need for adaptability. The fiat ability of the internal hierarchy to solve disputes points to an internal solution.

4. *Unified Governance:* self-sufficient organization to optimize idiosyncratic skills.

As shown in Figure 5.5, I/T services fall in the Bilateral Governance cell.

The question now turns to whether the governance structure should be with an internal or external supplier. The third parameter of this framework, uncertainty, is helpful in resolving this issue. As uncertainty grows, and the ability to adapt to events as they unfold becomes prominent, an internal hierarchy provides the maximum flexibility because of the use of fiat. We therefore conclude, again, that a hierarchy offers the best structure for delivering I/T services to internal business clients.

Game Theory

Some readers may be highly disappointed with the conclusion that an internal I/T organization is the superior I/T supplier structure. Having agreed with the diagnosis of economic dysfunction itemized in the prior section, they anticipated a free market structure as the preferred structure. The analysis we have concluded, driven by the organizational economic variables of performance ambiguity, goal incongruence, uncertainty, frequency of transactions, and investment characteristics, has concluded against that alternative.

Game theory provides another approach to explain why this is so. The organizational economic analysis indicates that the maximum benefit is derived from the structure that ensures the most extended cooperative relationship. "Extended" must be understood in terms of the number of collaborators, the time frame encompassed by the cooperation, and the ability to spontaneously order and reorder the relationship based on evolving times and circumstances. Game theory refers to this type of problem as the *prisoner's dilemma*.

The prisoner's dilemma refers to a game theory problem where each player would achieve maximum payoff by trusting and cooperating with the other players. Since trust is hard to come by, each player takes actions based on mistrust, and a less than optimal payoff is achieved. What the

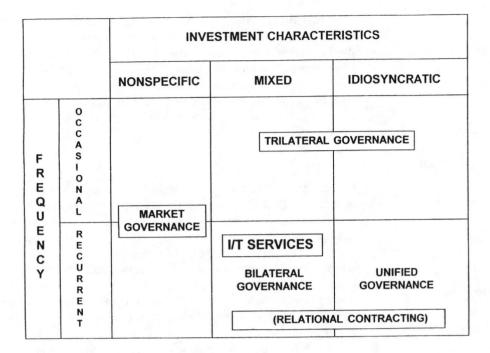

Figure 5.5   Superimposing I/T on Investment Characteristics Vs. Frequency Graph. I/T services are best delivered through bilateral governance.

organizational economic analysis is telling us is that the I/T supplier problem is a prisoner's dilemma game theory problem, and that the optimal payoff for the business occurs by an extended trusting relationship between supplier and customer. This is best achieved with an internal structural relationship. The critical organizational design variable is to construct a governance structure that encourages and builds trust between the users and the I/T providers.

Summary

This section has used organizational economics to assist in understanding how the trading relationship between the I/T organization and business unit customers should be structured. The use of two transaction cost analysis tools resulted in the same conclusion, that an internal relational governance mechanism is the preferred alternative. The internal relational governance mechanism permits the company to deal with the complexity and uncertainty of I/T in an adaptive and sequential decision-making manner. Problems can unfold and be dealt with in a bounded manner.

Outsourcing requires the specifying of a complete and exhaustive decision tree for all contingencies. Such a complete a priori knowledge is simply inconsistent with the nature of I/T assets and their use when devoted to supporting a war of global maneuver. The problem, then, is how to design an internal marketplace bounded by an internal hierarchy (I/T supplier and customer within the same business), but not lose the best features of a free market system that ensure value, service, and minimum opportunism.

An Aside

It is instructive that the preceding analysis supports the assertion made in Section 1.3 that the outsourcing of I/T services did not make strategic sense. As the speed of I/T change accelerates and the importance of I/T as the currency of advantage grows, performance ambiguity, goal incongruence, and the idiosyncrasy of I/T skills conspire against the outsourcing alternative. The real possibility of outsourcer opportunism is also quite important. While outsourcers portray themselves as strategic partners, few (if any) contracts personify the nature of a true partnership—shared objectives, shared strategic moves, and most important, shared financial reward or loss.

The outsourcing hoopla has suffered from confusing current events with history. For historical events, we know the outcome; for current events, the outcome is in motion. Much of the misinformation about the strategic efficacy of outsourcing is due to confusing what the outsourcing players say will happen with what is still to unfold. The problem with outsourcing rhetoric is best described by the word *prolepsis*, which means "the representation of a future act as if it has already been accomplished." Prolepsis is, unfortunately, quite common in the I/T industry literature.[4]

Machiavelli best expressed why you don't turn the basis of your security over to others:

> The arms on which a prince bases the defense of his state are either his own, or mercenary or auxiliary. Mercenaries and auxiliaries are useless and dangerous. If a prince bases the defense of his state on mercenaries, he will never achieve stability or security. . . . the reason for this is that there is no loyalty or inducement to keep them on the field apart from the little they are paid and that is not enough to make them want to die for you. . . . I conclude, therefore, that unless it commands its own arms, no principality is secure, rather it is dependent on fortune since there is no valor and no loyalty to defend it when adversity comes.[5]

As we move forward into the 21st century, we will be engaged in I/T fighting. Why would you voluntarily exchange your I/T warriors for I/T mercenaries?[6] We might even go so far as to say, in an antipodal equality, that outsourcing is as detrimental to the strategic well-being of the business as the development of a competent, loyal, and partisan I/T staff is beneficial.

5.4 PROPOSED I/T ECONOMIC SYSTEMS

The purpose of this section is to propose a governance mechanism to chaperon the efficient and effective exchange of goods and services between the I/T organization and its customers. Cooperation does not arise from an a priori assumption of harmony of interests, but from the creation of institutions that create enforced rules for collective action. In designing this economic system, we intend to alleviate the distortions identified in Section 5.2 and maximize the economic success factors identified in Section 5.1. The proposed governance mechanism is a regulated utility.

The I/T Regulated Utility

As shown in Figure 5.6, an independent regulator should be inserted to oversee the I/T to business marketplace. The regulator should perform the following functions:

1. *I/T Architecture:* the regulator, in concert with customers and the I/T organization, defines the rules of reach, range, and maneuverability for the business. The I/T organization delivers the architecture.

2. *Economic Measurement:* the regulator is responsible for defining and implementing processes to measure the economic results of the I/T organization. These measures have to be benchmarked against industry norms to ascertain their competitive position and set future goals. Of particular importance is the development of a rich customer satisfaction measurement system to judge the degree of customer satisfaction with the I/T organization. Again, benchmarking is required to judge and set performance metrics. Compensation of I/T management is correlated with economic and customer satisfaction measurements.

3. *Price Setting and Service Performance:* the regulator is responsible for establishing ceiling prices for goods and services consistent with graduated service levels. Benchmarking can be used to ascertain best market pricing and associated service levels. Pricing is then established, based on removing non-incurred expenses from prices. Service-level benchmarking leads to establishment of explicit service levels with guarantees. Financial penalties are imposed for fail-

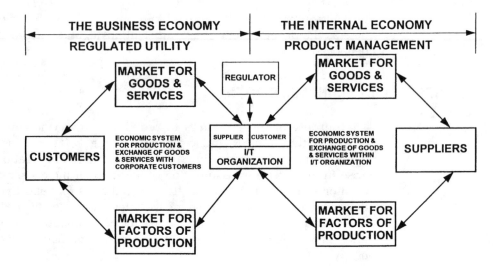

Figure 5.6 Governance Mechanisms. The relationship between the I/T organization and its customers should be regulated through a utility mechanism.

ing to meet service levels. The I/T organization can price up to, but not above, the benchmarked prices. This ensures customers the best prices and eliminates the need for market searching by them.

4. *Consortiums:* the regulator may serve as manager of consortium projects. When large cross-organizational systems are desired by management, the regulator can form the consortium and create a composite customer for the I/T organization.

In this closed market, exchange equity and value are ensured through benchmarking by a neutral third party.

The Business Economy

The following changes are suggested for the business economy (refer to Section 5.2):

1. *Allocation System:* each business unit negotiates an I/T budget in its own hierarchy (or as part of a horizontal process). The business units then purchase the services they want in the amounts that they want from the I/T organization. Business units, as appropriate, form buying consortiums for large cross-functional systems.

2. *Market System:* business units must buy from the internal supplier but equity and value have been assured by the regulatory body. The I/T organization delivers products and services in harmony with the I/T architecture.

3. *Budgeting:* all I/T expenses are charged back to the cost causer in the business units. There are no overhead taxes or global spreading of I/T expenses. The I/T organization receives revenue for its services and funds itself from that revenue. Major I/T investments are funded from I/T profits, specific project-associated expenses agreed to by a business unit, or loans/grants from the corporation. The I/T organization contracts and grows based on demand. There is never a backlog of projects as long as customers have budget dollars to pay for them.

4. *Supplier System:* the I/T organization grows by stimulating demand for advantageous I/T solutions. It proposes end-to-end solutions for customers, provides proposals, and bids fixed price or labor and materials as appropriate.

With equity and value assured, the business users and I/T organization engage in matching user needs to I/T product and services without the need for a political bureaucracy to decide priorities or funding. We would prefer to view the regulatory mechanism not as a new bureaucracy, but as a substitute for free market pricing, value determination, and service determination.

The last point deserves some elaboration. The user organizations, always suspicious of I/T opportunism, will seek marketplace bids so that they can evaluate the value and equity of internal services. The I/T organization, to demonstrate value and competitiveness, will have to engage in price and service benchmarking. An architecture, as we have discussed, is mandatory. So the regulatory agency is not so much a new bureaucracy as a neutral and efficient information broker, who can alleviate mutual suspicion and let the users and I/T turn their attention and focus to winning in the marketplace, rather than fighting with each other. The regulatory agency is *absolutely not* a central planning board; it is the arbiter of the rules of exchange and commerce consistent with the demonstrated a priori need for reach, range, and maneuverability across the enterprise. It is through the rules of commerce that an extended order of collaboration is achieved.

The Internal Economy

The internal I/T economy has to be reformed to adapt to the new realities. A strong notion of customer and supplier has to be ingrained into all

234   **Practical Steps for Aligning Information Technology with Business Strategies**

internal I/T exchanges. The self-serving vertical smokestack structure has to be replaced with a product management structure. In a product management structure, a product manager has end-to-end responsibility for the delivery of products and services to a customer. We suggest the following:

1. Budget control should be given to the product management function.
2. Product management should buy processes from process owners throughout the organization.
3. Process owners should buy needed functions from the various functional organizations. The functional organizations, analogous to object servers, advertise what services they can perform, and process owners string the services together to provide the end-to-end services needed to deliver the products.

Introducing market forces within the previously feudal I/T organization prods alignment by diffusing the goals of cost minimization and service/value maximization. Figure 5.7 illustrates this approach. Customers buy products; product managers deliver products throughout their life cycle by contracting for horizontal process with internal process owners. Process owners subcontract with functional organizations to do required services, and functional organizations consume resources in delivering the services.

This approach imposes a proper customer/supplier relationship within the I/T organization, inspires desired cooperative behaviors, and forces alignment through the funding of horizontal capabilities instead of vertical functions. Product managers can make customer satisfaction measurements and negotiate for required processes. Process owners can measure and negotiate for needed functions. Function owners compete for usage and focus on controlling expense. As a by-product of imposing this type of economy on the organization, the organization is well positioned to perform value chain analysis to improve productivity, time, or value added. By organizing in this manner, product managers would not only fund research/development (R/D) for their products, but they would also fund R/D for their processes; both product and process are subject to continual improvement.

In this manner, the same pressures and urgency that the line users feel on a daily basis are imposed on the I/T providers. There is a chain back to a real customer for all functional activities. I/T providers who do not deliver quality at prescribed costs will have a difficult time keeping their functional units funded.

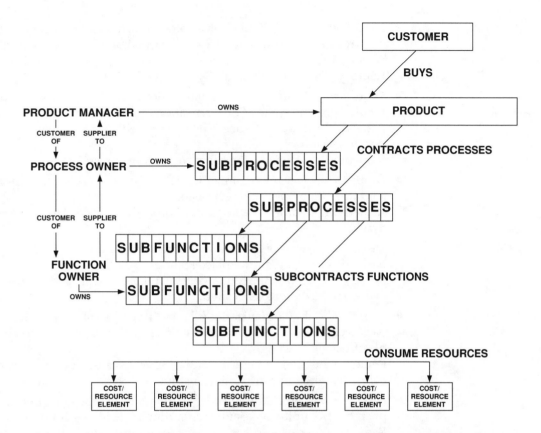

Figure 5.7   Internal I/T Customer/Supplier Relationships. Product mangers buy services from process owners, who buy functional delivery capability from functional units.

Alleviating Marketplace Deformities and Distortions

We believe that these remedies will alleviate the previously itemized marketplace distortions as follows:

- *Distortion 1:* Fulfillment of user needs is a result of politics by executives, rather than the wants of businesspeople close to the external customer.
  Remedy: Business units negotiate solutions directly.

- *Distortion 2:* Priorities are decided by an impersonal bureaucracy, rather than by the people with the need.
  Remedy: Each business unit sets its own priorities by allocating its own budget dollars.

- *Distortion 3:* The I/T budget creates an artificial cap on demand. This results either in covert use of technology or user frustration with I/T.
Remedy: There is no longer any cap on demand.

- *Distortion 4:* While the line organizations are under constant competitive pressures, the I/T organization is shielded from the unpleasantness of the marketplace. They share neither a sense of urgency nor the need for hustle.
Remedy: I/T units feel the same competitive pressures.

- *Distortion 5:* The I/T organization is focused on serving its supervisor rather than on serving its customer.
Remedy: I/T staff serve horizontal processes targeted to serve customers.

- *Distortion 6:* User organizations cannot dynamically shift demands based on changing marketplace realities.
Remedy: User organizations control their budgets and may shift demands allocations as desired.

- *Distortion 7:* I/T organizations have little motivation to innovate. New technologies are introduced on an I/T schedule, not on a schedule of business needs.
Remedy: Regulator benchmarking assesses best-in-class services being delivered to comparable customers.

- *Distortion 8:* The charging of I/T services to overhead or in indecipherable I/T units makes understanding costs impossible.
Remedy: All costs are charged back to the cost causer in meaningful business units.

- *Distortion 9:* There is no nimbleness in the process to support small, quick, advantageous projects.
Remedy: Customers can allocate budgets as they choose when they choose. Driven to earn revenue, the I/T organization is much more willing to reorganize spontaneously to meet revised revenue opportunities.

- *Distortion 10:* Not subject to competition or benchmarking, the internal I/T organization declares itself world-class but nobody really knows the truth of this claim. Users engage in subterfuge to hide expenses and hire external providers, resulting in growing distrust between I/T provider and customer.
Remedy: I/T organization is subject to extensive benchmarking. Equity and value of transactions is ensured; there is no need for users to engage in subterfuge.

The benchmarking of the eight criteria for evaluating an economic system (static efficiency, dynamic efficiency, level of output, rate of growth of output, customer satisfaction, composition of output, adaptability to change, and equity) will provide data to judge how well the governance mechanism is working, and appropriate tuning can be applied as events and results warrant.

Outsourcing and Free Market Governance Mechanisms

Though the analysis in Section 5.3 did not endorse these alternatives, if, after a number of iterations, satisfactory progress is not being made in meeting benchmark objectives, the regulatory structure allows you to adopt either alternative. Whichever you would choose, the architecture definition and benchmarking done by the regulatory mechanism will be invaluable in dealing with the external providers. The creation of the regulatory body is a prerequisite for outsourcing or free market I/T as well.

I/T Investment Valuation

A long-lived problem that has confronted and frustrated business executives has been placing a creditable value (return on investment) on the huge and seemingly endless sums of I/T expenditures. As illustrated in Figure 5.8, I/T investment continues to skyrocket, but research studies assert, for the most part, that I/T investment is a lemon, a bottomless pit that has overpromised and underdelivered.[7] This contradiction between I/T investment and measurable results is popularly referred to as the *productivity paradox*.[8] As Paul Strassmann, former Pentagon CIO, said, "There is no relation between spending for computers, profits and productivity."[9] The dissatisfaction with I/T evidenced in Figure 1.12 would not exist if executive management felt that they were getting a fair return for their staggering investments. There is no shortage of alternative ways to measure I/T investments. Proposed methodologies include the following:

- *Economic Approaches:* these approaches represent traditional accounting methods. Typical examples are net present value, internal rate of return, return on investment, and payback.

- *Cost Reduction Approaches:* these approaches represent traditional cost benefit, cost displacement, or cost avoidance methods. Typical examples of this approach are cost of quality, work value analysis, and cost displacement analysis.

- *Management Value Approaches:* these approaches attempt to place a value on the intangible business benefits of I/T. Typical examples of these approaches are Return on Management[10] and Information Economics.[11]

- *Strategic Approaches:* these approaches, generally qualitative, attempt to place a strategic value on the investment. This can be

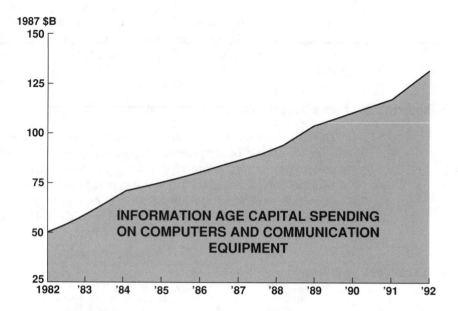

Figure 5.8   I/T Investment. In the last decade, I/T investment has grown by a factor of five. (Source: Commerce Dept.)

done using any combination of strategic frameworks. Typical examples are Sustainable Competitive Advantage and Competitive Response Analysis.

These measures are often used concurrently with allocated weightings to justify an investment.

While not a complete solution, the act of creating a proper economy with unambiguous customers and suppliers goes a long way to resolving the valuation problem. The I/T organization must make infrastructure and product investments just like any other supplier. It must decide what products and services at what investment levels will be attractive to customers. The customers, now in control of their budgets, make investment judgments by funding applications that have specific costs and benefits associated with them. The supplier invests to create value opportunities and the customer purchases to realize value.

The separation of I/T investment from user application investment removes much of the fog of I/T valuation. Each investment is independent and stands on its own merit. The I/T organizations can judge its success by its ability to sell its services, customer satisfaction measures, and benchmarking results. The users can assess their satisfaction with the services received. Since I/T has no indigenous value (it is only a means to an end), the value of I/T equates to the user's assessment of value received for the application portfolio. I believe that this is the way it normally works in everyday life, and it is the way it should work for I/T as well.

For making strategic I/T investments, the strategic approaches are the best methods to use. Many people are immediately dissatisfied with them because of their nonquantitative character. This, however, is a spurious criticism. If we insist on measurement as the criterion for making all decisions, then we robotically elevate measurement over relevance. If what can be measured is also the determining variable, that is the best of situations. However, if the determining variable does not lend itself to hard measurement (or at least to accurate measurement), then substituting what can be measured for measurement's sake and focusing on it rather than on the true strategic variable makes strategy a servant of measurement, rather than measurement a servant of strategy. So, in formulating strategic I/T investment decisions, measure. If you can't, however, qualitative assessment based on nonquantifiable strategic variables is far superior to quantitative assessment based on secondarily important but measurable variables.

A prudent way to resolve the dilemma between the traditional strengths of the economic approaches that exclusively emphasize cold cash flow analysis (net present value, discounted cash flow, return on investment, payback, etc.) and the more nebulous and nonquantifiable values associated with strategic I/T initiatives is to append economic valuation with option values.[12] Traditional investment control methods often reject strategically important I/T investments, because the cash flow analysis is not able to recognize the value of the embedded options within the initiative. The ability to be positioned for flexibility in a business environment of constant change, uncertainty, and competitive dynamics is certainly of immense value to the business. Nevertheless, traditional economic valuation ignores the current value of being able to alter strategy later in face of the emergent situation. This perspective is especially important given the importance we have given to reach, range, and maneuverability as the path to I/T business alignment. If I/T is to enable a war of movement and permit the business to exploit marketplace gaps, then I/T must preposition itself for the unforeseen. In other words, it must invest without assured cash flow returns for the option of later flexibility that will permit currently unknowable cash flow returns. Since economic valuation methods don't give value to adaptability (and in wars of maneuver, adaptability is more important then the strength of fixed positions), the economic methods must be altered to take into account option values that give proper worth to strategic maneuverability.

An option is the ability to take prompt advantage of opportunities at a later date that would not be possible without the earlier investment. Many of the I/T investments that are required to achieve a reach, range, and maneuverable architecture yield the business choices in the ability to scale, the ability to switch, and/or the ability to accelerate or decelerate plans. Exactly how the business will take advantage of these options is unknowable. The marketplace opportunities presented to the business will emerge and cannot be exactly planned for. Yet when they do emerge, I/T will have to have the reach, range, and maneuverability to take prompt advantage of them. Such flexibility will exist then only if you make a strategic investment in I/T now. So you are not buying predictable cash flows by your I/T investments, you are buying options for future unknown cash flows.

To do option value analysis, you basically do traditional cash flow valuation for the investment and then add the value that the investment gives you in terms of future flexibility. A premium should be given to the option value for uncertainty and time. The greater the uncertainty of the environment and the longer that the investment will provide you with choices, the greater the option value of the investment. In this way, I/T investments that have traditionally failed economic valuation and justification are quite justifiable, because you have finally included the most important value element of the I/T investment.

What is particularly attractive to the astute I/T strategist is that options are asymmetric financial instruments. While the cost is fixed in the cash flow analysis, the upside potential for future advantage is constrained only by future exploitation opportunities. Since our reach, range, and maneuverability theory provides us with an overarching framework for advantageous I/T investment, the issue is to use judgment and experience to decide which reach, range, or maneuverability investments now will yield the greatest option return later. Given the pressures on the business, how should you distribute your option buying dollars across reach, range, and maneuverability? Strategic I/T investments are equal to the net present value of cash flows plus the future value of options presented by the investment. By ignoring option value, you are valuating investments based on a war of attrition model. We know, however, that we will be fighting wars of maneuver. It is therefore necessary to invest both for the known (via predictable cash flows) and the unknown (via option values). In this way, you make strategic I/T investments that will position you so that you will surely prevail over those who have already lost by being chained to economic investment models that do not allow for nimbleness.[13]

Implementation

Implementation, moving from your current economic systems to your new economic systems, should be overseen by the following concerns:

1. *Dictating:* the change will have to be dictated from the top of the business. For better or worse, all the current power brokers know how to operate within the current system, and they will have a million and one reasons that it can't be done, not now, not ever. The change must be declared, a date set, and an executive responsible for implementation assigned ownership. You must commit yourself and your organization to the reformed economic system. Observe, in Figure 4.14, that the vestibule of Hell is reserved for the uncommitted.

2. *Modeling:* two models must be carefully developed: a model of the current economic system and a model of the new economic system. The new system should be judged to see that your distortions are remedied and new distortions are not introduced.

3. *Concurrency:* both economies must be changed concurrently. On a staggered basis, the order of change is: (1) introduce the regulatory authority, (2) reform the I/T internal economy, and (3) reform the business economy.

4. *Education:* business units and I/T staff have to be educated in the rationale for the change and the way the new system will work.

While some people worry about such massive change to the business economic systems and the reactions of the staff, the reality is that everybody knows exactly how to operate within the new model because they do it every day in their personal lives.

Conclusion

The prescriptions suggested herein are viewed by some as radical surgery. The reality is that the I/T organization is in a profound economic crisis and radical surgery is demanded. Alignment requires economic alignment to force daily reminders of who is the customer and why the I/T organization is here in the first place. Unless the economic system provides a daily wake-up call, the I/T organization, left to its own devices, will revert to its traditional monopolistic behaviors after the pep rallies are over. The ideas that have been presented here can serve as the foundation for you to build an economy that blends competitive fervor with relational hierarchy advantage. The time for economic reengineering is now; it is a prerequisite for successful strategic alignment of I/T with the business.

Though not often understood or analyzed as such, every business is confronted with an intractable and perennial dilemma. On one hand, in order to succeed, the business requires broad-based collaboration, cooperation, and alignment. It demands a collective competitive agenda. Conversely, Western culture admires and promotes individualism, entrepreneurship, distinctiveness, and self-motivated creativity. The sublimation of individualism to collective behavior requires the implementation of deliberate compulsive policies between enticement and overt coercion.

It is our assessment that the best solution to this irreconcilable dilemma is the design of the minimum possible compulsive act that yields the maximum quantity of alignment. Adam Smith taught in *The Wealth of Nations* that such an act is the free market system. The economy's invisible hand prods people, out of economic necessity, to work harmoniously together. We therefore assert that to successfully reengineer the I/T organization, one must reengineer the economy to provide the minimum coercion to guarantee the maximum cooperation. All the other prods and nudges, promotion and raise carrots, team-building junkets, slogans, reward and recognition programs, exhortations, and cultural norms are a hopelessly poor second to the simple compulsive act of designing the internal economic system to promote alignment transparently via its invisible hand.

5.5 CONCLUSION

This chapter has provided advice on how to reengineer the economic systems that govern I/T organization exchange of goods and services. It is our conclusion that the current system is a substantial hindrance to achieving I/T and business alignment, and that a relational hierarchy based on a regulated utility model will offer the best resolution for all the competing demands. The internal I/T economy must also be reformed to promote hustle, competitive fervor, and a constant reminder of service to the customer.

Table 5.1 summarizes some of the major design points in mapping out your governance system. An economy is like the pipe room next to a steam engine: there are hundreds if not thousands of valves for which a setting between wide open and completely shut must be chosen. As you set each valve, so you lay out the economy. As you lay out your economy, you design your organization's behaviors. The economic system of your business is much too important to be left to a haphazard collection of independent actions that have accumulated over the years.

There is a higher lesson in the study of organizational economics that transcends our immediate purpose. As indicated in the discussion of indirection in Section 2.4, the careful review and design of economic governance mechanisms is a mandatory component in the design of all strategic moves. Whether you're doing business reengineering, TQM, Baldrige, ISO 9000, or any type of major change, failure is 100 percent assured if your prescription is at odds with the prevailing economic system. Organizational behaviors will always necessarily conform to the economic system,

Table 5.1
Alternative Economic Systems. There are radical differences in how the economy works (or doesn't work) based on the choices you make.

Economic System Attribute	Economic Governance System			
	Free Market (Laissez-Faire)	Outsourcing	Traditional I/T Monopoly	Regulated I/T Utility
How does allocation system work?	Customer chooses projects	Settled in contract	Central committee	Customer chooses projects
How does market system work?	Customer chooses any supplier	Customer must use outsourcer	Customer must use I/T organization	Customer must use I/T organization, but value and equity ensured
How does budget system work?	Customer controls own budget and is charged for services	Settled in contract	Corporate tax allocated based on politics	Customer controls budget and pays for services at value prices
How does supplier system work? work?	Customer negotiates terms and conditions with each supplier	Settled in contract	I/T acts as monopolist	Control board sets major rules and conditions of exchange to ensure value and equity
Who is sovereign?	Customer	Settled in contract	I/T	Business
How is architecture coherence maintained?	Probably not maintained	Contract-determined	I/T organization chooses all technologies	Regulated utility sets architecture
How are major surprises or need changes managed?	Contract terms	Contract terms	Politics	Utility sets impartial mechanisms, including fiat
How are major cross-organizational consortia formed?	Probably not	?	I/T tries to form	Both utility and users form
What is the goal/performance framework position of this economy?	Impersonal market	Relational market	Impersonal hierarchy	Relational hierarchy
What is the investment character/frequency framework position of this economy?	Market governance	Bilateral governance	Unified governance	Bilateral governance

regardless of the elegance, righteousness, or farsightedness of your action. Neither deep and far-reaching nor shallow and nearsighted plans have a chance against the economic imprint on the staff's mind. Bertrand Russell, the foremost philosopher of the 20th century, said, "New doctrines that have any success must bear a strong relation to the economic circumstances of their age."

The destiny of your strategic moves can be foretold, and you need not be a sorcerer or witch to foresee the future. If you alter the economic system to serve your actions, they will succeed. If the economic system is left untouched and it is in disagreement with your aspirations, your aspirations will languish and go nowhere. You will actually make things worse as your exhortations for change confront an economic system that says no. Sooner or later, all problems reduce to economic problems. Do not leave congruence of the economic system with your actions to chance. Someone who looks at problems through an economic lens sees success. Someone who solves problems through the means of economic governance witnesses magic as the aims of each person coalesce and yield the maximum collective benefit for all.

Postscript

There is a symmetry between I/T architecture and the economic system that is subtle but conceptually important. The economic system defines the rules of governance for the exchange of goods and services between organizational trading partners. The I/T architecture defines the rules of governance for the exchange of information between I/T resources. In both cases, success demands collaboration. So by carefully designing both the economic systems and the I/T architecture, one can create conditions fertile and favorable to alignment.

NOTES

1. Engels, *Socialism: Utopian and Scientific.*
2. For a balanced analysis of both chargeback and overhead spreading of I/T costs, see G. Perry, "The Perils of Chargeback and Overhead," *Software Development*, April 1994.
3. The material presented herein on organizational economics is based upon the following articles:

    a. O. Williamson, "Transaction Cost Economics: The Governance of Contractual Relations," *The Journal of Law and Economics.*

    b. D. Bowen and G. Jones, "Transaction Cost Analysis of Service Organization-Customer Exchange," *Academy of Management Review* 11:2 (1986).

c. W. Hesterly, J. Liebeskind, and T. Zenger, "Organizational Economics: An Impeding Revolution in Organization Theory," *Academy
of Management Review* 15:3 (1990).

4. A most interesting example of prolepsis, in a most surprising source,
appeared in the January–February 1993 *Harvard Business Review.* In an
article entitled "How Continental Bank Outsourced Its Crown Jewels,"
Richard L. Huber, the Continental Bank outsourcing champion, explained
how the decision to outsource the bank's I/T to an IBM subsidiary (ISSC)
and Ernst and Young was a stirring strategic success. If we work backward from the publication date of January–February 1993, we would
deduce the following:

a. To be published in the January–February 1993 issue, the final draft
of the article must have been delivered by September–October
1992.

b. The article must have been submitted for review and referring
roughly three to four months sooner, June–July 1992.

c. Assuming that the original article must have taken three months of
a busy executive's time to write and edit, it must have been written
starting in April 1992.

Since the outsourcing contract went into effect on January 1, 1992, the
declaration of strategic success was essentially written three months after
the action.

Strategy is much more analogous to a marathon than to a 50-meter
sprint. When the article was written, only the earliest parts of the
marathon had been completed. It would seem that three things would be
required before you could declare the outsourcing act a success:

a. An appropriate time period would have to pass—perhaps three
years.

b. Continental would have to be benchmarked against banks that
were comparable at the time of the outsourcing and that kept their
I/Ts to see whose I/T was delivering better value three years later.

c. A neutral party, rather than the champion of the action, would have
to judge the act's success.

I do not know the current status of Continental's outsourcing decision,
and it may in fact have been an excellent action for the bank. I do not
believe, however, that the status of a strategic action three months after its
initiation is evidence of its success or failure. Three months into a deep
and far-reaching strategy, an ultimate failure may be doing wonderfully,
or an ultimate success may be muddling along. The article should there-

fore not be understood as an example of a strategic outsourcing success, but as an example of prolepsis.

Note: As this book went to print, Bank of America was set to buy Continental Bank and it was anticipated that the outsourcing contract would be cancelled so in a perfect final act, this example of successful strategic outsourcing "never happened"!

5. Machiavelli, *The Prince.*

6. For an excellent analysis of outsourcing, see M. Lacity and R. Hirschheim, *Information System Outsourcing* (John Wiley & Sons, 1993). Also see Tom Peters, "The Quaint Ideas of Absolute Mastery," *Forbes ASAP,* 28 February 1994, in which Peters labels I/T not only a core competence for most companies, but a "towering competence." He is also dismayed at the I/T outsourcing phenomenon and blames it on executive I/T illiteracy. In a later *Computerworld* article on 28 March 1994, Peters adds, "I can't imagine outsourcing IS. The idea of shucking this off to outsiders as if running the IS function were like running the company cafeteria is a crock."

7. See Richard Due, "The Productivity Paradox," *Information Systems Management,* Winter 1993; M. C. Augustus van Nievelt, "Managing with Information Technology: A Decade of Wasted Money?" *Information Strategy,* Summer 1993; Gary Loveman, "An Assessment of the Productivity Impact of Information Technologies," Sloan School of Management (MIT), July 1988; Gary Loveman, "Cash Drain, No Gain," *Computerworld,* 25 November 1991; Jim Manzi, "Productivity: Faith Isn't Enough," *Computerworld,* 4 May 1992; James Krohe, Jr., "The Productivity Pit," *Across the Board,* October 1993; McKinsey & Co., "Service Sector Productivity," 1992.

8. Some defenders of I/T argue that the problem of poor I/T productivity is not inherent in I/T, but is due to implementation shortcomings (see "Viewpoints: Plug in for Productivity," *New York Times,* 27 June 1993). I agree completely; the problem is the absence of alignment.

9. Paul Strassmann, "The Business Value of Computers" (Information Economics Press, 1990).

10. *Ibid.*

11. Marilyn Parker, "Information Economics: Linking Business Performance to Information Technology."

12. For more information on option values, see D. Sharp, "Uncovering the Hidden Value in High Risk Investments," *Sloan Management Review,* Summer 1991, and L. Trigeorgis, "Real Options and Interactions with Financial Flexibility," *Financial Management,* Autumn 1993.

13. This positive view of option values is certainly not universally held. Stephen Roach of Morgan Stanley & Co. says, in a February 1994 *CIO* magazine article referring to I/T investment in the service industry, "Don't waste your money if you can't measure the productivity before you do the installation. If you can't quantify it, don't buy it, period."

6

Application Development

The purpose of this chapter is to analyze ways to reengineer the I/T organization to dramatically improve the alignment of the application development process. Development alignment means that applications are built quickly and at minimum cost, are of the highest quality, and meet customer requirements. Customers want applications; they really couldn't care less about database management systems, SQL, fourth-generation languages, objects, frame relay, or any other of the technological wonders that get the I/T staff so excited. What users want is instant systems at no cost that are perfectly malleable, work flawlessly, and exactly meet their requirements.

Improving application development, speed, quality, and cost remains a puzzle. In spite of the existence of an endless processional of approaches to close the application development gap—inspection techniques, rapid development methodologies, structured everything (analysis, design, and coding), CASE, cost estimation tools, measurements systems, and developer tool chests—customers remain grossly dissatisfied with the results. It is not possible to address aligning I/T with the business without attacking the problem of application development.

The remainder of this chapter will analyze ways to narrow the development gap, as follows:

- *6.1. Object-Oriented Technologies*
  This section performs a strategic analysis of object-oriented technologies. Objects, in all their flavors (analysis, design, programming, database, and interoperability frameworks), offer great promise for radically altering the development process and elevating software development from an artisan endeavor to an engineering discipline.

- *6.2. Data Servers*
  This section analyzes the importance of creating data servers to provide shared information to applications. The use of data servers can dramatically reduce development time and cost by eliminating the need of each project to define its own data and create redundant and expensive proprietary data stores.

247

- *6.3. Application Prototyping Revisited*
  This section analyzes the contribution that prototyping, the building of software models, can make to improving customer satisfaction. While commercial application prototyping is now at least ten years old, there remains a community of development organizations that have not adopted this proven technique. The continual introduction of ever more dynamic user interfaces (i.e., GUI, voice, sight, virtual reality, etc.) promotes prototyping from a choice to a necessity.

These proposed development initiatives complement the other alignment actions that have been proposed. The architecture provides the infrastructure on which the applications run. Technology forecasting and planning provide a flow of ever-improved technologies to build applications with. The economic system provides incentives to drive the developers with the same competitive fervor that affects the line organizations. One can go so far as to assert that architecture, planning, and economy design are prerequisites for successfully reengineering the development process.

6.1 OBJECT-ORIENTED TECHNOLOGIES

The purpose of this section is to analyze the strategic importance of object-oriented technologies to aligning information technology with the business. It is not an exaggeration to assert that object-oriented technology, in its myriad of flavors (analysis, design, programming, database, and interoperability frameworks), is the most significant event for application development in the last 30 years. It far overshadows structured techniques (analysis, design, and programming) in its potential to radically transform development from an artisan hand-crafted model of development to a software engineering fabrication and assembly methodology.

Objects

Figure 6.1 illustrates an object. An object is a self-enclosed container of private data, private functions (logic), and public services (or functions). The functions define the behaviors of the object. To reuse an object, one need only know the interfaces (named service and data parameters) and send a message to the object. The invoker is completely shielded from the internal mechanisms of the object. An object should be fathomed as a *reusable part*.

Figure 6.2 shows an aggressive time line for the assimilation of object technologies, and Figure 6.3 illustrates the predicted market growth. The reason for this is that object-oriented technology offers the greatest promise of concurrently reducing application life cycle cost, improving software quality, and accelerating development speed. This is because

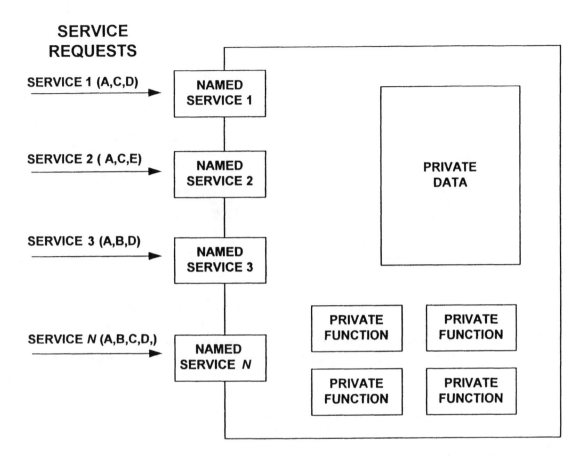

Figure 6.1   An Object. An object consists of private data, private functions, and external
service interfaces.

1. Object-oriented technology provides a uniform modeling para-
    digm for analysis, design, and programming. This provides a con-
    sistent framework for attacking all the major steps of software
    development, focuses training and skills, and eliminates the com-
    munication problems between analyst, designer, and programmer.
    The fog of hand-off between steps is eliminated.

2. Objects, in every sense of the engineering metaphor, are parts. They
    can be developed, quality-tested, certified, advertised, and reused
    as parts. This has extraordinary productivity, speed, and quality
    implications to the software craft, where everything is hand-crafted
    from scratch. The greatest implication, of course, is that developers
    assemble applications rather than coding them. They assemble
    them with pretested and certified components that merely have to

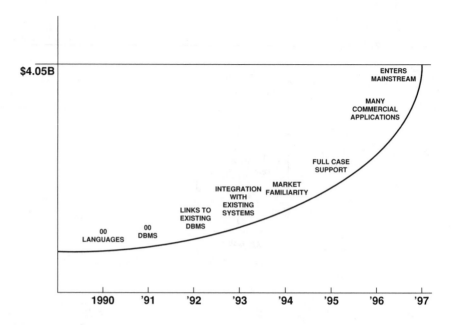

Figure 6.2   Object Technology Time Line. It is predicted that object-oriented technology will be commercial mainstream technology by 1997. (Source: Ovum Ltd.)

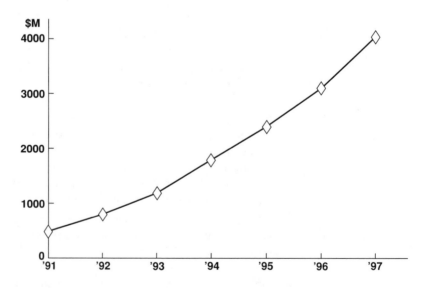

Figure 6.3   Object-Oriented Market. The object-oriented market will grow by a factor of eight in six years. (Source: Ovum Ltd.)

be plugged into the specific application logic controller. Since object notions are completely recursive, objects can invoke other objects and assemblies. Super-assemblies and super-super-assemblies of objects can be created that embody tremendous certified functionality, but to the invoker, they are simply a service request with a well-defined set of data parameters. Figure 6.4 illustrates an assembled object program.

It is important to understand that reusability is an attribute of object-oriented analysis and design as well as programming. This further improves productivity and positions the assemblers to reuse code by virtue of reused designs. The notion of cut and paste is brought to the entire application life cycle.

3. The nature of objects simplifies the cost of software maintenance. Changes can be isolated and the structure of the software can be altered by unplugging a part or plugging in new parts.

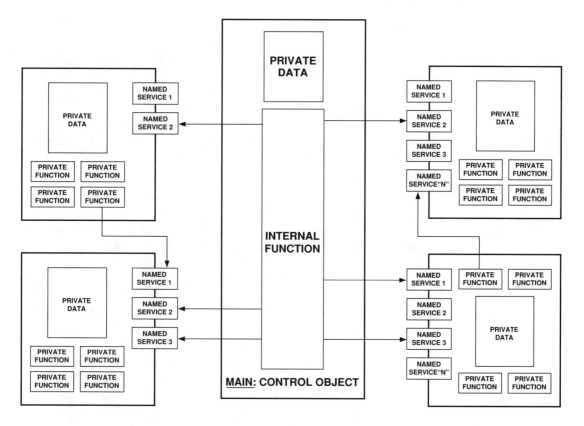

Figure 6.4 Object-Oriented Program. An object-oriented program consists of an object-oriented control module that invokes other object-oriented modules.

4. Objects are decoupled from each other and communicate through well-defined messages. This enables objects to be distributed across an architecture yet be reused. Object technology compounds benefits by being fully compatible with network computing architectures.

5. There is no difference to the invoker between requesting a service and manipulating data. The developer does not have to deal with incompatible semantics between a programming language and a data manipulation language.

To obtain dramatic changes in software development productivity, a paradigm shift would have to occur. This occurs with objects through the alteration of the unit of productivity, which moves from writing a new line of code to plugging in a certified part.

Key Object Concepts

Object technology is best understood as a way to create self-contained parts with six key qualities:

1. *Objects:* an object is a thing or entity—for example, a person, a store, or an account. An object has a name, internally maintained data fields (attributes) that describe the state of the object, and procedural logic that defines the behaviors of the object. Some of the procedural logic is accessible to external objects (i.e., public services), and may be invoked by name with a set of data parameters through a message.

2. *Class:* a group of like objects.

3. *Encapsulation:* the quality of an object that it hides its internal data structures and procedures from other objects. The only thing open about an object should be the names of public services and the required data parameter strings for innovation. Encapsulation results in the public services acting as connectors to the outside world while the object's internal world remains fully hidden. This quality makes objects independent of each other and permits changes to be made in isolation, so long as the integrity of the interface is preserved.

4. *Messaging:* objects communicate with each other by sending messages. This decouples the objects from each other and positions objects for distribution across a network computing architecture.

5. *Inheritance:* the ability of a class to have subclasses that inherit data and procedures from the superclass and add or delete data and procedures at the subclass level.

6. *Polymorphism:* objects in different classes may respond uniquely to the same message.

Object technology provides a way to build software with connectors, just like a microprocessor or any other piece of hardware is built with connectors.

Understanding Object-Oriented Technology Strategically

Object technology is of strategic interest because it offers realization of the strategic themes of leverage and reuse, speed, productivity, quality, and maneuverability through one technology. While this is difficult to prove quantitatively,[1] it is discernible through a combination of common sense, business sense, technology sense, empirical observation, experimentation, engineering analogy, and faith. There is significant strategic vulnerability incurred by not adopting object technology.

To analyze the strategic risk of not adopting objects, we will use the Competitive Response analytical framework. To apply this framework, we

- Assume the validity of the strategic attributes of object technology.
- Look at the business through various strategic lenses.
- Assess the competitive consequences of nonadoption.

The net disadvantage of neglecting object technology is computed for each strategic view. If the summation of disadvantages is small, it may be ignored, but if the disadvantage is great, it may be disregarded only at strategic peril.

The Competitive Response analysis will be done using the following format:

- *Strategy framework:* the name of the strategic analytical method used as the lens.
- *Description:* a brief synopsis of the framework.
- *Analysis:* an assessment of the strategic disadvantage accrued to the business when the competition adopts object-oriented technology but you don't.

A disadvantage summary will be provided at the end.

1. *Strategy Framework:* Reach, range, and maneuverability architecture.
   Description: The manifest destiny of I/T is the realization of a perfect reach, a perfect range, and a perfect maneuverability architecture (see Figure 2.6). As illustrated in Figure 1.11, as the reach, range, and maneuverability of the I/T architecture matures, so does the state of I/T–business alignment.
   Analysis: Object technology markedly increases range and maneuverability. Objects are units for reconfiguration and porting. Data-

bases may also be treated as objects (whether an object DBMS is used or not), and this decouples data from the applications, increasing the sharing and reusability of data. Since objects may be remote from the requester, objects support the sharing of services across the network computing architecture. The competitive disadvantages of not adopting object technology are inferior maneuverability and an inferior range of service and data sharing or reusability.

2. *Strategy Framework:* Value chain (see Figure 6.5).
   Description: Value chain analysis is a method for classifying, analyzing, and understanding the translation of resources through processes into final products and services. It is used to analyze how to improve cost structure, speed, quality, and value added as products move through the chain of steps from supplier to customer.
   Analysis: Value chains have parallel information chains that mirror the movement of products and services. Object-oriented technology improves the ability of the information chain to maneuver quickly in response to desired changes in the value chain. Object-oriented technology enables reconfiguration of value chains by permitting the information chain to sway in harmony with the value chain reengineering efforts. The competitive disadvantages of not adopting object technology are inferior maneuverability and inferior speed of response.

3. *Strategy Framework:* Bottleneck analysis (see Figure 6.6).
   Description: Bottleneck analysis is a special form of value chain analysis where the value chain is specifically surveyed to discover bottlenecks that block the efficient and effective flow of products and services.
   Analysis: Bottlenecks present vulnerabilities for competitors; they are your performance gaps. The competitive disadvantages of not adopting object technology are inferior maneuverability, inferior speed, and increased cost in eradicating these problems.

4. *Strategy Framework:* Leverage.
   Description: Leverage is the design element of a strategic action that is the multiplier, amplifier, and accelerator of the benefits of the action. It is the means to maximize the benefits of an action for a given investment. The vocabulary of leverage includes words such as reusability, sharing, open accessibility, linkage, replicability, duplicability, economies of scale, economies of scope, synergy, cascading, modularity, and dispersion.
   Analysis: Object-oriented technologies provide leverage in the following ways:

   a. *Reduced development cost:* as shown in Figure 6.7, as the number of shareable objects increases, development progresses from writing lines of code to assembling programs and systems.

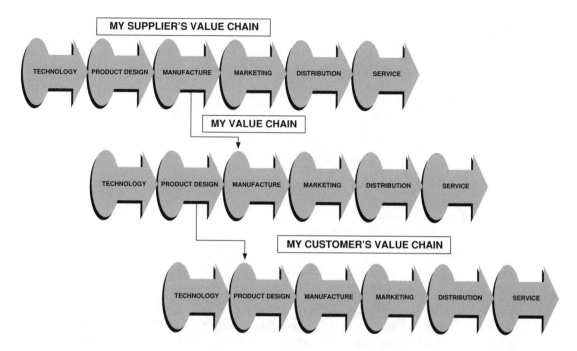

Figure 6.5   Value Chain Analysis. Examine the value chain to discover opportunities to improve speed, cut costs, or add value. (Source: *The Art of Strategic Planning for Information Technology*, Bernard Boar, John Wiley & Sons, 1993)

      b. *Change transparency:* as shown in Figure 6.8, maintenance is isolated to the object manager, so that newer technologies can be taken advantage of without disrupting the integrity of each user application.

      c. *Object reuse and sharing:* as shown in Figure 6.9, not only do multiple applications reuse the same object part, but when the object

Figure 6.6   Bottleneck Analysis. Examine processes to discover bottlenecks between you and the consumer and eradicate them.

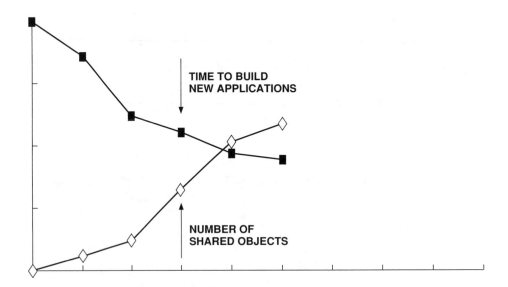

Figure 6.7   Reuse. As the number of objects increases, reusability increases and development time decreases as certified parts are substituted for error-prone hand-crafted coding. (Source: *Implementing Client/Server Computing: A Strategic Perspective*, Bernard Boar, McGraw Hill, 1993.)

is amended, the new functionality becomes available to all client applications.

The competitive disadvantages of not adopting object technology are inferior maneuverability and reduced reuse.

d. *Strategy Framework:* Pivot position.
    Description: Pivot positions are strategic positions that are taken at crossroads to permit rapid adaptability to events as they unfold and the fog of competition lifts.
    Analysis: The rationale for pivot positions is that the marketplace, customers, and competitors will always be full of surprises. Pivot positions permit one to be flexible and dynamic in responding to the vagaries of the market. The competitive disadvantages of not adopting object technology are inferior maneuverability and inferior speed.

e. *Strategy Framework:* Sustainable competitive advantage (see Table 3.1).
    Description: Sustainable competitive advantages are the resources, capabilities, skills, assets, and competencies that provide distinct attraction to customers and unique advantage over competitors.

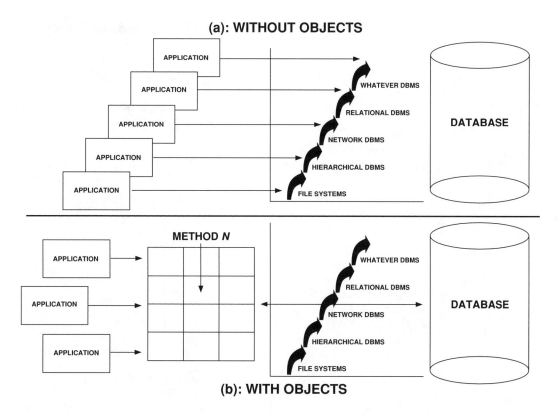

Figure 6.8 Shielding Change. The application interface remains inviolate as DBMS technology or physical media is altered to take advantage of newer technologies.

Analysis: As was discussed in Section 3.1, five of the attributes of a sustainable competitive advantage are durability, transparency, accessibility, coordination, and replication. Object-oriented technology can contribute to all of these attributes. The competitive disadvantages of not adopting object technology are inferior maneuverability, inferior speed, reduced quality, and increased cost.

f.   *Strategy Framework:* Kano methodology (see Figure 6.10).
Description: The Kano methodology is a strategic framework with the intent to create dislocations in the marketplace (see Section 1.3). The heart of the methodology is to partition customer satisfiers into three categories:

1. *Threshold attributes:* basic and important satisfiers.

2. *Performance attributes:* satisfiers for which there is a dollar-for-dollar return in investment for customer satisfaction.

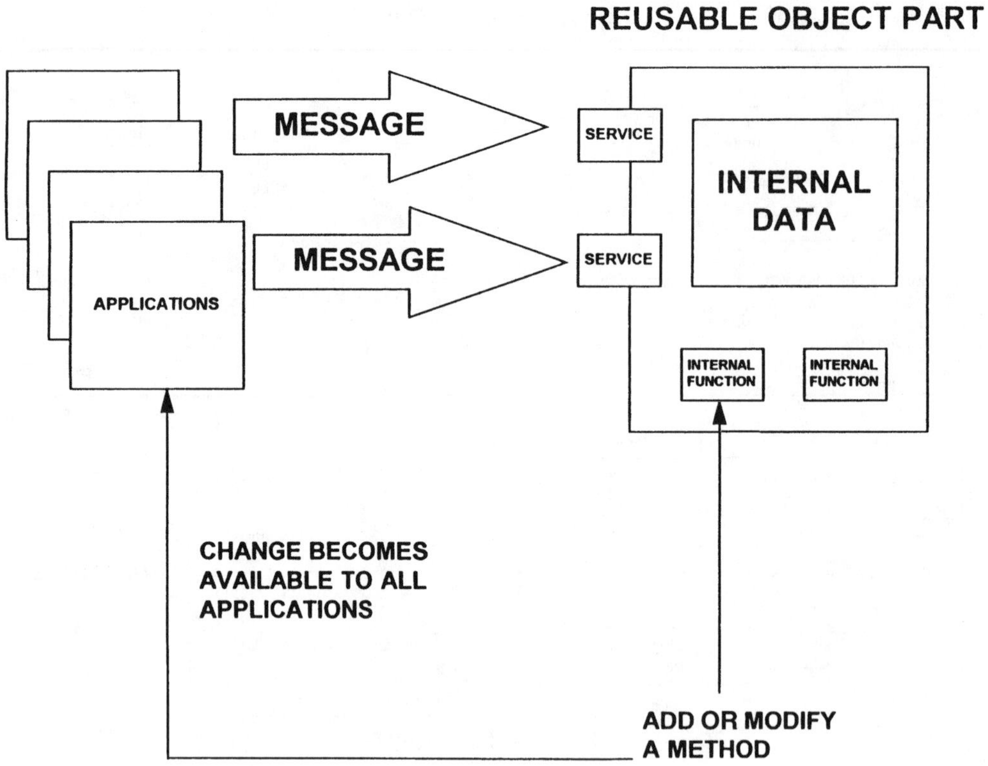

REUSABLE OBJECT PART

Figure 6.9   Propagating Change. An addition or modification to a part is available to all users of the part.

3. *Excitement attributes:* satisfiers that yield an exponential return in customer satisfaction per unit of investment.

The trick is to identify the excitement attributes and rapidly implement at the highest quality to change the perception of this attribute to a threshold attribute. Since you can perform it and your competitors can't, you will have created strategic distance between yourself and your opponents.

Analysis: Kano-driven success depends on the ability to rapidly take advantage of excitement gaps in the marketplace. The competitive disadvantages of not adopting object technology are inferior maneuverability and inferior quality, which prevent you from creating dislocations.

g. *Strategy Framework:* Artisan to engineer (see Figure 6.11).

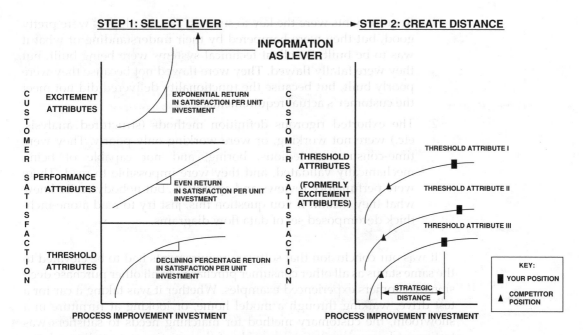

Figure 6.10   **Kano Methodology. The Kano methodology demands speed and dexterity to take advantage of excitement attribute gaps in the marketplace.**

Description: The artisan-to-engineer framework acknowledges the evolution of a discipline from magic to science, based on the formalization of knowledge and methods.

Analysis: Engineering disciplines are typically driven by applying proven and reliable methods to trade-off cost, quality, and value.[2] The competitive disadvantages of not adopting object technology are increased cost and reduced quality.

h. *Strategy Framework:* Five forces (see Figure 6.12).

Description: The five forces framework is a method used to analyze competitive position by virtue of your strengths and weaknesses relative to five forces and their factors.

Analysis: The theme of the five forces framework is the fundamental necessity to be able to maneuver, both to find a better position within the five forces and to parry the thrusts of others. The competitive disadvantage of not adopting object technology is maneuverability; this means that you are unable to respond to the dynamics of competitors, suppliers, and customers.

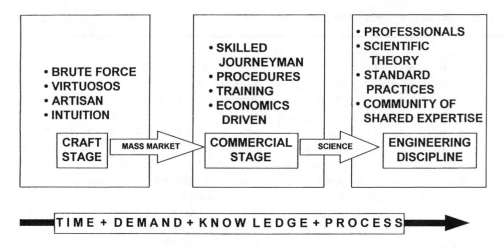

Figure 6.11   **From Artisan to Engineer, from Magic to Science. The attributes of traditional software development exemplify a craft, while those of an object-oriented environment exemplify an engineering discipline. (Source:** *Implementing Client/Server Computing: A Strategic Perspective,* **Bernard Boar, McGraw Hill, 1993.)**

Most important, object-oriented software provides the appropriate software response for a business that has adopted a maneuver marketplace style. Objects provide a collection of formless parts that can be rapidly assembled into new or modified business applications. In this way, the strategic configuration of software power is endlessly reconfigurable to the precise demands of the times and circumstances. Objects will permit business applications to rapidly take on endless forms. Is this not the notion of maneuver perfectly applied to the domain of software?

It is fair to assert that Competitive Response Analysis indicates a significant risk of severe competitive disadvantage if object-oriented technologies are not adopted and your competitors do adopt them. This risk cannot be ignored. Table 6.1 summarizes the Competitive Response findings.

Implementation

Implementing object-oriented technologies is a major technology transfer program, because you are advancing software development from the artisan paradigm to the engineering paradigm (see Figure 6.11). It must be approached with considerable attention and forethought, because who-

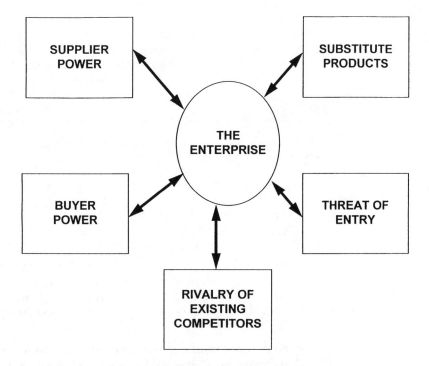

Figure 6.12   The Five Forces. The moral of the five forces is the primacy of maneuverability to deal with the intrigue of the marketplace.

ever has the superior implementation, you or your competitors, will collect the advantage.

Rather than repeating the normal litany of steps and caveats that are normally recited in support of implementation efforts (executive commitment, implementation ownership, pilot projects, measurement, etc.), I would prefer to discuss four issues specific to object-oriented success:

1. *Education:* it is obvious that the staff will have to be reeducated in the discipline and techniques of object-oriented technologies. What is not as obvious is that object education is the second type of reeducation they will require. The first training that is needed is to teach them the principles and methods of engineering. Does your staff understand what engineering means? Do they understand the notion of parts and assembly? Do they appreciate the discipline of parts, engineering change control, and configuration management? Do they have an appreciation of engineering economics or value engineering? I suggest that there is strong reason to suspect that they don't.

Table 6.1
Competitive Disadvantage Summary. Failure to adopt object-oriented technologies will leave your business at a significant competitive disadvantage.

Strategy Framework	Competitive Disadvantage Consequence of Not Adopting Object-Oriented Technology
Reach, Range, and Maneuverability Architecture	1. Reduced Maneuverability 2. Reduced Reusability
Value Chain	1. Reduced Speed 2. Reduced Maneuverability
Bottleneck Analysis	1. Greater Cost 2. Reduced Speed 3. Reduced Maneuverability
Leverage	1. Greater Cost 2. Less Reuse
Pivot Positions	1. Reduced Maneuverability 2. Reduced Speed
Sustainable Competitive Advantage	1. Reduced Maneuverability 2. Reduced Speed 3. Reduced Quality 4. Increased Cost
Kano Methodology	1. Reduced Maneuverability 2. Reduced Quality
Artisan to Engineer	1. Increased Cost 2. Reduced Quality
Five Forces	1. Reduced Maneuverability

To upgrade them from being spaghetti or structured developers to software engineers, you must invest in teaching them object technologies, but only after you have prepared them by teaching them engineering. The chasm between where they are and where you wish them to be is extraordinarily wide. It is akin to teaching witch doctors modern medical procedures. Before the witch doctors can apply modern medical technology, they must first understand the fundamental principles that govern modern medical practice and forsake their primitive ideology. They must adopt a new mental model; they must be modernized. So it is with object-oriented technology. If object-oriented technology is treated merely as today's technology transfer effort, you will benefit substantially less than you anticipated. This is because they will treat the new methods with the attitudes of an artist rather than with the discipline of an engineer. Your object-oriented reengineering effort must first create engineers; only then will the remarkable advantages of object-oriented technology be fully realizable.

2. *Economy design:* the economic system must be refined to encourage the development, use, and growth of objects. We suggest the following exemplary approach:

   a. Create an internal unit, an object repository group, that is in the object business. Fund this unit as an investment. The unit's mission is to create or buy objects, and to support the extensive reuse of these objects on all development projects. The domain of this group would be general objects of broad horizontal value.

   b. To encourage the use of objects initially by your development projects and eventually by the maintenance efforts, announce that after a threshold critical mass of objects is created, you will lower your rates to reflect the improved productivity from using objects. Developers then have two choices: they will either use objects to meet the improved productivity bogeys (the means of getting your return on investment), or they will not meet the accelerated productivity requirements. The economic incentive here is obvious.

   c. By vertical application domain, domain-specific objects should be created and supported. The same approach as in (b) above should be applied.

   d. Developers should be free to sell the objects they create to the object repository groups. The repository groups with a finite budget to create objects, buy objects externally, or buy objects internally then have the proper incentive to negotiate for the best trade-offs in object price and quality.

   In this way, those who change best and most quickly to the new object paradigm are those for whom the economic system provides no choice.

3. *Object repository:* to maximize reuse, it is self-evident that objects must be accessible to developers in order for them to assess suitability, and users must be registered so that updates can be appropriately distributed. The selection and design of the repository system, an object inventory, and a distribution system are thus of critical importance. It should also be remembered that the objects

being inventoried for reuse are not only program objects; they also include reusable analysis and design objects. The earlier in the development life cycle the point of reuse, the greater the ultimate program level reuse accrued. Spend time, money, and intellect on designing your repository system.

4. *Target applications:* target the reengineering efforts that have selected your most important capabilities as the candidates for object-oriented technology roll-out. These applications are the most important to enable with object advantages.

These four issues are especially important in implementing object-oriented technologies. While all the normal technology transfer caveats and procedures apply, you should be particularly attentive to engineering education, economy design, repository design, and target applications.

Conclusion

From the customer's perspective, alignment may well equate to application development. Whatever you do, regardless of excellence, it will be of little value, and it will be dismissed if the customer concludes that your development is excruciatingly slow, premium priced, of inferior quality, or hopelessly unresponsive to business dynamics. Object technology is one of those few opportunities that comes along once in a career to transform things radically for the better; this is what reengineering is all about. Object-oriented technology is a technology of alignment. With it, you can improve speed, quality, cost, and maneuverability, all with a single technology.

To approach the issue of adopting object-oriented technology a little more crudely, you don't exactly have many other alternatives or an outstanding track record to coast on. If we apply a poker analogy, five-card stud, and look back at Figure 1.12, you are playing with a hand that couldn't beat an opponent's hand with a pair of deuces. If you look at Table 6.2, it is clear that object-oriented technology offers therapy for most of the critical issues. There is every reason to pick the object card and add it to your hand. Conversely, if you pass on object, what will you do? Do you have reason to believe that more structured this and more structured that will yield more than a marginal improvement?

Yes, object is not yet mature; yes, all the tools are not yet here; yes, there is confusion and debate over whose methods are best; yes, you can find or create endless reasons to procrastinate. You must, nevertheless, proceed with the understanding and assurance that Thomas Kuhn provides us on the nature of paradigms shifts:

Table 6.2
Object-Oriented Therapy. Object-oriented technologies provide high-leverage therapy
for most of the critical issues identified by I/T executives.

CIO Critical Issues from Figure 1.12	Strategic Themes Enabled by Object-Oriented Technology (Primary Two Themes Per Issue)			
	Speed	Quality	Cost	Maneuverability
1. Reengineering	X	X		
2. I/T Business Alignment	X		X	
3. System Development		X		X
4. Cross-Functional Applications		X		X
5. Utilizing Data		X	X	
6. Cost Control	X		X	
7. I/T Architecture	X			X
8. Update Obsolete Systems	X			X
9. I/T Strategic Plan		X		X
10. Change I/T Platforms	X			X
11. Integrate Systems	X			X
12. I/T Human Resource				
13. Dispersed Systems		X		X
14. Capitalize on I/T			X	X
15. I/T for Competitive Advantage	X			X
16. Connecting to Customers and Suppliers			X	X
17. Leadership Skills				
18. Educating Management				
19. Open Systems			X	X
20. Promoting I/T				

Paradigm debates are not really about relative problem solving abilities, though for good reasons they are usually couched in those terms. Instead the issue is which paradigm should in the future guide research on problems, many of which neither competitor can yet claim to solve completely. A decision on alternative ways of practicing science is called for, and in those circumstances that decision must be made less on past achievement than on future promise. The man who embraces a new paradigm at an early stage must often do so in defiance of the evidence provided through existing problem solving. He must, that is, have faith that the new paradigm will succeed with the many large problems that confront it, knowing only that *the old paradigm has failed* with a few. A decision of that kind can only be made on faith.[3]

As shown by Figure 1.12, the old paradigm has failed, and object offers a reasonable promise of success.

The simple reality is that object is the only card in the deck. Either you go object or you stand pat with your Figure 1.12 hand. While almost miraculous hardware price and performance improvements have become all but routine, and the speed and flexibility of communications grows beyond many people's wildest imaginations, there remains a pronounced poverty of thought and a dearth of innovative ideas on how to dramatically improve software development. Understood this way, your choice of action is predetermined. As shown in Table 6.3, your minimax (minimize maximum loss) decision is achieved by selecting the object strategy. After all, it is not in your power to choose your competitor's action, but it is in your power to implement object technology better than others and achieve perfect alignment. Sun Tzu said, "In ancient times, skillful warriors first made themselves invincible and waited for vulnerabilities in their opponents."[4] You have much to win and little to lose. What is the superior alternative action?

6.2 DATA SERVERS

The purpose of this section is to analyze the advantages accrued by separating data definition and management from specific applications and positioning data as high-reuse data servers. The advantage of creating a data architecture like the one in Figure 6.13 have long been known. By creating a set of subject databases to run the business and a set of decision support databases to analyze the business (a.k.a. a data warehouse), not only can the quality and integrity of the data resource be dramatically improved, but significant productivity improvement can be obtained by treating data as a reusable part.

Table 6.3
**Payoff Matrix. Any rational minimax player will choose to adopt
object-oriented technology to minimize her maximum loss and strive
for excellence in implementation to maximize payoff. The value in
each cell represents your payoff based on the intersection of your
action and your competitor's action.**

		Competitor Action	
		Adopt Object-Oriented Technology	**Not Adopt Object-Oriented Technology**
Your Action	Adopt Object-Oriented Technology	From −250 to +500 (Payoff Value Is a Function of Who Has Superior Implementation)	+1,000 (Big Win)
	Not Adopt Object-Oriented Technology	−1,000 (Big Loss)	0 (Shared Continued Muddling Through)

If one empirically observes actual software project reuse behaviors, one notices an interesting phenomenon. Development teams, naturally without prompting or coercion, will engage in vertical reuse. As if led by an invisible hand, they will unquestionably reuse a set of platform givens—operating system, DBMS, transaction monitor, compilers, linkage editors, and so on. Nobody would suggest that for their typical business applications, they need to write a compiler or create a proprietary DBMS.

On the other hand, developers abhor and resist horizontal reuse. They tend to avoid reusing routines, call libraries, or copy libraries provided by their peers. The reasons for this are a combination of concerns about quality, support, functionality, and robustness, as well as the not-invented-here syndrome. In any case, they typically don't view application-level presentation logic, processing logic, or data manipulation as givens, so they rewrite over and over again rather than reusing existing components.

The strategy of creating data servers is to make the data resource a given. Just as developers wouldn't contemplate rewriting the operating system, it is a given that they shouldn't question reusing the data server. Since most commercial applications are data-intensive, making the data layer reusable can generate a vast productivity improvement of increased development speed and improved quality of applications. That is, it is extraordinarily faster to plug in the data than to create a database and write

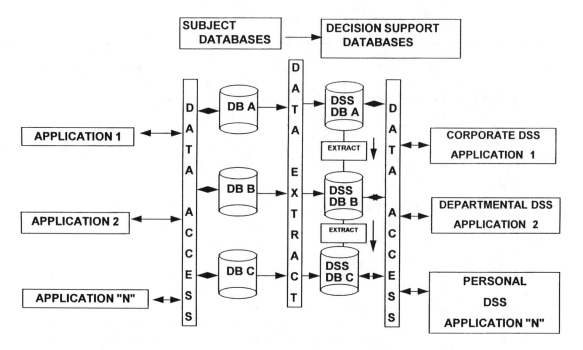

Figure 6.13   Data Architecture. An optimal data architecture consists of a family of shared subject databases to run the business and a set of shared decision support databases to analyze the business. (Source: *Implementing Client/Server Computing: A Strategic Perspective*, Bernard Boar, McGraw Hill, 1993)

all the access methods. As illustrated in Figure 6.7, the overriding strategy of data servers is to create object data servers that eliminate the need to create application-specific data solutions, and thereby accelerate application development, improve its quality, lower its cost, and ultimately yield more satisfied customers. Data should be a given for the developers, just as languages, interactive debuggers, and report writers are.

Problem Definition

For the most part, data has traditionally been managed at the application level. As shown in Figure 6.14, whether management was done at first by use of file management systems or later through database management systems, the data was owned by the application, and convoluted spaghetti interfaces were required to move and translate data between applications. It was recognized and recommended that if data architectures such as that shown in Figure 6.13 (dual database architecture) were built, the following benefits would be accrued at a pragmatic level:

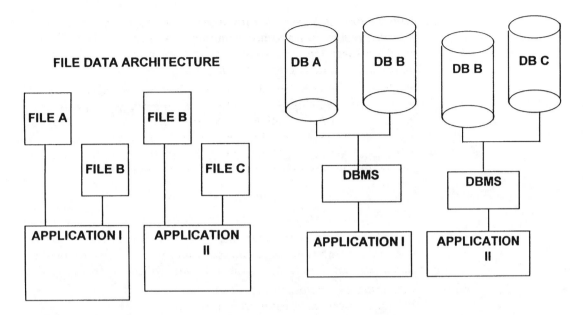

Figure 6.14 Closed Data Environments. In traditional closed data environments, each application owns its own data.

- Maximize data quality
- Maximize data accessibility
- Maximize data sharing
- Eliminate unplanned data redundancy
- Simplify building cross-functional collaborative systems
- Ensure data standardization
- Maximize life cycle application productivity
- Accelerate new application development through data reuse
- Enable the creation of centers of excellence in data management to protect the data asset

However, the technology did not exist to make decoupled data easily accessible to dispersed processing layers of multiple applications.

The perennial problem, then, was that before one could accomplish massive reusability of data, one would have to have a processing architecture that would support partitioning data from the application but permit transparent access. This is exactly what client/server computing does. Concurrently, one would like access to data to be semantically consistent with all other application service requests. This is what object-oriented technology does. When one puts these two ideas together, as shown in Figure 6.15, with object data servers, one can:

- Create data stores that are reusable parts.
- Eliminate the need to create application-dependent data.
- Vastly improve the productivity and quality of the application development process.

What was desirable has become possible.

Data Server Advantage

The reengineering of databases to create subject data servers and tiered decision support data servers is a critical component of aligning application development with the business. How better to improve productivity and quality than by eliminating one of the most time-consuming and

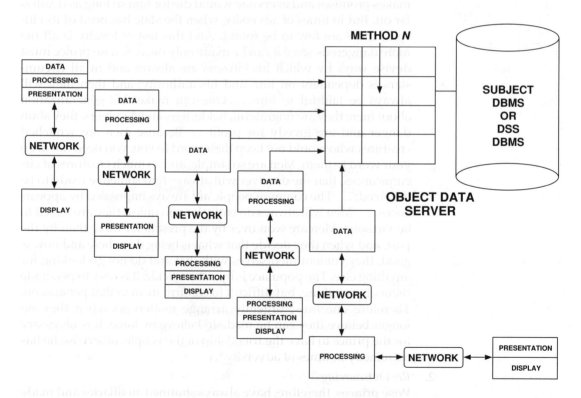

Figure 6.15   Object Data Servers. Object data servers permit applications to access shared data, regardless of their architectures.

labor-intensive parts of the development process? If data sits as a part ready to be connected, and processing components sit ready as reusable parts to deliver application functionality, new application development is reduced to writing user interfaces and control programs that integrate and manage the processing and data reusable parts.

A data server environment creates a high-leverage environment. The core competency model can be used to illustrate this point. As shown in Figure 6.16a, with the core competency model, competencies are multiplied into multiple core products. These are fed into multiple business units, which in turn are multiplied into numerous end products. From a few core competencies, multiple products for multiple markets are created. Core competencies yield high leverage.

As shown in Figure 6.16b, the same is true for a shared data server environment. Data elements are used in multiple data servers, which are accessed by multiple systems used collaboratively by multiple users. A relatively small number of data servers can meet the needs of most critical applications. Data servers yield high leverage.

If we look at this a little more closely, as in Figure 6.17, object data servers yield leverage in two ways:

1. The server is reused by multiple applications. It thereby eliminates all the redundancies of having each application define and maintain its own data.

2. As methods are added or modified to the data server, they become available to all clients. This also reduces individual application work and increases productivity.

If we revisit Figure 6.4 but modify it to include object data servers (see Figure 6.18), we believe that an extraordinarily high-productivity, high-quality, and rapid application environment is created. It is the consequence of moving not only processing logic to objects, but data to object servers as well. This is doable by joining the notions of network computing with object-oriented technology.

I/T Architecture Revisited

Data servers are illustrated on a Mulciber drawing as resources, as per Notion 14 in Section 3.3. Data servers would normally be drawn as subarchitecture diagrams that connect to client requesters, using the connection technique documented in Notion 15 in Section 3.3. As per Figure 6.13, the Mulciber drawings can be partitioned into those that run the business and those that analyze the business. In this way, data architecture can be bridged to the processing architecture that is documented with the Mulciber drawing technique.

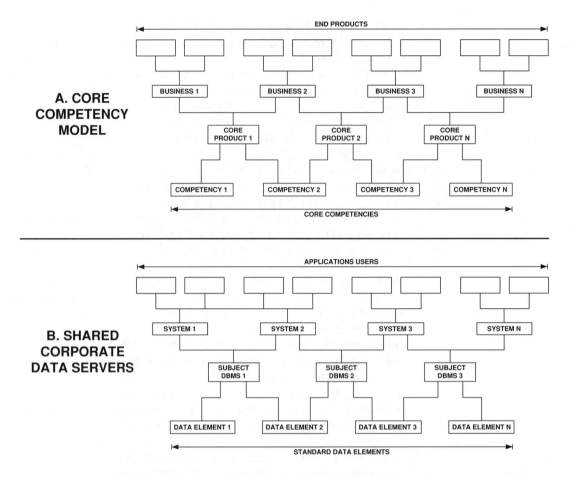

Figure 6.16 Data Server Leverage. The leverage created by data servers is analogous to the leverage created by core competencies.

Implementation Strategy

As was the case with object-oriented technologies in the previous section, no value is added by repeating a perfunctory litany of project dos and don'ts. As with object-oriented technology, the key to successful implementation may once again rest with the economic design of the implementation. Specifically, implementers should consider the following:

1. Have the regulated utility function as an object server sponsor, and form consortiums of users to fund the creation of high-payoff (highly reusable) data servers. The utility should take over funding of the individual application data stores.

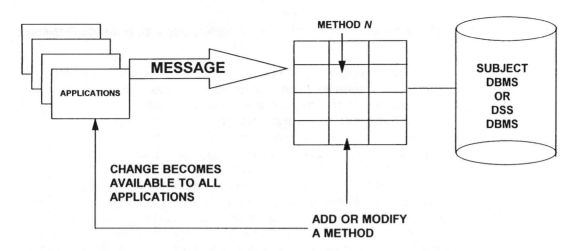

Figure 6.17   Data Server Advantage. Changes made to the data server methods are available to all clients.

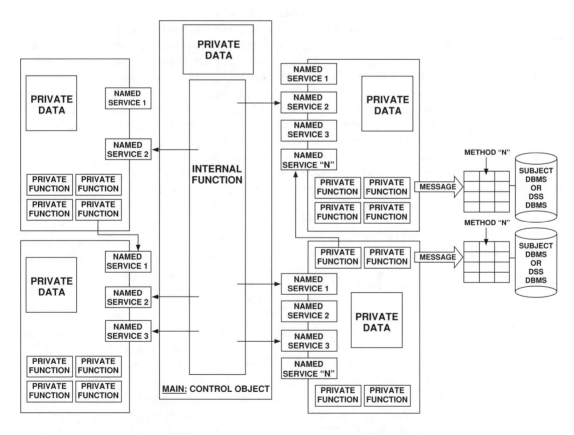

Figure 6.18   Object-Oriented Program Revisited. An object-oriented program that accesses data servers would be transparent to the programmer or program assembler.

2. When ready, schedule the conversion of the user applications to the server. As they are converted, cease funding the data portions of the individual applications. Applications that are slow to convert should have the data portion of their funding cut off. This provides a proper incentive to convert.

3. All new applications must use the data server. It is a given.

To implement something of the magnitude, consequence, and value of data servers, it is important in the economic design of the action to demonstrate not only how the action is funded, but how the recovery of the investment is ensured. This is done through the mechanism of the utility to fund the new servers and cease the funding of the private data stores.

Summary

As shown in Figure 6.19, data is and will remain the I/T asset with the highest value to the corporation. Processes change, software comes and goes, and hardware is becoming a commodity, but data remains a relatively constant store of value. By reengineering application development to rely on data servers rather than on application-specific data stores, one moves briskly toward alignment. One move toward alignment because one increases development speed, improves quality, and minimizes cost. This is exactly what the customer demands. This is accomplished by making data a given.

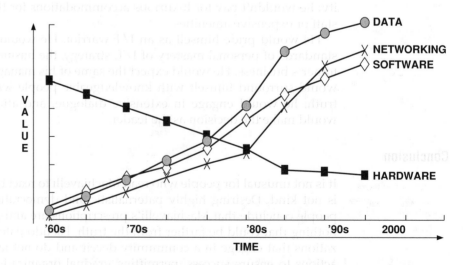

Figure 6.19   I/T Asset Value. Data has the highest I/T asset value.

6.3 APPLICATION PROTOTYPING REVISITED

The purpose of this section is to analyze the contribution that application prototyping can make to software development, and to provide a revision of my original thoughts on the subject. In 1984, I published what is now the seminal work on prototyping, called *Application Prototyping: A Requirements Definition Strategy for the 80s*. I was a little shortsighted in my title, as prototyping has grown in relevance and necessity far beyond my original 1980s vision. Prototyping has grown astronomically in its acceptance and practice since then, because it works, and so has an appreciation of its strategic contribution to success. There exist numerous testimonials in the press, books, and seminar circuit as to its efficacy. We will first review what prototyping is and then analyze how a proper strategic understanding of it can help foster business–I/T alignment.

Definition

Application prototyping is a strategy for determining user requirements wherein user needs are extracted, presented, and refined by building a working model of the ultimate system, quickly and in context. Rather than engaging in a tedious, slow, and often futile review of paper requirements documents, requirements definition focuses on developing and testing an animated model of the application. Through iteration of the model, the ultimate requirements are discovered by successive refinement rather than prespecification. Having experienced the prototype, users are assured that the developed application will exactly meet their needs, and developers can proceed, confident that what they deliver will be in harmony with actual user needs. The users already have experienced the animated prototype, rather than having to imagine how the system will operate from lifeless paper models.

During its developmental period, application prototyping was alternatively referred to as modeling, heuristic development, evolutionary development, simulation, or successive refinement. In the 1990s, prototyping is often referred to as rapid application development, structured prototyping, and evolutionary prototyping. All of these terms refer to a requirement (and sometimes iterative development strategy) wherein the core of the approach centers on experiencing a model of the application to gain understanding through experimentation, rather than attempting to create a perfect but inert paper statement of need.

Origin of Prototyping

In the early 1980s, there were two things that were obvious to those involved in application software development:

1. Requirements were the key to success. The developers were pretty good, but they were hampered by their understanding of what it was to be built. Excellent technical systems were being built, but they were fatally flawed. They were flawed not because they were poorly built, but because the functionality delivered did not meet the customer's actual requirements.

2. The exhorted rigorous definition methods (structured analysis, etc.) were not working, or were working only poorly. They were time-consuming, tedious, boring, and not capable of being mechanically validated, and they were impossible to read. There were perfunctory reviews and approvals, but nobody really knew what they meant. If you question this, just try to read a one-inch-thick decomposed set of data flow diagrams.

It was our conclusion that software requirements had to be elevated to the same status as all other consumer purchases. In all other purchase decisions, customers experienced examples. Whether it was taking a car for a test drive, walking through a model home, or looking at furniture in a showroom, the customary method for matching needs to satisfiers was testing and experiencing an example of the satisfier, not reading a long-winded technical specification of it. This analysis led us to the conclusion that prototyping would be a superior method for doing requirements, as illustrated in Figure 6.20. This was fully consistent with the experience of other engineering disciplines, where prototyping was a standard part of the product development cycle. One could go as far as to infer that the absence of prototyping provided prima facie evidence of the immaturity of software development as an engineering discipline; all established engineering disciplines had long ago given up trying to develop perfect products without the iterative learning and experiential benefits of prototypes.

With the advent of tools that permitted one to build applications very quickly, our early experiments were most rewarding. Customers rejoiced that finally someone was speaking to them in terms they could understand, and progressive developers were swept up in the excitement of rapid iteration with models. It was a victory for common sense and the engineering metaphor. It worked beyond our wildest dreams. The only ones unhappy about prototypes were the structured community, whose bland response was "You can't do that."

The reason for the resistance was a combination of vested interest and frozen mental models (a.k.a. psychological maps or mental schemas). There was a large intellectual, skill, and temporal investment in the structured techniques that conveyed mystical powers of analysis to the analysts. The prototypers were much more humble and mundane. We simply

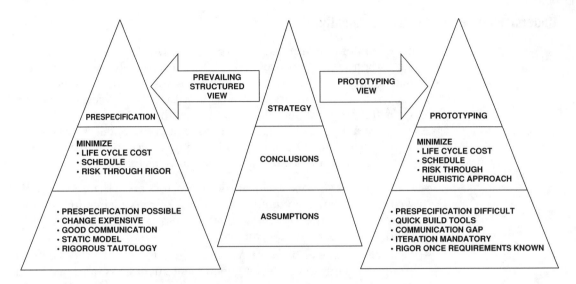

Figure 6.20 **The Logic of Prototyping. Prototyping originated in a very different set of assumptions about the nature of the requirements-gathering process.**

showed them our best guess of their requirements and asked them what they wanted changed. There was exactly zero magic to it.

At the same time, I believe that many of the prototyping detractors did not really understand that rather than disregarding engineering practices, we were implementing engineering practices. Our intent was to use prototypes to develop a rich comprehension of requirements, and then use standard methods to develop the actual application. The prototypes were designed to be thrown away. (We will discuss this more later.) In actuality, unlike many others, I was a very conservative proponent of prototyping, in that I didn't envision or recommend that the prototypes be turned into the actual systems.

Prototyping has survived its period of controversy. It ran the gauntlet of dissenters, and today is a fully accepted and standard part of most modern software development practices. There exists an excellent document entitled "A Classification and Bibliography of Software Prototyping"[5] that provides a complete taxonomy of prototyping literature according to the classifications shown in Table 6.4. If anything, the rise of more dynamic and participatory user interfaces, such as GUIs, three-dimensional real-time, gesture recognition, voice recognition, full multimedia, and virtual reality, have all conspired to make prototyping mandatory. It is literally impossible to convey the mechanics of such interfaces within the confines of a cold and inert paper document.

Understanding Prototyping Strategically

The conclusion of our prototyping experiment was "Why take the risk of prespecification when you could experience a relatively fast, cheap, and animated model?" Our understanding of its success, in 1984, however, was restricted to the empirical observation that it worked. We had no strategic insight into the significance of the methodology.

As it is now a decade later, 1994, our strategic consciousness has grown. A strategic spin can now be put on prototyping. Prototyping may be interpreted using four strategic analysis frameworks, as follows:

- *Critical success factors:* Critical success factors are what you must do well to succeed. They are the mandatory prerequisites for success. Prototyping addressed the critical success factors of participation, validation, risk reduction, and communication.
- *Value chain:* The application value chain is the set of processes that you go through to convert a general statement of system need to a production application. Prototyping offers opportunities to cut the costs of the value chain by moving iteration to the front of the chain, where it was relatively cheap, to learn from the back of the process, where rework was very dear. (See Figure 6.7.)
- *Bottleneck analysis:* Bottleneck analysis prescribes that the way to improve productivity is to search for blockages in the value chain and eliminate them. The greatest hurdle to successful development was the absence of meaningful communication between the players. Prototyping provided a requirements dialogue in a common medium that all participants could understand, so they could work collaboratively to develop an excellent statement of needs. (See Figure 6.8.)

Table 6.4
Prototyping Literature. There is today a rich set of experiences on which to design prototyping initiatives.

Classification of Literature on Prototyping				
Techniques	**Paradigm**	**Domain**	**Process**	**Miscellaneous**
Mockups	Object	OLTP	Concept	Road maps
Executable specs	Functional	Real-time	Evolution	Tools
4th GL	Knowledge-based	Distributed		Survey
Reusable modules		User interfaces		
Code		Knowledge-based		
Graphical				

- *Kano methodology:* Prototyping was a customer excitement attribute. The only word to describe the consumer reaction to prototyping was joy. Developers who adopted prototyping created a strategic gap between themselves and their well-intentioned but inwardly focused structured colleagues. Customers who experienced prototyping would never again settle for the confusion and dullness of the passive paper specification approach. Prototyping is an example of identifying an excitement attribute, developing a process to address it, delivering it, and then making it the standard against which other methods must compete. (See Figure 6.10.)

Our modern strategic understanding of prototyping is that prototyping solves the elemental problem of requirements definition, which is meaningful communication. By solving this problem, prototyping offers strategic advantage by increasing development speed, improving the quality of applications, and reducing cost. Prototyping is an overt manifestation and exemplary model of the learning organization in execution.

Prototyping and I/T–Business Alignment

While providing a means to solve the communication problems of development is, by itself, a great gift to alignment, the value of prototyping has actually grown due to the other development ideas, object-oriented technology and data servers. When I developed prototypes, they were not translatable into the actual application, because they were hand-crafted, rapidly built, and of questionable production quality.[6]

The advent of objects and data servers radically changes this equation. If you build prototypes by assembly, most of your prototype is already certified. While the control logic needs to be rigorously validated and tested, most of the software is valid a priori. This means that translating the prototypes into the actual application, thereby further accelerating speed, reducing cost, and improving customer satisfaction, is entirely plausible. What this means, even more profoundly, is that prototyping will evolve from being a development add-on to being the fundamental method of software development. By the turn of the century, we should anticipate that prototyping will be the standard software engineering method for doing application software development. In an interesting 20-year twist of fortune, structured methods will become interesting artifacts in software museums, along with vacuum tubes, and prototyping will ascend to become the dominant method of application development.

So prototyping continues to grow in stature. Used as the arrow tip of a customer satisfaction strategy, prototyping can be augmented with objects and data servers to create a rapid application development environment that exceeds customer expectations. Exceeding customer expectations is the way of alignment.

Conclusion

Though not usually understood as such, a software application is a product. Though often not understood as such, the user is a customer. In the real world, customers experience products before they buy them. This is what prototyping means to software development. The resulting alignment of the I/T developers with the customers can only be described as joyful.

The success of prototyping addresses all four of the major risks inherent to software development. By building software models, the development team can reduce the risk of cost overruns, schedule slips, misunderstanding of requirements, and incomplete technical specifications. There is little more that can be asked of any development technique. All this and it's fun, too.

My advice in 1984 was that the requirements definition strategy is solvable if you just take advantage of the available solution. My advice in 1994 is that the requirements definition strategy is solvable if you just take advantage of the available solution, and you get strategic benefits and joyful alignment gratis. If you are using prototyping today, congratulations on your wise decision, and continue to invest in improving your process. If you are not, why not? What are you doing, and what are you waiting for?

6.4 CONCLUSION

It is difficult to contemplate a state of I/T–business alignment without taking actions to dramatically improve the speed, cost, and quality of application development. There are, fortunately, specific actions to be taken to address this important issue. Object-oriented technology, data servers, and prototyping work both individually and together to satisfy the customer insistence on I/T for an application development process that responds to "I want it quick, I want it cheap, and I want it to work perfectly." Figure 6.21 summarizes the thrust of the actions recommended in this chapter. It is broadly acknowledged that application development takes too long, is too costly, and is of poor quality. This current strategic position of application development is depicted by the large triangle in Figure 6.21. Object-oriented technology, data servers, and prototyping provide an integrated way to attack these problems and move to a superior strategic position, as portrayed by the shaded triangle in Figure 6.21.

Economic theory teaches that there are only three generic ways to improve cost, quality, and speed:

- *Change in individual effort:* you change the attitude, motivation, zeal, willingness, cooperation, or skill of the worker.

- *Change in factors of production:* you change the materials used to develop the product.
- *Change in methods of production:* you change the process of production.

The ideas we have submitted for your consideration in this chapter cross all of these approaches. Prototyping affects individual effort, data servers change the factors of production, and object-oriented technology radically changes the methods of production. We have therefore offered a balanced approach to addressing the problem of aligning application development.

The speed at which you reengineer this movement arbitrates the competitive advantage earned. If you move too slowly, you will be a laggard and be a net advantage loser. If you move with the wave, you will achieve parity. If you move quickly, you can be the guide and create lasting strategic distance. It is an exaggeration, but only slightly so, that your plan can't be too bold in expediting your development process to the superior position illustrated in Figure 6.21.

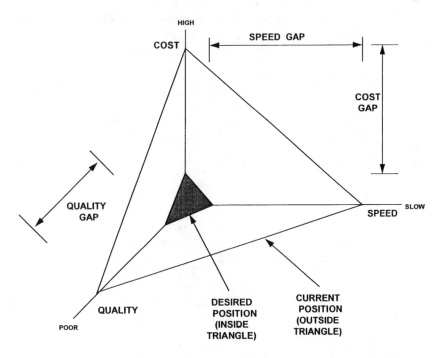

Figure 6.21   Collapsing the Application Development Gap.
Object-oriented technology, data servers, and prototyping provide
a collaborative way to reduce development cost, improve quality,
and accelerate speed.

NOTES

1. See the article "How Effective Are Software Engineering Methods" by N. Fenton in *Journal of Systems Software* 22 (1993), 141–146, for a searing indictment of the state of software productivity measurement.

2. Admittedly, software engineering is unlike traditional forms of engineering. The traditional engineering disciplines are founded on the physical laws that govern the subject area, while software is founded on the abstract disciplines of mathematics and logic. The software engineer is not constrained by physical limits. Nevertheless, there is no logical reason that best practices cannot or should not be implemented. A continued ad hoc approach to software development offers no hope or opportunity for consistently improving cost, quality, and speed.

3. Thomas Kuhn, *The Structure of Scientific Revolutions* (University of Chicago Press, 1970). Italics added.

4. Sun Tzu, *The Art of War.*

5. Software Engineering Institute, Carnegie Mellon University, document number CMU SEI-92-TR-013.

6. In support of this view, see Alan Davis, "Software Lemmingineering," *IEEE Software,* September 1993.

7

Management Philosophy and Style

The purpose of this chapter is to turn our attention to the most daunting reengineering problem of all: the question of what is to be the management philosophy and style, and how that translates into human resource policies. One can apply technology fixes, such as object-oriented technology, or economic fixes, such as creating a regulated I/T utility to resolve the misalignment problem, but sooner or later, one must also create a people fix. After all, nothing happens without the effort of the staff, yet motivating and aligning staff efforts toward a far-reaching and unified agenda is the most incalculable task of all. Almost any obstacle is easier to overcome, and any uncertainty or risk more easily controlled, than providing sustained charismatic leadership for the staff. As Herculean as they are, the tasks of technology and economic fixes shrink in comparison to the people fix problem.

As discussed in Section 2.5, there is no shortage of theories on how to manage. Currently in vogue are the notions of empowerment and teams. Some of the presentations on these subjects are so idyllic that if it were not for the absence of cherubim singing hymns of praise in the background, one would have every reason to believe that one had found management paradise. While self-directed, naturally formulated, dynamically rotating, customer-focused and empowered teams are certainly appealing, one must wonder whether they are here to stay, or are simply limping along the management theory life cycle that was introduced in Figure 2.14.[1]

It will be our approach to study the management philosophy, style, leadership, and personnel policies of the two greatest I/T strategists of all times: Machiavelli and Sun Tzu. They are the greatest I/T strategists because I/T strategy is 80 percent strategy and 20 percent I/T; they remain unchallenged in their claim to leadership in strategic thinking. To go forward, we will look backward and try to learn from the greatest teachers, rather than from fleeting contemporary theorists. While some of what they suggest in their writings is incongruent with modern ideas, it is certainly worth discussion, so that from a blending of their ideas with modern theories, a workable approach to I/T management can be formulated.[2]

How would Machiavelli or Sun Tzu as Chief Information Officer run an I/T organization in the turbulent 1990s and forward?

The structure of this chapter is as follows:

- *7.1. Machiavelli: CIO*
  This section reviews the teachings of Machiavelli on management philosophy, style, leadership, and personnel policies.
- *7.2. Sun Tzu: CIO*
  This section reviews the teachings of Sun Tzu on management philosophy, style, leadership, and personnel policies.
- *7.3. Strategic Issues*
  This section suggests how an imaginary CIO who has embraced the teachings of Sun Tzu and Machiavelli would approach the strategic issues confronting a contemporary CIO.
- *7.4. Conclusion*
  This section summarizes the primary points of this section.

There is no place better to begin the task of building a superior management philosophy than with the thoughts of the greatest strategists. It is from this perspective that we proceed.[3]

7.1 MACHIAVELLI: CIO

Niccolo Machiavelli was the author of many books on politics and political strategy, but without debate, he is best known and remembered for his classic book on political realism, *The Prince*. Machiavelli was a Florentine who lived between 1469 and 1527. It was a time of great political unrest and warfare in a disunited Italy, and Machiavelli wanted a strong leader to arise to unify Italy against all the foreigners engaged in Italian politics and intrigue. He wrote *The Prince* for Lorenzo De'Medici, prince of the city-state of Florence, in the hope that Lorenzo would rise to unite Italy. While Machiavelli is recognized as one of the premier political philosophers of all time, he has earned a much undeserved bad press. Most who critique him and cite him have never read him, yet the label "Machiavellian" translates to "evil" in everyday speech. His books in general, and *The Prince* in particular, provide extraordinarily deep insights into the psychology of leadership. They are not so much immoral or moral as amoral. They recount Machiavelli's exhaustive study of political history. Machiavelli, the first political scientist, analyzed events and then gave advice based on what people who led successfully did in practice, rather than simply what they espoused.

It is the cold candor with which Machiavelli recounts what leaders do that is the source of Machiavelli's infamy. It is not necessarily clear, however, whether the repugnance with which Machiavelli's cold and amoral advice is greeted is due to moral affront, or merely to a preference that the charade be maintained. In either case, one cannot help but be challenged by the directness of the uncompromising and crisp advice provided. Whether you like the advice or are shocked by it, it is presented with naked crystal clarity and directness; if you wish to accomplish that, then this is what you must do.

The Prince has remained relevant for over 500 years, because it was intended be read symbolically rather than literally. *The Prince* is not so much about how a prince in 15th- or 16th-century Italy should rule as it is about how a leader in any large organization confronted by political opposition and turbulent times should reign if (s)he wishes to succeed.

A representative set of Machiavelli's thoughts on management are as follows:

1. *Re: The Nature of the Staff*
   When things are quiet, everyone dances attendance, everyone makes promises and everyone would die for him so long as death is far off. But in times of adversity, when the state has need of its citizens, there are few to be found. And this test of loyalty is all the more dangerous since it can be made only once. A wise prince must devise ways by which his citizens are always and in all circumstances dependent on him and his authority; and then they will always be faithful to him. . . . One can make this generalization about men: they are ungrateful, fickle, liars and deceivers, they shun danger and are greedy for profit. . . . Because men are wretched creatures who would not keep their word to you, you need not keep your word to them. Men are so simple, and so much creatures of circumstances, that the deceiver will always find someone ready to be deceived. . . . The common people are always impressed by appearances. . . . Men will always do badly by you unless they are forced to be virtuous. Men are won over by the present far more than by the past; and when they decide that what is being done here and now is good, they content themselves with that and do not go looking for anything else. The populace is by nature fickle; it is easy to persuade them of something, but difficult to confirm them in that persuasion. Therefore one must urgently arrange matters so when they no longer believe they can be made to believe by force. It is necessary for the prince to have the friendship of the people; otherwise he has no remedy in times of adversity.[4]

2. *Re: Outsourcing*
   Wise princes, therefore, have always shunned auxiliaries and made use of their own forces. They have preferred to lose battles with their own forces than win them with others, in the belief that no

true victory is possible with alien arms. . . . Friendship that is bought with money and not with greatness and nobility of mind is paid for but it does not last and it yields nothing.

3. *Re: Core Competencies*

    A Prince, therefore, must have no other object or thought, nor acquire skill in anything, except war, its organization and its discipline. The art of war is all that is expected of a ruler. . . . we find that princes who have thought more of their pleasures than of arms have lost their states. The first way to lose your state is to neglect the art of war; the first way to win a state is to be skilled in the art of war.

4. *Re: Organizational Learning*

    As for intellectual training, the prince must read history, studying the actions of eminent men to see how they conducted themselves during war and to discover the reasons for their victories or their defeats, so that he can avoid the latter and imitate the former.

5. *Re: Strategic Planning*

    All wise rulers must cope not only with present troubles but also with ones likely to arise in the future and forestall them. When trouble is sensed well in advance, it can easily be remedied: if you wait for it to show itself any medicine will be too late because the disease will have become incurable. . . . Political disorders can be quickly healed if they are seen well in advance (and only a prudent ruler has such foresight); when, for lack of a diagnosis, they are allowed to grow in such a way that everyone can recognize them, remedies are too late. . . . A wise prince must observe these rules; he must never take things easy in times of peace, but rather use the latter assiduously, in order to be able to reap the profit in times of adversity. Then, when his fortunes change, he will be found ready to resist adversity.

6. *Re: The Character of the CIO*

    It would be splendid if one had a reputation for generosity; nonetheless if you do in fact earn a reputation for generosity you will come to grief. . . . A prince acting in that fashion will soon squander all his resources . . . he will lay excessive burdens on the people, his subjects will hate him and he will be generally despised. . . . So a prince must think little of it if he incurs the name of miser. . . . A prince must want to have a reputation for compassion rather than for cruelty; nonetheless, he must be careful that he does not make bad use of compassion. By making an example or two he will prove more compassionate than those who, being too compassionate, allow disorders which lead to murder and rapine. These nearly always harm the whole community, where as executions ordered by a prince only affect individuals. . . . From this arises the following question: whether it is better to be loved than feared, or the reverse. The answer is that one would like to be both but because it is difficult to combine them, it is far better to be feared than loved if you cannot be both . . . nonetheless, he must make himself feared in such a way that if he is not loved, at least he escapes being hated. . . . I conclude that since men love as they please but fear when the prince pleases, a wise prince should rely on what he controls, not on what he cannot control. He must only endeavor, as I said, to avoid being hated. . . . A prudent ruler cannot and must not honor his word when it places him at a disadvantage and the reasons for which he made his promise no longer exist but one must know how to color one's actions and to be great liar and deceiver. . . . To those seeing him and hearing him, he should appear a man of compassion, a man of good faith, a man of integrity, a kind and a religious man and there is nothing so important as to seem. Men, in general, judge by their eyes rather than by their hands; because everyone is in a position to watch, but few are in a position to come in close touch with you. Everyone see what you appear to be, few experience what you really are. . . . He must avoid anything that will make him hated and despised. He will be despised if he has a reputation for being fickle, frivolous, effeminate, cowardly, irresolute; a prince should avoid this like the plague and strive to demonstrate in his actions grandeur, courage, sobriety and strength. When settling disputes between his subjects, he should ensure that his judgment is irrevocable and he should be so regarded that no one dreams of trying to deceive or trick him. . . . A prince also wins prestige for being a true friend or a true enemy, that is for revealing himself without any reservations in favor of one side against another. This policy is always more advantageous than neutrality. . . . A prince should always show his esteem for talent, actively encouraging able men, and honoring those who excel in their profession. The prince should reward men who increase the prosperity of their state.

7. *Re: Commitment*
   He should put policies agreed upon into effect straight away and he should adhere to them rigidly. Anyone who does not do this is ruined by flatterers or is constantly changing his mind because of conflicting advice: as a result he is held in low esteem.

8. *Re: Benchmarking*
   Men nearly always follow the tracks made by others and proceed in their affairs by imitation even though they cannot entirely keep on the tracks of others or emulate the prowess of their models. So a

prudent man must always follow in the footsteps of great men and imitate those who have been outstanding. If his own prowess fails to compare with theirs, at least it has an air of greatness about it.

9. *Re: Economic System—Budgetary Control*
    We must distinguish between innovators who stand alone and those who depend on others, that is between those who to achieve their purposes can force the issue and those who must use persuasion. In the second case, they always come to grief, having achieved nothing; when, however, they depend on their own resources and can force the issue, then they are seldom endangered. This is why all armed prophets have conquered, and unarmed prophets have come to grief.

As we suggested and as is evidenced by these quotes, Machiavelli was shrewd, blunt, and piercing in his analysis, and he did not let pleasantries interfere with passing judgment on what is to be done to be successful.

Analysis

We can safely assume that Machiavelli would take actions to preposition the I/T organization for success. He would attempt to be farsighted in anticipating changing technologies, and would engage in deep and far-reaching strategic planning; he is definitely a charter member of the design school of strategy. He would not try to protect or embalm any existing technologies, but would view all I/T strictly as a temporary means to achieving the constant goal of business success.

Machiavelli would shun outsourcing of all but the most operational aspects of I/T. He would view I/T as a core competency, and endeavor to make the organization ever more proficient in translating I/T to business solutions. He would make major investments in training and awareness programs, recognizing that the way to lubricate the continuous introduction of newer and better technologies is to kill resistance before it emerges. While Machiavelli would engage in benchmarking, he would aspire to always be the one benchmarked against. He would see it as defeat to have to emulate others rather than to be the innovator who is emulated.

Machiavelli would reward the worthy and create strong financial and other incentives to motivate behaviors consistent with his aims. In particular, he would recognize that the future staff will require more horizontal, renaissance people and fewer vertical, in-depth people. Conversely, he would make examples of those who consistently blocked the achievement of his plans; better that a few should suffer than that an entire organization go through the pain of massive downsizing and layoffs because some players didn't wish to have their fiefdoms altered. He would be ruthless and relentless in effecting change by whatever means necessary.

He would empower teams, but with well-defined objectives. He would not support aimless empowerment, hoping that skunkworks would magically produce results. He believed in strong and visionary leadership, and would never abrogate that leadership role. He would not believe that modern management theory has rescinded the bell curve, and would not leave decision making to the whims of organizational democracy.[5]

Machiavelli would invest generously in winning the personal loyalty of the staff. He believed that results are a function not of verbal exhortations, but of personal loyalty and respect. That is one of the reasons that he would have had such little faith in outsourcing. When and if times and circumstances brought misfortune to the organization, he would count on the staff's personal loyalty and dedication to help survive the period. Machiavelli would design the economic system to promote cooperative behavior. He believed that people acted only in their immediate self-interest, and would therefore arrange the economic system to align self-interest with his own interest. He would engage constantly in a game of minimax, wherein he would set up the game payoffs to align individual decision making with the business goals. Before making decisions, he would question himself as to his real commitment. He would take on major challenges either with his complete devotion or not at all; halfhearted efforts are doomed to failure.

Machiavelli would run an extremely lean organization. He would see cost control as a means to keep the staff from growing fat and lazy. He would, however, invest based on strategic value, relying on visionary foresight instead of being a servant of net present value or other cost justification methods. He would invest in skill building, learning, and flexibility; he wouldn't pay for luxurious accommodations for the management staff or expensive amenities.

He would pride himself as an I/T warrior. He would set the highest standards of personal mastery of I/T, strategy, the business, and his customer's business. He would expect the same of his management staff. He would surround himself with knowledgeable people who told him the truth, he would engage in extensive dialogue, and after reflection, he would make the decision as the leader.

Conclusion

It is not unusual for people who read Machiavelli to react by saying that he is not kind. Desiring highly paternalistic and democratic organizations, people conclude that Machiavelli's prescriptions are anti-people. There is nothing that could be farther from the truth. Pseudo-paternalistic organizations that engage in a community deceit and do not take the required actions to ensure success, permitting gradual organizational rot, are the organizations that are not kind. The massive downsizings by supposedly paternalistic organizations like IBM and DEC are prime examples of unkindness. Coldly assessing reality and prompting the organization to do what must be done to ensure a viable business is the first and last kindness.

An excellent example of paternalistic unkindness appeared in the article "If Mainframes Are Dinosaurs, Why Is IBM Creating a New Generation?"[6] The article commented on the forthcoming announcement of a new generation of microprocessor/CMOS-based mainframes that would reduce the price/performance of mainframes by two thirds and vastly improve their competitiveness; it said: "Remarkably, IBM had started working on the technology a decade ago but stopped because the new computers would have resulted in massive layoffs in mainframe factories. . . . The new chip technology requires fewer designers, workers and production space." Rather than ensuring their dominance (did they believe that nobody else would figure it out?) and a viable organization by managing the transition, they chose to protect their employees. As we all know, ultimately they have been most unkind, as they have terminated tens of thousands and destroyed more than half of the market value of IBM's stock. It is ultimately always kinder to be propelled by pragmatic strategy than by a fixed ideology.

In a world of intense competition, kindness starts and ends not with empty rhetoric, but with continued employment and the opportunity to increase one's welfare. That is what Machiavellian-based strategy makes possible. A growing and viable Machiavellian-based organization is much kinder than a moribund pseudo-paternalistic organization.

Machiavelli would be an extraordinary CIO to work for. He would be consumed with getting things done, and by getting things done, he would bring prosperity to the organization and the business. What more can be asked for?

7.2 SUN TZU: CIO

Sun Tzu is the author of the most highly acclaimed and influential book on strategy in the world today, *The Art of War*. This acclaim cannot be over-emphasized. *The Art of War* presents an incredibly insightful treatise on the philosophy of managing and resolving discord, and is orders of magnitude beyond the next work in its profoundness and enduring value. While overtly a book about military strategy, it is written in such deep and profound metaphor that it is relevant to mastering the psychology, economics, politics, and physical confrontational aspects of all types of conflict and competition. *The Art of War* is a philosophy of strategy, not merely a procedural handbook.

Sun Tzu was a warrior–philosopher who lived approximately two thousand years ago during the Warring States period of ancient China, from the fifth to the third century B.C.E. It was a period of destabilization and interminable warfare between feuding and rival warlords. While some modern scholars question whether there was a Sun Tzu or whether multiple people authored the book, from a clinical perspective what matters is the book's existence and wisdom, not the academic scholarship question of its lineage. Consistent with its Taoist influence, *The Art of War* often finds the answers to problems in their opposites; the greatest warriors are those who win without fighting, and those best at resolving problems are those who prevent them in the first place. The greatest victories are those won at the minimum cost of lives and property. Great strategists win through superior strategy that makes victory an anticlimax.

As is true of all timeless books, *The Art of War* conveys knowledge in proportion to your worthiness and preparation to receive. As one's mastery of strategy matures, so does the meaning of the aphorisms in the text. It never ceases to amaze how you can reread the book over and over again and how, each time, it provides ever greater insights based on your superior ability to understand the teachings. It is not an exaggeration to suggest that if a modern pundit gives advice that conflicts with the teachings of Sun Tzu, you should carefully consider getting another pundit. Much of all modern strategic thinking, often presented as new and revolutionary, is merely a footnote to or an elaboration of *The Art of War*.

A representative set of Sun Tzu's thoughts on management is as follows:

1. *Re: The Nature of the Staff*
   Confront them with annihilation, and they will then survive; plunge them into a deadly situation, and they will then live. When people fall into danger they are then able to strive for victory. . . . When they have fallen into dire straits, they obey completely. . . . Put them in a spot where they have no place to go, and they will die before fleeing. If they are to die there, what can they not do? When warriors are in great danger, then they have no fear. When there is nowhere to go, they are firm. If they have no choice, they will fight. When people are desperate, they will fight to the death. . . . It is said that where there are big rewards, there are valiant men. If people know they will be richly rewarded if they overcome the opponent, they will gladly go into battle. . . . It is easy to get people to act by means of the force of momentum, whereas it is hard to demand power in individual people. The able have to choose the right people and let the force of momentum do its work. . . . If soldiers are punished before a personal attachment to the leadership is formed, they will not submit, and if they do not submit they are hard to employ. . . . Consistent means all along: in ordinary times it is imperative that benevolence and trustworthiness along with dignity and order be manifest to people from the

start, so that later, if they are faced with enemies it is possible to meet the situation in an orderly fashion with the full trust and acceptance of the people.

2.   *Re: Organizational Learning*
Test them to find out where they are sufficient and where they are lacking. Do something for or against them, making opponents turn their attention to it, so that you can find out their patterns of aggressive and defensive behavior.

3.   *Re: Strategic Planning*
In ancient times, skillful warriors first made themselves invincible. . . . It is easy to take over from those who do not plan ahead. . . . Those who are good at getting rid of trouble are those who take care of it before it arises. . . . Those who face the unprepared with preparation are victorious. . . . A victorious army first wins and then seeks battle, a defeated army first battles and then seeks victory. . . . Be prepared and you will be lucky. . . . Compare the strength of the enemy with your own and you will know whether there is sufficiency or lacking. After that, you can assess the advisory of attack or defense. . . . If you know others and know yourself, you will not be imperiled in a hundred battles; if you do not know others but know yourself, you will win one and lose one; if you do not know others and do not know yourself, you will be imperiled in every single battle . . . The considerations of the intelligent always include both harm and benefit. As they consider benefit, their work can expand; as they consider harm their troubles can be resolved. . . . Attack what can be overcome, do not attack what cannot be overcome. . . . To advance irresistibly, push through their gaps. . . . So when the front is prepared, the rear is lacking, and when the rear is prepared the front is lacking. Preparedness on the left means lack on the right, preparedness on the right means lack on the left. Preparedness everywhere means lack everywhere. . . . Attack where there is no defense.

4.   *Re: The Character of the CIO*
What the aware individual knows has not yet taken shape. If you see the subtle and notice the hidden when there is no form, this is really good. What everyone knows is not called wisdom. A leader of wisdom and ability lays deep plans for what others do not figure on. . . . The multitudes know when you win but they do not know the basis. Everyone knows the form by which I am victorious, but no one knows the form by which I ensure victory. The science of ensuring victory is a mysterious secret. Victory is not repetitious, but adapts its form endlessly. . . . A general must see alone and know alone, meaning that he must see what others do not see and

know what others do not know. Seeing what others do not see is called brilliance, knowing what others do not know is called genius. . . . If you can always remember danger when you are secure and remember chaos in times of order, watch out for danger and chaos while they are still formless and prevent them before they happen, this is best of all. . . . The lives of the people and the order of the nation are in the charge of the generals. . . . When their assistance is complete, the country is strong. When their assistance is defective, the country is weak. . . . Act when it is beneficial, desist if it is not. Anger can revert to joy, wrath can revert to delight; but a nation destroyed cannot be restored to existence, and the dead cannot be restored to life. Therefore an enlightened government is careful about this. This is the way to secure the nation. . . . What enables an intelligent leader to overcome others and achieve extraordinary accomplishments is foreknowledge. All matters require foreknowledge. . . . If you see the subtle and notice the hidden so as to seize victory when there is no form, this is really good . . . Harmony among people is the basis of the Way. The Way means inducing the people to have the same aim as the leadership, so that they will share death and share life. If people are treated with benevolence, faithfulness and justice, then they will be of one mind and will be glad to serve. The Way means humanness and justice. Share both the gains and the troubles of the people, then the troops will be loyal and naturally identify with the interests of the leadership. . . . Leadership is a matter of intelligence, trustworthiness, humanness, courage and sternness. . . . Good leadership rewards merit.

5. *Re: Commitment*
   When an army goes forth and crosses a border, it should burn its boats and bridges to show the populace that it has no intent of looking back.

6. *Re: Alignment*
   Those whose upper and lower ranks have the same desire are victorious. . . . Those skilled in strategy achieve cooperation in a group so that directing the group is like directing a single individual with no other choice. . . . Employ the entire force like employing a single individual. . . . Strategy is a problem of coordination, not of masses.

7. *Re: Competition*
   What causes opponents to come of their own accord is the prospect of gain. What discourages opponents from coming is the prospect of harm. . . . So the rule is not to count on opponents not coming, but to rely on having ways of dealing with them; not to count on opponents not attacking, but to rely on having what can't be

attacked. . . . What motivates competitors is profit . . . what restrains competitors is harm. . . . Wear enemies out by keeping them busy and not letting them rest . . . make them rush about trying to cover themselves, they will not have time to formulate plans. . . . To keep them from getting to you, attack where they will surely go to the rescue.

8. *Re: Organization Design*
   Structure depends on strategy. Forces are to be structured strategically based on what is advantageous.

As we suggested and as is evidenced by these quotes, Sun Tzu believed that strategy should first and foremost be deep and far-reaching. Victory goes to those who win through intelligence and leave nothing to chance; victory goes to those who position themselves so that they will have won before the engagement. The greatest victories go to those who have positioned themselves with such daunting superiority that the opponents surrender or retreat. Strategic acumen is unquestionably the most important quality of leadership in Sun Tzu's system.

Analysis

The heart of Sun Tzu's approach to I/T management is strategic thinking. Thinking strategically is not something that is superadded to an individual, but something that is an essential part of a leader. Thinking, acting, assessing, judging, revisiting, altering, and monitoring things always in terms of their strategic dimension is the way to success. A Tzuian strategist is immersed in strategy.

Sun Tzu's view of the leader is crisp: "Those who know strategy do not wander when they move. They act in accord with events. Their actions and inactions are matters of strategy, and they cannot be pleased or angered." A leader "knows" strategy as she knows nothing else. Wandering is wasteful, potentially dangerous, and evidence of strategic incompetence. Leaders look at events neither narrowly nor superficially, but always with depth and breadth. Strategic actions are not something done occasionally. All actions emanate from a mix of dynamic and reflective strategic assessment of the situation. Situations are always considered as they are in truth, never as one would wish them to be. The leader sees things and analyzes them with cold detachment. Emotional involvement clouds thinking. One must do what is dictated by times and circumstances, not ever by wishful thinking, tradition, or what one would prefer the situation to be.

Sun Tzu can be considered the founder of the design school of strategy. While he vigorously endorsed speed, adaptability, experimentation, surprise, and the unorthodox, he saw them happening within the context of an overall carefully assessed and designed strategic framework. He would view the ready-aim-fire school of strategy as absurd, and the emergent school as executing strategy at the lowest common denominator. He would view those who embrace real-time strategy as extraordinarily easy to manipulate and control.

In studying the teachings of Sun Tzu, the following themes stand out:

- The primacy of strategic thought as the basis of all actions.
- The responsibility of the leadership to lead.
- The importance of preemptive actions.
- The importance of developing excellent relationships between the leadership and the staff based on justice, benevolence, and caring. Sun Tzu would adduce that the crisis with worker involvement is not that workers feel alienated, but they do not feel anything, and that the solution to that indifference is rooted in demonstrating persistent and caring leadership by example.
- Analysis and synthesis based on facts, not opinion or wishful thinking.
- Prescience based on a deep understanding of the environment.
- Ceaseless vigilance.
- Competitors will come; one must exploit times of prosperity and tranquility to prepare for the inevitability of opponents.
- Generous reward for the worthy.[7]

Sun Tzu wouldn't engage in outsourcing, would only empower teams with well-defined objectives and feedback mechanisms, would design an economic system that demands individual and team alignment with business objectives, and would view strategic technology planning as a mandatory investment. Sun Tzu would make I/T investments based on his assessment of the far-reaching consequences of the investment to his position, and be neither slave nor servant to economic (ROI, ROE, payback, etc.) justification methods.

In a Tzuian managed organization, the realization of strategic benefit would be a continual event. As shown in Figure 7.1, strategy creation and maturation are not isolated or episodic events. Rather, concurrently and continuously, strategic actions are being born, growing, and maturing. The actions are deliberately designed to engage in strategic calving, whereby benefit spin-offs occur intermittently throughout the action's life cycle. The nurturing of strategic advantage does not start and stop; it is a continuous spawning activity without lull. This is in stark contrast to the common state of what-is worship that is endemic in many I/T organizations.

Sun Tzu's *Art of War* imposes the requirement of "mastery" on the leadership. The CIO must develop preeminent skill in the domains of strategy,

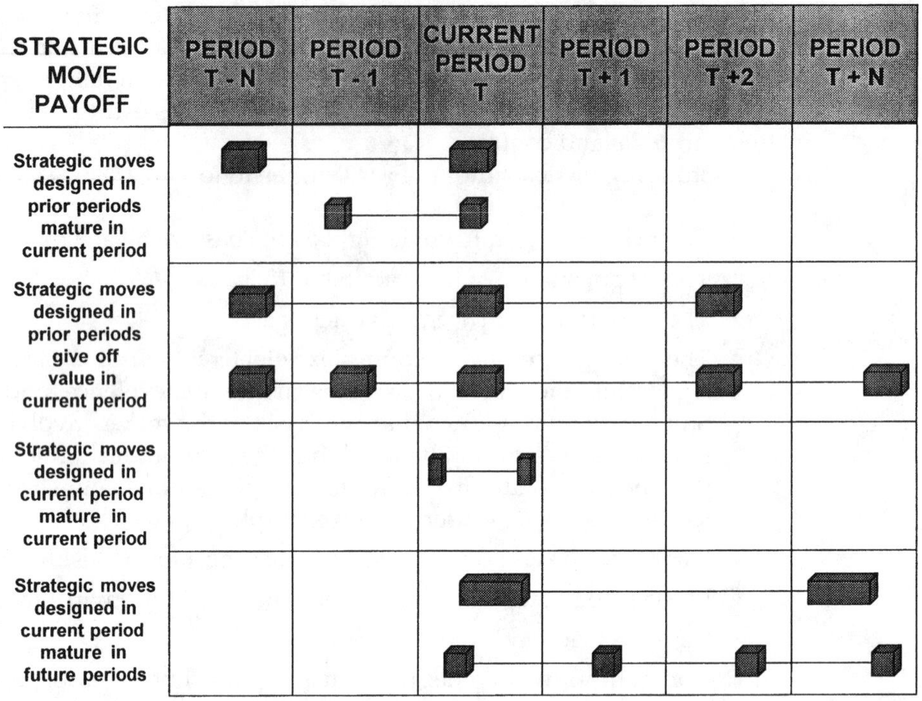

STRATEGIC MOVE PAYOFF	PERIOD T - N	PERIOD T - 1	CURRENT PERIOD T	PERIOD T + 1	PERIOD T + 2	PERIOD T + N
Strategic moves designed in prior periods mature in current period	■	■	■			
Strategic moves designed in prior periods give off value in current period	■	■	■	■	■	■
Strategic moves designed in current period mature in current period			▪—▪			
Strategic moves designed in current period mature in future periods			■	■	■	■

Figure 7.1   Strategic Payoff. A Tzuian strategist designs a constantly evolving family of strategies that are in different stages of maturity and deliver strategic value on a graduated basis.

the I/T industry, her business, and her customers' business. Mastery itself demands a derivative commitment to continuous learning, experimentation, prototyping, and willingness to revise plans based on actual events. It is not an accident that the book is called The *Art of War*, not the Algorithm of War. While Sun Tzu's strategic philosophy promotes long-term strategic thinking, he clearly recognized the inverse relationship between time and precision. Strategy must ultimately be constructed on the artful characteristics of creativity, intuition, and an almost extrasensory ability to see the formless and cull the essence from chaos.

Conclusion

The two most prominent lessons taught by Sun Tzu are that the supreme weapon for marketplace victory is the mind and that the most crucial asset to be deployed in achieving victory is the loyalty of the staff. The actual situation in many I/T organizations is therefore quite disheartening.

Many I/T leaders study and master strategy only as an accident. As evidenced by outsourcing, organizational downsizing, and the casual treatment of the staff, many leaders view the I/T staff as the nouveau lumpen proletariat. How will you win when your vision is shortsighted and shallow and your means of execution, the staff, is disdainful of you?

Tzuian strategy provides a path to success, and Sun Tzu would be the most extraordinary CIO to work for. He would be the mentor of mentors, because one would have the opportunity to learn from the greatest strategist who ever lived—it would be like learning music from Mozart. Blessed many times is the organization that has a CIO who walks in the path of Sun Tzu.

7.3 STRATEGIC ISSUES

The purpose of this book is provide advice on how to dramatically improve the state of alignment between the business and the I/T function. If you refer to Figure 1.12, you will recall that those 20 items represent the key strategic I/T issues that don't go away; they have been, since 1980, intractable. Alignment requires that you address and resolve each one.

If we could imagine a CIO who walked in the paths of Sun Tzu and Machiavelli, it would be interesting and instructive to conjecture what actions that CIO would take. While it is somewhat presumptuous to assert what such great strategists would do, it is beneficial to stretch and attempt to envision their response to the issues. In this way, we can develop a set of therapeutic actions to purge the alignment gap.

Strategic Issues

A CIO trained in the teachings of the greatest I/T strategists, Sun Tzu and Machiavelli, might respond to the top-ten Figure 1.12 I/T strategic issues as follows:

Issue 1: Reengineering Business Processes Through I/T

CIO Response: The CIO would focus first on understanding the strategic themes that the customers wish to infuse in their processes—speed, productivity, quality, maneuverability, customization, and so on. She would then carefully select development methodologies and enabling technologies that align exactly with the desired strategic themes. In particular, the CIO would work with her counterparts to discover how the reengineering efforts could contribute to creating a marketplace dislocation. The I/T organization would serve as a counselor to the user community, explaining the possibilities and the trade-offs of various solutions, but always keeping in mind that what delivers the true business value is the depth and breadth of the reengineering ideas, not the technology deployed.

Issue 2: I/T and Business Alignment

CIO Response: All I/T organizational processes would start with the customer. Process owners would be charged with the responsibility of tuning their processes to synchronize with customer satisfiers. The entire I/T organization would focus on improving the reach, range, and maneuverability of the I/T architecture, so that the I/T resource would never block or hinder a business initiative.

Issue 3: Improving System Development

CIO Response: The organization would adapt a software life cycle measurement system, implement object-oriented technologies, create given object data servers, utilize prototyping, utilize packaged software for nonstrategic business systems, off-load decision support system development to empowered users, and charge for all services. Benchmarking would be used to demonstrate competitive pricing and value.

Issue 4: Instituting Cross-Functional Information Systems

CIO Response: The I/T organization would develop a core competency in data server development and management. By separating data from specific application ownership, multiple functional applications could access the shared data resource. The reach, range, and maneuverable architecture would provide the means for wide access. A corporate data policy would be published and serve as the highest-level rules of governance for the data resource. The CIO would work with his counterparts to create a consortium that would be a customer and pay for the cross-functional applications. The consortium would take ownership of the shared database.

Issue 4: Utilizing Data

CIO Response: The dual database architecture would be implemented. Data administration would be implemented to standardize the definition of corporate data elements. Users would be encouraged and enabled to be self-sufficient in developing decision support and information center–type applications.

Issue 6: Cutting I/T Costs

CIO Response: All I/T process owners would annually submit plans to reduce process costs (single-year and multi-year efforts) as part of the annual planning cycle. Agreed-to investments in cost reduction of processes would be preprogrammed into rate structures. Products and services would be available in both bundled and unbundled versions; there would not be cross-subsidization of products and services. Products and services would survive or perish based on customer willingness to pay for value received.

Issue 7: Create an Information Architecture

CIO Response: This is an item of the highest priority. The economic system would permit the imposition of a pollution tax on organizations or developers who violated the architecture. Routine benchmarking would be done to ensure that the architecture remains competitive with the best in the marketplace.

Issue 8: Updating Obsolete Systems

CIO Response: The I/T organization would provide a variety of differently priced and featured approaches to update the aging system portfolio. Working collaboratively with customers, a systems plan based on willingness to pay and system business value would be developed that matched method (replace though new development, buy package, new front end, migrate to different platform, etc.) to customer business requirements.

Issue 9: Developing an I/T Strategic Plan

CIO Response: The design school approach to strategic planning would be used. Due to the current volatility of both the general business environment and the I/T environment, a strong emphasis would be placed on achieving pivot positions in a selected strategic area, such as architecture, customer satisfaction, capabilities, supplier relationships, or core competencies. Given the current business world, one would anticipate an I/T strategic plan driven by the strategic themes of cost, quality, speed, and maneuverability.

Issue 10: Changing I/T Platforms

CIO Response: Platform selection and design would be incorporated into the I/T architecture. Specific attention would be paid to the key success factors of scaleability, portability, reconfigurability, interoperability, openness, and heterogeneity.

An overriding characteristic of the Tzuian- and Machiavellian-schooled CIO would be that she would be both unimpressed and undeterred by the current situation. While recognizing that established frameworks, conceptualizations, and paradigms mediate our interpretation and categorization of events, she would endeavor not to be imprisoned by them. Organizational cultures perpetuate themselves. The perpetuation is not a rational process; it is a process driven by inertia for the status quo. The CIO would first break and then reinvent I/T culture as demanded and without reservation to ensure a viable organization.

Maneuver-Based Strategic Planning

As a foundation for addressing all these problems, a Tzuian/Machiavellian CIO would implement a strategic planning processing that is in harmony with maneuver-based competition. This would involve design changes to the strategic planning process introduced in Section 1.2 and very specific changes to human resource management. The purpose of these changes would be to infuse maneuverability into strategy formulation and into the character of the I/T organization, as follows:

1. *Strategic Planning Process*

   The Strategic Planning Process (see Section 1.2) would be adjusted to provide a clear and shared strategic agenda while empowering implementation teams. This would be done as follows:

   - The entire strategy in general, and strategic moves in particular, would focus on the intent of the strategy and the desired outcome of the strategy, but would leave open the methods of attainment. Strategic moves would be designed with the absolute minimum implementation program parameters (see Table 1.4). One might explain this as by saying that the teams are being given open-ended orders, as opposed to detailed orders. The strategy focuses on the ends, leaving the means to the implementation teams.

   - Flexibility, adaptability, latitude, innovation, entrepreneurship, and customization are thereby given to the people who are closest to the actual situation. Executive management focuses on strategy, while implementation teams focus on the means of realization.

   - Maintenance of overall cohesion is accomplished by a clear and shared strategy that informs all of what is to be accomplished and why, but not how. Empowerment, push-down decision-making, teams, and layers of leaders are now possible, because all can act independently while maintaining fidelity with a clear and grand intent. Dispersed but coordinated and synchronized strategic execution is therefore possible.

2. *Human Resource Management*

   To engage in maneuver warfare, an organization must internalize speed, adaptability, rapid decision making, and dynamic coordination. In dispersion of action, there must remain cohesion and unity of purpose. Unfortunately, the human qualities that permit this— trust, confidence, friendship, and morale—cannot be improvised; they must be built over time. An I/T organization that was run by *detail orders*—that is, central command, tight control, and explicit detail—would simply be too slow. New human resource policies and training consistent with a maneuver strategy would be implemented as follows:

   - Risk-taking would be rewarded.

   - Training would focus on dispersed decision-making and adaptability.

   - Teams would be formed based on the principles of mutual respect, trust, esprit de corps, and permanence.

   - Leadership development would be pushed down.

- The primary value of a judgment would be in its prudence. It is better to take an improper but prudent action than none at all.

Interestingly enough, teams and empowerment would be implemented, but with a clear bounding strategy. The entire staff would be mobilized to implement the strategy, which would be based on cohesion and unity of purpose. There would be empowered teams, but none would be aimless, nor would they be permitted to wander.

Strategy provides the anchor for a maneuver-based organization, and empowered people provide the means of attainment.

Summary

It is the certainly the case that some people expect strategy always to be awesome, remarkable, and completely unexpected. While it sometimes has such attributes, it just as often equates simply to applied common sense. Much strategic success is rooted in simply executing the mundane with excellence. The issues that we have discussed do not require arcane approaches. What they do require is clarity of thought, breadth of thought, depth of thought, commitment, embracing change, an overwhelming desire to serve the customer, and envisioning all actions within the context of the teachings of Sun Tzu and Machiavelli.

7.4 CONCLUSION

I have been asked on several different occasions why I have chosen Machiavelli and Sun Tzu as my reference strategists instead of modern business or I/T strategists. Wouldn't it make more sense to build strategy based on the teachings of James Martin or Dr. Michael Hammer or Dr. Michael Porter or Dr. C. K. Prahaldad?[8] Why construct late 20th-century I/T strategy on teachings that are 500 (Machiavelli) and 2000 (Sun Tzu) years old?

An important but unstated assumption in this assertion is that what is current is automatically better. In certain fields, this is certainly the case. One cannot help but marvel at the progress that has been made in 20th-century science, engineering, biology, medicine, and auxiliary natural sciences and engineering disciplines. The I/T industry itself is the apotheosis of this remarkable progress. However, without consideration, one often projects similar accomplishments to other fields, assuming that they also share such miraculous progress and improvement over all that preceded modern thinking.

My study of strategy indicates that this is not the case. As in many disciplines—aesthetics, art, music, and metaphysics—the classicists have superiority over the modernists. The classical strategists, Sun Tzu and

Machiavelli, have not been surpassed in the depth and breadth of their understanding of strategy.[9] As we noted in Chapter 2, much of today's strategic thinking can be reduced to fads that enjoy a predictable life cycle. While many modern strategists often offer good advice, the efficacy of that advice is normally short-lived because it is easily devalued through imitation. In 1990, the business journals screamed that the key to success is reducing cycle time. Two years later, the same journals lamented that competing on cycle time is an endless and hopeless treadmill.[10]

The strategic teachings of Machiavelli and Sun Tzu share ageless insights into the nature of strategy, strategic thinking, and the character of the strategist. I find it remarkable that many who practice and teach strategy have not read or studied their teachings. It cannot be too strongly recommended that if you wish to manage a truly exceptional I/T organization, you and your I/T management team must strive to be excellent students of Tzuian and Machiavellian strategy. What chance do you have of success, and how will you compete, if you are not employing this strategy and your competitors are? Do you have to believe that you have found a superior source of strategic wisdom?

The root cause of I/T–business misalignment is not a mystery: it has been and continues to be an absence of an I/T organization driven by strategy. The I/T organization has been driven by everything else over the years—suppliers, politics, self-aggrandizement, wishful thinking, hubris, and monopoly mind-sets—but never by strategic thinking. If alignment is to be achieved and is to persist, then the I/T organization must be driven by deep and far-reaching strategy. Such strategy will have its philosophical underpinnings in the teachings of Machiavelli and Sun Tzu. Their teachings have beaten time and survived endless imitators, and they provide unrivaled guidance for modern I/T strategy formulation and execution.

NOTES

1. See Thomas Kiely, "Group Way," *CIO Magazine,* October 1993, for an interesting interview with Professor Abraham Zaleznick of the Harvard Business School. Zaleznick suggests that the fascination with teams and collaborative decision-making methods is eroding leadership. This could be an early sign that teams are beginning to enter the disenchantment stage of the management theory life cycle.

While I think that the move to teams and empowerment signals a democratization of the workplace, I do not believe that either Machiavelli or Sun Tzu would find these solutions acceptable as a replacement for strong and visionary leadership. Machiavelli would reject them because their assumptions about the nature of the staff are inconsistent with his own. Sun Tzu would reject them because they would compromise his view of the roles and responsibilities of leadership. It will be interesting to see whether teams go the way of the management theory life cycle or revolutionize business operations.

2. I would like to make it clear that I do not agree with all of Machiavelli's ideas, but it is nevertheless very worthwhile to consider their merit. I believe that Machiavelli is most important not for his particular ideas, but as an example of using analysis and synthesis to confront and understand reality. One of the most important realities that Machiavelli helps us confront is that human actions are, for the most part, the product of enlightened self-interest, not altruism or corporate patriotism, and that reengineering actions must carefully consider how the change management program will motivate self-interest convergence with the goals of the business. Wherever and whenever you look, you find the same kinds of people. Knowing how people have behaved in the past provides a way to predict how they will act in the future, and Machiavelli was an astute observer of people.

3. All of the Sun Tzu and Machiavelli quotes in this chapter are from *The Art of War* and *The Prince*.

4. As pejorative and uncomplementary as Machiavelli is in his assessment of the staff, there are worse. A very interesting treatise, which includes a section on the tyranny of the technical elite (he calls them "learned ignoramuses"), is in Jose Ortega Y Gasset, *The Revolt of the Masses* (W. W. Norton, 1962).

5. Joseph Schumpeter, in his *Theory of Economic Development*, argued that while many could be adaptive and thereby deal with incremental change, few had the entrepreneurial ability of being creative. He labeled that small minority who could lead into the unknown as "the elite," and said "to act with confidence beyond the range of familiar beacons and to overcome resistance requires aptitudes that are present in only a small fraction of the population and that define the entrepreneurial type as well as the entrepreneurial function." The only qualification to enter the community of the elite was to be innovative, to be able to overcome, and to get things done. By definition, teams involve the masses; they entail decisions through consensus, which compromise true entrepreneurial leadership. Will team members, encumbered by human baggage (pride, ambition, jealousy, envy, conceit, avarice, etc.), embrace and follow the high-risk entrepreneurial team member who is only their peer, or will they oust her for not wishing to abide by the more subdued team rules?

In his other book, *The Discourses*, Machiavelli said, "One might be quite certain that it is better to entrust an expedition to one man of average prudence than to give to two men of outstanding ability the same authority." When no one is designated as the leader, in accord with modern team theory, then all are the leaders and the result is foretold. While technology changes ever more quickly in the foreground, human desire and passion are as constant as pi in the background. So teams are excellent for fact finding, tactical management, and execution, but are not the path to entrepreneurial-based strategic thinking and leadership.

Lest we be misunderstood, our view is as follows:

a. All are equally human and entitled to all human rights, treatment, and respect.

b. Though all are equally human, the talents of each are apportioned in a wide variety of combinations and degrees of perfection.

c. Excellence in strategic thinking is apportioned to only a select few; excellence in strategic thinking, formulation, and execution is exceedingly rare.

Sun Tzu said, "Victory by means of formation [strategy] is unknowable to the multitudes. Everyone knows the form by which I am victorious but no one knows the form by which I ensure victory. . . . Ordinary people see the means of victory but do not know the forms by which to ensure victory." In all fields, anything the multitudes can do is called "average." It would be most interesting to see how strategy, leadership, and entrepreneurship will fare under a corporate ochlocracy.

6. *Wall Street Journal*, 4 April 1994.

7. Rewarding the worthy is getting increasingly expensive. The 10 March 1994 *Wall Street Journal* reported that John Akers, former IBM chairman and CEO, received severance pay of more than $3 million. This was in addition to his $1.2 million pension and 100,000 stock options he was granted at exit. This occurred after his resignation from IBM on 25 January 1993. During Akers's tenure, IBM recorded its first operating loss and recorded more than $15 billion in charges, and the market value of IBM stock declined by approximately $28 billion. One can only imagine what would be a worthy reward had IBM broken even or had a profit.

8. For an interesting perspective on management theory fashion setters, see "The Good Guru Guide: Take Me to Your Leader," *The Economist*, 23 December 1993. The author analyzes many current gurus by the dimensions of influence, originality, intellectual coherence, and devotion of followers. Interestingly enough, he also acknowledges the importance of stagecraft, showmanship, charisma, and self-promotion in achieving and maintaining guru status. I would rate myself as being in the "pre-guru" stage, as I have no influence and even less of a following.

9. A reviewer commented that I have a "predilection for historical strategy." This analysis is incorrect. What I have is a "predilection for winning strategy," and the best winning strategy is rooted in the historical teachings of Sun Tzu and Machiavelli. I will be most amenable to switching to a newer and more fashionable strategy teacher when one of greater wisdom appears. Any suggestions?

10. It is perhaps overly cynical, but I find that the proliferation of strategy, wherein everyone proclaims herself a strategist, has had the consequence of leveling strategic thinking and actions to mediocrity. An excerpt from a poem by an Argentine poet, E.S. Disoepolo, entitled "Cambalache (Junkshop)" expresses my pessimism.

Todo es igual!	/	All is the same
Nada es nejor	/	Nothing any better
Lo mismo un burro	/	A donkey the same
Que un gran profesor.	/	As a great professor.

8

Finale

The purpose of this section is to provide some summary thoughts on the actions required to align I/T with the business. This will be accomplished as follows:

- *8.1. Pixie Dust*
  This section reviews some ways that the basic strategic actions can be enhanced to increase their utility. However well thought out and well intentioned the actions are, there will be numerous obstacles to overcome. By spicing the actions with additives, the efficacy and acceptance of the actions can be markedly increased.
- *8.2. Reprise*
  This section summarizes the main ideas of the book.
- *8.3. Epilogue*
  This section provides a closing thought on strategic alignment and I/T reengineering.

The most simple but elegant definition I have ever heard for strategy is "the art of devising a way short (the shorter the better) of brute force to accomplish your ends." This final chapter provides some final advice on how to do that.

8.1 PIXIE DUST

When my daughter was much younger, we went to see the play *Peter Pan*. As you may recall, Peter Pan, Wendy, Michael, and John all fly off to Never-Never Land in the first act. My daughter asked me how it was that they could fly. I told her that they had harnesses under their costumes and were carried by an almost invisible but very strong wire. She thought about this awhile and then, with the knowing smile of someone who has solved a complicated puzzle, she said, "But Daddy, they still first have to be sprinkled with the pixie dust."

Strategy, like flying, is greatly benefited by being sprinkled with some magical pixie dust. Implemented in raw form, regardless of merit, most strategic actions will encounter a legion of barriers and not find safe passage through the quagmire of change. It is much wiser to take time and sprinkle your implementation design with some strategic pixie dust to ease the passage. We would suggest the following types of dust to choose from:

- *Indirection:* the attempt to achieve one's ends by taking a circuitous path. We discussed indirection in Chapter 2, but would like to reemphasize its importance. Unless you have control of the budget and the political powerhouses, and are in the midst of a deep crisis where all are praying for a messiah, the types of actions we have recommended will meet stiff resistance. It is worth the time to consider ways to chip away at the resistance, rather than contesting it head-on. As a practical matter, one often has to do both. It is, however, much easier to execute the direct move once the indirect actions have had some time to dissipate and soften the resistance.

- *Commitment:* the demonstration of resolve to execute a strategy. The staff is extraordinarily perceptive in detecting contradictions between what is espoused and what is enacted. In the game of pretend, the staff are experts. If you pretend to believe in the strategy, they will pretend to enact it. Having seen so many new programs introduced with fanfare, only to go even more quickly than they came, the staff is understandably jaded, skeptical, and cynical. It is therefore vitally important, before you start down a new strategic path, to ask yourself honestly, "Do I truly believe in these actions, and how will I demonstrate resolve to win and sustain the organizational commitment to them?"

- *Change Management Plan:* a supporting plan to each major strategic action that accounts for anticipated obstacles and the methods to preemptively overcome those obstacles. There will be resistance to any action of significance. Some will resist based on well-reasoned objections; most will resist, albeit even if only by benign neglect, because the change is a perceived threat to their position. Time, consideration, and resources must be given to discerning who will resist, why they will resist, and how that resistance can be nullified.

- *Bluffing:* the art of creating the illusion of possessing something that you do not, in fact, possess. In corporations, what people bluff about is breadth and depth of knowledge. Most managers are caught in a dilemma. On one hand, it is almost humanly impossible to acquire and sustain substantive knowledge about all the subjects about which you are called upon to give opinions and pass judgments. On the other hand, it is unseemly to admit ignorance publicly. The resolution of this dilemma is bluffing—anything from a harmless pretense to a bold charade of knowledge.

The motivation for this bluffing is well intentioned. There is no evil intent to engaging in a self-serving con or deceit; what is motivating the bluffing is pragmatic survival in a world where there is a hopeless abyss between the depth and breadth of information that must be mastered and the time and energy available to master it. The solution is to bluff, and since all (or at least most) are also bluffing, everyone plays the game by the primal rule that you do not challenge anyone to the point of exposing the bluff. Calling a bluff is taboo. After all, if you expose another, your turn may also eventually come, and you will no longer be protected by the unspoken code.

The implications of this on strategy implementation are very important. If many people whom you have to convince are bluffing, then the way to reduce resistance is to perform the famous *double bluff*—that is, don't be bluffing. You should be a master of your strategy, its justification, its payoff, and its implementation. You should always speak first at meetings, demonstrate extreme and unquestionable mastery, and welcome debate. This will establish the ground rules for debate—ground rules that are clearly in your favor. Most will have neither the time nor the inclination to play the game when mastery is the ante. In playing the game in this manner, you have not called anyone else's bluff. You have played by the rules, but you have outbluffed them by not bluffing. The double bluff, renaissance competence, is the best bluff of all for the to-be-successful strategist.

- *Learning:* Learning, as a systematic process, is a critical component of strategy formulation from a number of perspectives. First, how can you hope to improve if you have not learned anything new? Without learning, all you can do is alter things cosmetically, with the inevitable consequence of putting only a temporary bandage on a wound that will soon bleed again. Masked, the wound will grow worse, later requiring even more dramatic measures to heal.

  Learning needs to be incorporated into strategy in all of the following ways:

  1. *Preemptive:* use learning as a means of indirection to reduce resistance. If you constantly teach and challenge the staff, new ideas are not alien, and their gradual adoption is not a threatening surprise.

  2. *Monitoring:* use learning from the results to date of your implementation to revise and adapt the implementation strategy. The probability of correctness of an implementation plan is inversely proportional to the time of conception to action. It is not an embarrassment to revise a plan based on more current information.

It is an embarrassment to continue on an incorrect path because it was in a plan.

3. *Mastery:* use learning as a continual method to update and refine your knowledge of the subject areas that are critical to your success. As we suggested before, a CIO must be a perpetual student of strategy, I/T, her business, and her customer's business.

Learning from one's own experience is good, but one's own experiences are extremely limited. It is much wiser to read, attend seminars, participate in industry groups, benchmark, and in all other ways learn from the experiences, good and bad, of others.

- *Holistic Thinking:* Holistic thinking is the act of looking at a problem from all possible angles and considering all the implications. It is normal and necessary to decompose problems to make them manageable and permit analytical focus. Having chosen an action to address that decomposed problem, it is necessary to go back up the decomposition tree and ask yourself, "If I take that action, what other actions are necessary to maintain alignment and synergy between areas?" Since everything in a business value chain is inevitably connected, if you do not take collateral strategic actions, you will create as many problems as you correct. You will, by virtue of your neglect, create next year's strategic problems.

  Consider the implications of implementing a reach, range, and maneuverable architecture. The holistic approach demands that you ask what changes must be made to supplier relationships, what changes must be made in personal policies, what changes must be made in capabilities, and what new competencies are needed. If you fail to attack problems holistically, as you fill one sink hole, you will be creating the next. Your strategic thinking must have not only depth in the area of focus, but breadth in its impact on ancillary areas.

- *Will:* Will is persistence through determination and strength of mind, character, and spirit to overcome obstacles and maintain effort in spite of incredible friction. The mathematics of implementation equate to how much budget and how many people you will have, but success often means having the persistence through will to overcome all the setbacks, frustrations, false starts, and interim failures before success is achieved. Liddell-Hart said, "In war, the chief incalculable is the human will." You must develop the strength of character to *will* success. Those who will success experience failing, like all others, but do not equate failing to failure. They equate failing to learning, and see it as a necessary step to success.

  The friction most often encountered and the most difficult to overcome is the denial of the need for change. Consider the following anecdote:

B borrows a car from A. Upon its return, A tells B that the fender is now dented. To this, B replies, "When I borrowed the car, the fender was already dented, and in any case, it was not dented when I returned it, and this is all irrelevant since I never borrowed the car."[1]

This type of denial, where reason is fragile, is often encountered in reengineering situations. Will is required to overcome denial.

- *Judgment:* Judgment is the final arbiter of strategic actions. There will always be uncertainty, unknowns, and risks. If this were not the case, then computers could and would make all the decisions. Making no decision or postponing a decision is also a decision, and almost any reasonable decision is better than none. Leadership cannot abrogate its responsibility for making judgments and decisions in a timely manner. The tempo of your decision making is, in fact, a basis for advantage. Those who can apply judgment more quickly can accrue time-based superiority.

  One way to compensate for the fog of strategic decision making is through the use of pivot positions. Take paths to your objectives that transverse crossroads. That way, if changes are required, you can back up to a point where a new path is easily taken. Just as you wish to enable dramatic maneuverability for the business through I/T, design your actions with options so that they are infused with maneuverability.

- *Dilemma:* In dealing with opposition, particularly strong politically based opposition, it is advisable to find ways to place your opponents on the horns of a dilemma. If they do not completely understand where and how you will proceed, they will not be able to amass their forces against you. If you can set up payoff matrices, where the minimax leads to supporting you even though their inclination is to oppose, they will stand confused and immobile while you proceed without interference. If you can provide them with the prospect of some gain in the midst of loss, they will agonize over whether to accept the new benefits or resist to maintain the old order. The creation of dilemmas for an opponent is an integral component of maneuver warfare, and it is invaluable in dealing with internal political opposition.

- *Falsification:* It is extremely frustrating in dealing with opponents to strategic initiatives to watch them repeatedly bring up opposing arguments, refute them, and then assert another argument in endless opposition. One is caught in a hopeless and eternal game of "but what about that?" They are trying to break your will through a war of argument attrition.

Science has dealt with this problem by the notion of *falsification*. In presenting a theory, one should state not only the premises, assumptions, and conditions of the theory, its derivative hypothesis, and proofs, but also the grounds for falsifying the theory—what evidence would have to be presented to prove the theory wrong. When you play the science game, you must be willing to state under what conditions you would abandon your theory.[2]

This would seem to be an excellent approach to dealing with hard-core resistance. Rather than engaging in an useless game of one-upmanship, publicly request a statement of what evidence they require to get them to change their minds and positions. What would convince them of the viability of your actions and the futility of maintaining the status quo? One could then work at providing the necessary final evidence.

Once this answer is presented, one of two things may occur. If they are fair-minded people, they will be convinced by virtue of your having met their own demands, and will cease resistance and become your allies. If they are disingenuous, they will ignore the evidence and continue their opposition. In the latter case, one is left with no alternative but to hold them up to public ridicule for the contradiction of their actions.

I believe that these ten examples provide a good sampling of pixie dust. There are others, as well, and it is incumbent on the strategist to sprinkle the strategy with a custom combination for the specific challenges presented. In this way, like Peter Pan and the others, your strategies will also be able to fly.

8.2 REPRISE

In *The Art of Strategic Planning for Information Technology,* I wrote, "Strategy is inspired by vision and guided by reason."[3] Vision determines an end worthy of a deep and far-reaching commitment, and reason provides the most advantageous means to that end. As both vision and reason are endlessly extensible, so an ever better strategy can be imagined.

The vision we propose for I/T is a state of perfect strategic alignment with the business. I/T is no longer viewed as a strategic bust or a necessary but burdensome expense; rather, it is viewed as the primary resource to be applied for achieving business ends. At this point, through a reach, range, and maneuverable architecture, I/T is able to reshape and reconfigure itself, on request, to meet or set the accelerating tempo of the business environment. At this point, I/T architecture provides the business with the maximum possible degree of freedom for information movement and management.

This is no longer just a vision, it is feasible. We have suggested five elementary actions that need to be taken to translate potential to reality:

- Implement a reach, range, and maneuverability I/T architecture.
- Design both of your economic systems properly.
- Align technology planning with business needs.
- Take actions to dramatically reduce the cost and increase the speed and quality of application development.
- Implement a realistic management philosophy and style.

Architecture provides the glue to hold the multitude of advantageous information technologies together, and it serves as the flash point of business alignment by providing the means to create marketplace disruptions. Technology planning provides the means to keep the architecture fluid and current. Application development provides the means to satisfy immediate customer needs. The economic system provides the basic means to align individual and group decision making with the aims of the leadership. Management philosophy and style provide the leadership to make everything else possible. What would constitute a more pragmatic plan?

Reengineering the I/T organization is clearly not just a technology transfer problem. Reengineering the I/T organization is a technosocioeconomic problem. All aspects of the I/T organization must be redesigned; technology transfer, the fun part, is only part of the problem. If you do not do a holistic job, you will plant and cultivate the seeds of your future strategic problems. Left to their own devices, entropy will cause horizontal dysfunction between the reengineered and legacy aspects of your business. There are many who will strive to cause you strategic grief; why bring it upon yourself?

Table 8.1 restates Table 2.8, but illustrates our treatment plan. Since it is a systemic problem that is causing our sorrows, the absence of strategy, our therapy is aimed at the root cause level. Actions taken at any other level will offer only fleeting relief.

You are competing in an era of hypercompetition, an era in which advantage has shifted from being based on size and deep pockets to being based on agility and novelty. The key to success in this era is continuously increasing customer satisfaction and concurrently disabling your competitor's ability to do the same. This is accomplished through lightning speed, paralyzing surprise, nonimitable actions, and the atomizing of the competitor's will and ability to respond. To accomplish this, you must align I/T with the business.

Table 8.1
Therapy. The prescriptions in this book provide therapy for the systemic problems that are afflicting the I/T organization.

Root Cause Analytical Model	I/T–Business Analysis	Therapy: Treatment Plan
Symptoms: External Signs and Indications of a Problem	Figure 1.12 Recurrent Critical Issues	
Immediate Problem: Malfunctioning Part/System/Etc.	1. Business Demands on I/T 2. Technology Change 3. Competition	
Root Cause: The Ingrained and Systemic Failure	Absence of I/T Strategy Aligned with the Business	Align I/T with the Business 1. I/T Architecture 2. Technology Planning 3. Economy Design 4. Application Development 5. Management Philosophy

You really do not have a choice. You may either align or decline. The I/T organization is at a crossroads: As Sun Tzu said, "There is a way of survival which helps and strengths you; there is a way of destruction which pushes you into oblivion."[4] One does not need to imagine the future versions of Figure 1.12. Table 8.2 shows the 1994 version of the strategic issues study that was published as I completed this book. Again, the card deck of strategic I/T issues is shuffled, but the strategic absurdity remains; we will endlessly work the same strategic issues, year after year after year. This year (1994) is particularly dispiriting, because it's the first year in which the exact same set of issues from the prior year is repeated. This folly must be brought to an end. The time for alignment is now, and we have argued the means.

As is common with anyone who participates in the public debate on such an emotional topic as I/T strategy, there are those who are displeased with my analysis, diagnosis, and prescriptions. I recall, on more than one occasion, colleagues who, after reading what I wrote or hearing me speak, told me that I had paid absolutely no attention to their appraisal. Frustrated by the absence of inclusion of their ideas, they accused me of being stubborn, close-minded, and insular. How could I ignore their well-reasoned arguments?

Nothing could be further from the truth. I listen carefully to everyone, read profusely, and spend an inordinate amount of time thinking, conceptualizing, integrating, and reflecting on all the information I have accumulated. When I ignore or contradict the opinions of others, it is not

Table 8.2
1994 Strategic I/T Issues. All the perennial favorites are back.

Issue	1994	1993	1992	1991	1990	1989	1988
Reengineering Business Processes	1	1	2	1	1	11	N/R
Aligning I/S and Corporate Goals	2	2	1	2	4	2	1
Utilizing Data	3	4	4	5	7	6	7
Cross-Functional Systems	4	4	6	3	3	7	N/R
Information Architecture	5	7	3	8	9	5	5
Systems Development	6	3	9	4	6	13	12
Updating Obsolete Systems	7	8	18	N/R	13	N/R	18
Integrating Systems	8	11	13	9	16	12	6
I/T Human Resource	9	12	5	13	11	8	8
Changing I/T Platforms	9	10	N/R	N/R	N/R	N/R	N/R
I/S Strategic Plan	11	9	10	6	5	4	2
Cut I/S Costs	12	6	11	11	10	14	17
Capitalize on Advances in I/T	13	14	19	20	N/R	17	N/R
Managing Dispersed Systems	14	12	15	19	N/R	16	13
Use I/T for Competitive Breakthrough	15	15	14	12	8	1	4
Connecting to Customers and Suppliers	16	16	20	15	19	N/R	N/R
Moving to Open Systems	17	19	N/R	N/R	N/R	N/R	N/R
Educating Management on I/T	18	18	16	14	2	3	3
Promoting the I/S Function	19	20	17	17	15	N/R	N/R
Improving Leadership Skills of I/S Management	20	17	7	10	N/R	N/R	N/R

Source: CSC/Index.

because I didn't consider them, it is because I did. I discount them because

- Those ideas would cause you to wander.
- Those ideas do not lead to deep and far-reaching strategy.
- Those ideas do not position you so that you will surely win.

- Those ideas are not in harmony with the times and circumstances.
- Those ideas do not represent things as they are in real truth; rather, they represent things as they are imagined.

Recall the wisdom of Machiavelli:

My intention is to say something that will prove of practical use to the inquirer, I have thought it proper to represent things as they are in real truth, rather than as they are imagined. Many have dreamed up republics and principalities which have never in truth been known to exist; the gulf between how one should live and how one does live is so wide that a man who neglects what is actually done for what should be done learns the way of self destruction rather than self preservation.[5]

It is and always was my intention to meet the standards set by Machiavelli. The precepts contained herein offer a path to self-preservation. What more can advice offer you? Many organizations have, understandably, become cost-obsessed, and have reacted by taking a slash-and-burn attitude toward their I/T assets. Frustrated by the intractable chasm between I/T promises and reality, and under immense pressure to improve productivity, they have reduced I/T to an expense line to be mercilessly pinched like housekeeping. This is surely a path to ruin.[6] Even if successful in the short run, one cannot run a business in the long run on a strategy of saving money rather than making it. Cost reduction, while forever important, is a self-limiting strategy. The more successful you are in your early efforts, the sooner the value of new opportunities approach zero. The purpose of a business is to make money, not to save it. It therefore follows that I/T investments should not be slashed, but focused on carefully increasing reach, range, and maneuverability so that the business is positioned to take advantage of open-ended growth opportunities as they present themselves. How will you grow and prosper if you eliminate the asset (I/T) that enables your success? It is therefore not a coincidence that the lower purposeful uses of I/T, functional systems, and cross-functional systems on Figure 1.11 serve primarily to save money, while the higher uses, imagineering the business and creating opportunities through dislocations, serve primarily to make money. (Reengineering is a transitional stage.)

It is interesting to observe that when you follow a reach, range, and maneuverability strategy, cost savings fall out as if by accident. When you undertake direct I/T cost saving opportunities, the cost saving effort is taken, the money is saved, and the opportunity ends. Savings is an event. When you implement a reach, range, and maneuverability architecture, you position yourself in a tremendously flexible state where you are continuously able to take advantage of cost reduction opportunities. Savings occur systematically as a by-product of your positioning, not as a singular event. So, not surprisingly, a deep and far-reaching strategy positions you not only for growth, but for opportunistic savings opportunities, as well.

By the Power Invested in Me

I grant to each and to all a pardon. Your sentence is commuted; your penance is completed; your sins are erased; the curse is lifted; the power of the hex is annulled. You need no longer be a modern-day Sisyphus. Your slate is wiped clean. The power of my absolution is awesome. There is, however, a price: you must use what you have learned to do it right next time.

I can imagine a conversation, a few years from now, between a CIO who did not choose wisely and an I/T consultant. The CIO asks, "What should I do now?" The consultant, in a moment of unrestrained honesty, replies, "It is too late; what you need to do now needed to have been done then." Fortunately, then is now.

8.3 EPILOGUE

The scene is repeated on a daily basis in conference rooms throughout the world. It is repeated in the offices of public corporations, government agencies, universities, and other institutions. The multidivisional task force has completed the final presentation to the VP of Information Technology (a.k.a. CIO or Chief Technology Officer). The best minds of the business have assessed the situation and reached the irrefutable conclusion that their I/T organization is in serious trouble.

Even those with the greatest ability for denial have conceded the reality. Customer satisfaction is in free fall, they are having gargantuan difficulties in managing the transition to network computing, and system integrators are winning more and more of the new application development business. A 15-minute break is called, during which the VP thumbs through the overheads and ponders the readout. The task force members have followed the instructions perfectly; they have coldly assessed things as they are in truth, not as they would wish them to be. The break concludes and all eyes anxiously turn to the VP. The VP asks of one and all, "Ladies and gentlemen, what should we do now?"

I have shared with you what I think they should do now. They must devote themselves to achieving a state of strategic alignment with the business. To accomplish this, they must reengineer their organization to dramatically reverse its misfortune. They can accomplish this through the actions that have been presented. As shown Figure 1.11, reengineering is a dual activity. Business processes can be reengineered so that they can create marketplace dislocations, and I/T must be coincidentally reengineered to enable processes to become powerful. So a single framework, Figure 1.11, summarizes a deep and far-reaching vision of alignment that can assure you that you will surely prevail over those who have already lost. What will you do now? If you do not follow the path that has been outlined, how will you create a superior strategic configuration of I/T power?

Postscript

It is sometimes the case that despite one's best efforts and most resolute intentions, one fails to adequately convey one's message. As I believe my message to be of the utmost urgency, I will risk the imperfection of repetition to ensure that the essence of my ideas is concisely conveyed. Businesses enter markets not to engage in expensive, time-consuming, and exhausting battles with fierce competitors, but to win profits. A maneuver style of marketplace behavior permits one to economically achieve the latter while deftly avoiding the former. Given our previous conclusion that an excellent maneuver fighter will best an excellent attrition fighter, one does not need to be a soothsayer to foretell which choice of style—attrition or maneuver—will be increasingly selected by astute business leadership. As illustrated in Figure 8.1, they will migrate from an attrition style to a maneuver-centric style. They will then demand that I/T resources be reoriented to support this new approach to the marketplace.

The business demand on the I/T organization is therefore obvious. A business is one massively parallel information-processing entity. It is implausible that the business will be able to engage in maneuver behaviors unless the I/T assets are themselves perfectly malleable. The business must have an I/T asset that permits maximum freedom of action. Only when an I/T organization can deliver reach, range, and maneuverability can it be in alignment. Through I/T, the business can attack anywhere and defend everywhere. As shown in Figure 8.2, not only can I/T be the root of advantage for the business, it can be the wellspring of disadvantage for the competition.

In a business world that is accelerating toward total entropy, of this you may be absolutely certain. There are only three types of I/T organizations:

1. Those that are adapting themselves to maneuver-based competition.
2. Those that will adapt themselves to maneuver-based competition.
3. Those that will cease to exist.

The ideas in this book provide guidance for those in the first two categories.

SECONDARY STYLE

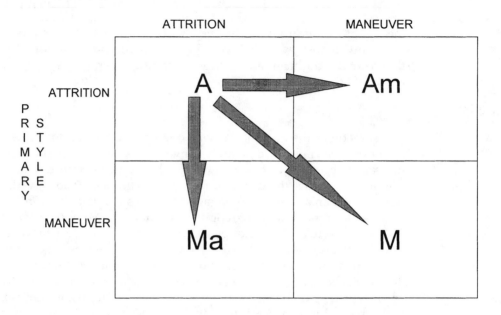

Figure 8.1   Marketplace Style. As we move toward the year 2000, most companies will migrate to a marketplace style that emphasizes maneuver over attrition behaviors.

NOTES

1. This anecodote is a variation from Pierre Vidal-Naquel, *Assassins of Memory* (Columbia University Press, 1992).

2. An excellent example of falsification is provided by Charles Darwin's famous theory of natural selection. In *The Origin of the Species,* Darwin exhaustively itemizes plausible objections to his theory, addresses them, and acknowledges that proof of the objections would compromise his theory. How refreshing it would be if I/T pundits provided similar integrity for their theories.

3. Bruce D. Henderson, former chairman of the Boston Consulting Group, in "The Origin of Strategy" (*Harvard Business Review,* Nov.–Dec 1989), said, "imagination and logic make strategy possible."

4. Sun Tzu, *The Art of War.*

5. Machiavelli, *The Prince.*

6. After WWI, the French built the Maginot line on the French/German frontier. Built as a series of fortresses with connecting tunnels, the Maginot line was intended to prevent any future German attack against France. To

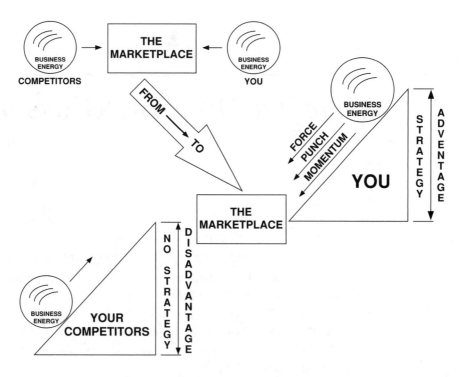

Figure 8.2   Marketplace Advantage. I/T will achieve its maximum value to the business when it can be used not only to create advantage, but to create disadvantage as well.

save on the cost, the line was never completed, and the gun emplacements were fixed facing east. When the Germans in WWII attacked France through Belgium, the Maginot line was taken from behind without a shot in defense (the guns were immobile). So in retrospect, as designed to save money, the Maginot line was prodigal at any price, but had it been able to preserve French liberty, it would have been inexpensive regardless of the price.

A

Mulciber Drawing Glossary

And Service Path   A service path in which a subpath is taken, returned, and then another subpath is followed.

Application   The name of an application running in a program layer.

Building Block Configurations   Five basic configurations from which any other configuration for a platform can be created.

Bundled   The application code from more than one program layer is intertwined and cannot be separated.

Commit Group Name   The name of a two-phased commit group that this resource participates in.

Complex Service Path   A service path that splits into multiple subpaths.

Configuration   A platform on which 1 to n program layers are executing.

Configuration Instance #   The number of instances of this configuration in the architecture.

Device Type   A specific type of ITD.

Distributed Data   Interoperability between two data program layers.

Distributed Interoperability Event   Interoperability between two program layers of the same type.

Distributed Presentation   Interoperability between two presentation program layers.

Distributed Processing   Interoperability between two processing program layers.

DT   A data program layer.

Geography   The physical location of a configuration.

Header Service   A service directly invoked by a program layer.

Information Technology Device (ITD)   Any kind of information appliance, computer, network station, or dumb terminal that may participate in an architecture.

Insular Service Path   A service path that does not involve interoperability between program layers.

Internetworking Diagram   A string of network diagrams.

Interoperability Domain   Defines an execution space in which program layers may interoperate.

Interoperability Event   A series of darkened circles that show the information flow between interoperating program layers.

Interoperability Role   Defines the role that a program layer takes when it invokes an interoperability service path.

Interoperability Service Path   A service path that involves interoperability between program layers.

Intraconfiguration Interoperability   Interoperability between two program layers on the same configuration.

Layer Instance #   A unique integer that distinctly identifies a program layer on a configuration.

Layer Type   A type of program layer.

Middleware   A set of services that enables and oversees interoperability between program layers on the same or different platforms.

Middleware Box   Defines the middleware, transaction support, networking speed range, and internetworking diagram for an interoperability event.

Mulciber Architecture Diagram (MAD)   An architecture drawing that follows all of these conventions except the MID.

Mulciber Drawing   A MAD, MID, and associated tables.

Mulciber Internetworking Diagram (MID)   An internetworking diagram.

Network Diagram   A diagram that identifies the network speed, network name, and OSI levels 1 to 4 for a network.

Network Name   The name of a network.

Network Resource   Any type of resource (typically a DBMS) on the architecture.

Network Speed   The speed of a network.

Networking Speed Range   Identifies the low and high speeds of the networks that information will traverse for an interoperability event.

OSI Reference Model   A layered set of seven generic functions that networking must fulfill.

Platform   An ITD with an associated operating system (if applicable).

PN   Presentation program layer.

PNPR   Bundled presentation and processing program layers.

PNPRDT   Bundled presentation, processing, and data program layers.

Portability   The ability to perform scaleability but to do it at the source code level.

PR   Processing program layer.

PRDT   Bundled processing and data program layers.

Program Layer   Any I/T application should be understood as consisting of three basic program layers that can interface with each other. These layers are:

- *Presentation layer (PN):* the layer that handles application logic with regard to collecting, preparing, and presenting data.
- *Processing layer (PR):* the layer concerned with application business logic. Also known as the function layer.
- *Data layer (DT):* the layer concerned with data management (addition, deletion, selection, and modification of data records).

This partitioning is the basic structure of all software systems.

Program Layer Area   The part of a platform that is reserved for program layers.

Reconfigurability   The ability to selectively choose a layer (at the program layer level), reconfigure its relationships with associated layers, port the layer to a different platform, and maintain all interoperability.

Remote Data   Interoperability between a nondata program layer and a data program layer.

Remote Interoperability Event   Interoperability between two different types of program layers.

Remote Presentation   Interoperability between a nonpresentation program layer and a presentation program layer.

Remote Processing   Interoperability between a nonprocessing program layer and a processing program layer.

Resource Name   The name of a network resource.

Resource Type   Uniquely identifies a type of network resource.

Scaleability   The ability to move program layers, in total, with associated service paths and interoperability at the binary (load, execution) level from one platform to another and maintain all interoperability.

Service   A major software function invoked by a program layer through an application program interface (API).

Service Area   The part of a platform that is reserved for service paths.

Service Interface The application program interface or protocol that is invoked to make use of a service.

Service Interface Level Defines the location and protocol transparency of the service interface.

Service Path A concatenated string of services.

Service Prefix Defines the interoperability domain and interoperability role of an interoperability service path.

Service Provider Identifies the software that embodies the service interface.

Service Request An instance of a service.

Service Type A specific class of services.

Simple Service Path A service path containing only one path.

Sink An unknown configuration that participates in the architecture and is a receiver of information.

Source An unknown configuration that participates in the architecture and is a sender of information.

Source/Sink An unknown configuration that participates in the architecture and is both a sender and receiver of information.

Source Language The source language that an application is written in.

Tier # Identifies the tier of a configuration.

Transaction Support Identifies whether the middleware supports transactions.

B

Mulciber Drawing Templates

This appendix contains templates of the basic constructs of Mulciber drawings. Each figure consists of two parts:

- An annotated template that identifies the variables for the template.
- A blank template.

Templates are provided for the following constructs:

Figure	Mulciber Construct	Explained in Section 3.3, Notion Number
B.1	Information Technology Device	1
B.2	Platform	2
B.3	Program Layer	3
B.4	Configuration	4
B.5	Service	6
B.6	Service Prefix and Service	8
B.7	Middleware Box	11
B.8	Network Diagram	12
B.9	Internetwork Diagram	12
B.10	Resource	14

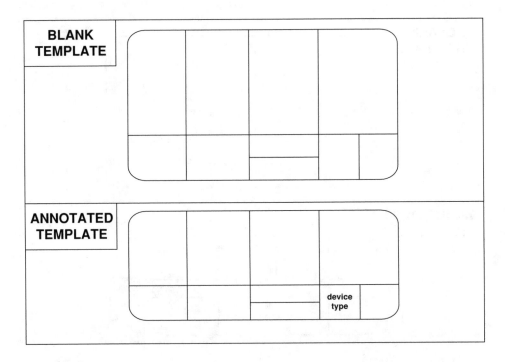

Figure B.1   Information Technology Device. Any kind of information appliance, computer, network station, or dumb terminal that may participate in an architecture.

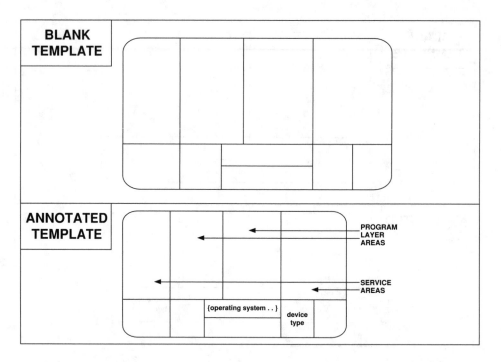

Figure B.2   Platform. An ITD with an associated operating system
(if applicable).

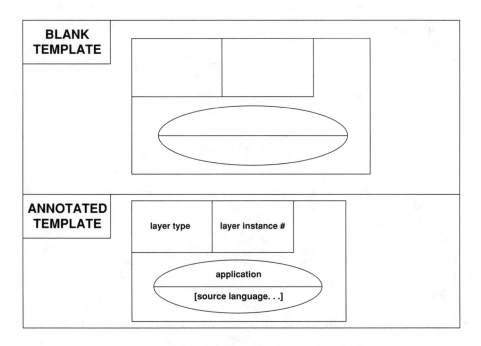

Figure B.3   Program Layer. Any of three basic program layers that can interface with each other.

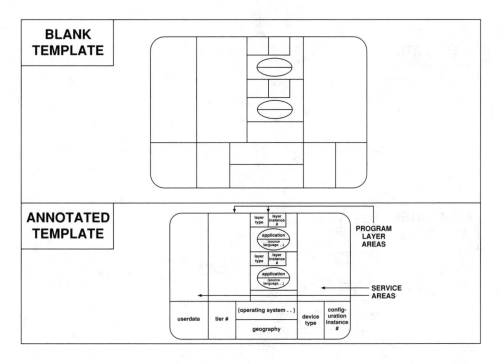

Figure B.4   Configuration. A platform on which 1 to *n* program layers are executing.

327

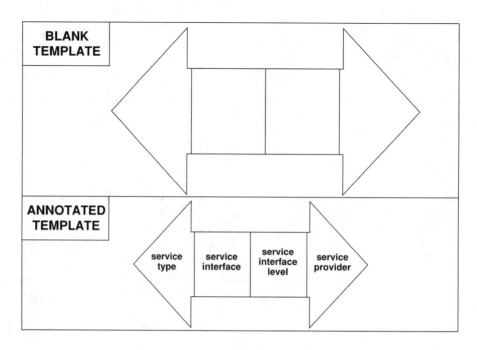

Figure B.5   Service. A major software function invoked by a program
layer through an application program interface.

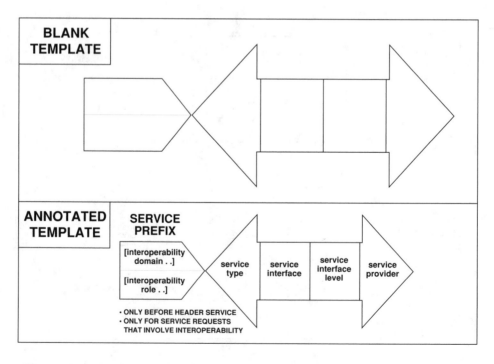

Figure B.6   Service Prefix. Defines the interoperability domain and interoperability role of an interoperability service path.

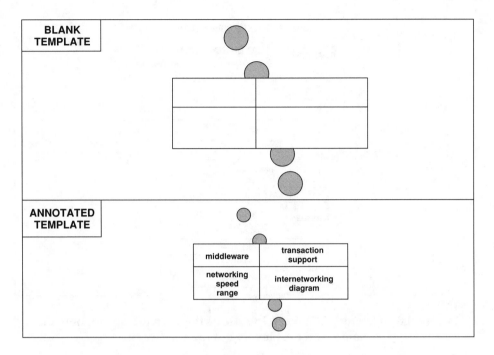

Figure B.7   Middleware Box. Defines the middleware, transaction support, networking speed range, and internetworking diagram for an interoperability event.

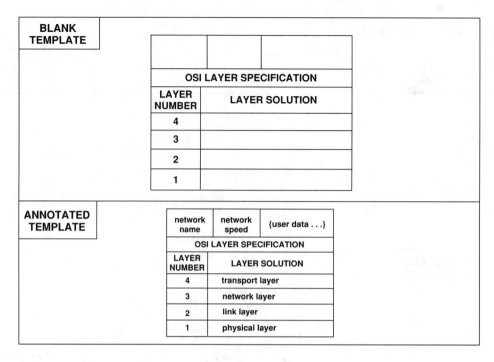

Figure B.8   Network Diagram. Identifies the network speed, network
name, and OSI levels 1–4 for a network.

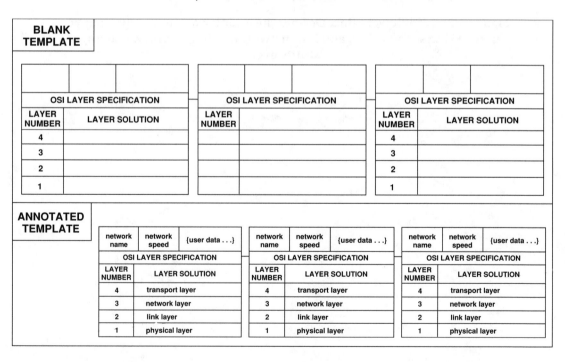

Figure B.9   Internetwork Diagram. A string of network diagrams.

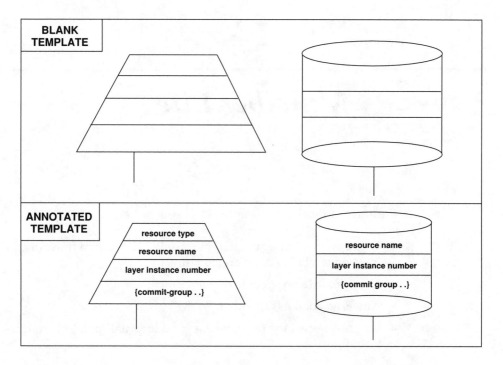

Figure B.10   Resource. Any type of resource (typically a DBMS) on the architecture.

C

Mulciber Lite

In the body of this book (Chapter 3), I argued that:

- Conceptual architecture diagrams only serve the purpose of conveying a general idea of an architecture.
- They provide no specificity value.
- Any is as good as any other.
- It is not necessary to formalize a conceptual architecture drawing technique.

Everyone should be free to bluff in a manner that she is most comfortable with. Users of Mulciber (its customers and market) have nevertheless indicated that they would like a simpler and higher-level drawing version that can be used to quickly sketch conceptual architectures. Bowing to the pressures of the marketplace, I propose *Mulciber Lite* as a conceptual drawing technique that is much simpler than Mulciber drawings, conveys the essence of an architecture, and is formal. Figure C.1 shows a Mulciber Lite drawing. The variables, all defined in Section 3.3, are as follows:

- Device type: see Notion 1
- Operating system: see Notion 2
- Application: see Notion 4
- Service type: see Notion 6
- Middleware: see Notion 11
- OSI network layer 3: see Aside 3

A Mulciber Lite drawing shows either the business application architecture or the OA&M architecture; it does not show both concurrently. The

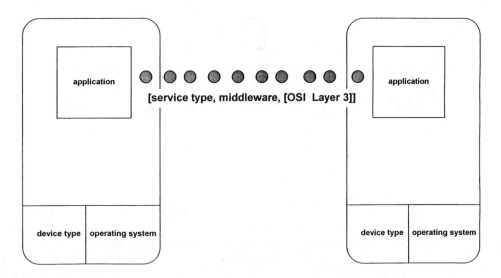

Figure C.1 Mulciber Lite. Mulciber lite provides a simple way to sketch conceptual architectures.

diagram conveys at a high level the essence of interoperability; it identifies the platforms (device type and operating system) and the players (applications) and specifies how they communicate (service type, middleware, and OSI network layer 3).

D

Drawing Network OA&M

A colleague who is quite adept at drawing Mulciber drawings once remarked, "It can get pretty ugly pretty fast." Having used Mulciber to document existing incoherent architectures, she found that the drawings rapidly deteriorated into unconnected disorder as she attempted to blueprint the real-world I/T chaos. Mulciber cannot magically transmute lead architectures into gold architectures. It can merely show that they are indeed lead.

In recognition of the general complexity of documenting even well-designed architectures, let alone the prevailing mess, it was stated in Section 3.3: Aside 3 that the diagramming technique would not encompass the detail drawing of either the networks or the network elements. As presented, the networking is summarized by a network diagram (see Figure 3.33a) or an internetworking diagram (see Figure 3.33b) that treats the networks at a macro level. The advantage of this is simplicity, but at the price that the OA&M of the networks, which may be of prime architectural importance, is not included in the Mulciber drawings.

For those who wish to include network OA&M in their drawings, we would like to suggest three alternative ways to diagram it in increasing levels of complexity:

1. *Level 1: Simple Network OA&M*
   As shown in Figure D.1, include in the Mulciber Architecture Drawing a network diagram with the associated OA&M interoperating with it, while treating the network diagram as a source or sink (Section 3.3: Notion 17). At the point where the interoperability darkened circles meet the network diagram, we identify the type(s) of network device that are being managed.

2. *Level 2: Mulciber Network OA&M Diagram (MNOD)*
   The idea behind an MNOD is to draw a selective explosion of the elements composing the network with their associated OA&M. Since each communication device within the network can be treated as a computer, a hard-wired device (e.g., equivalent to a

334

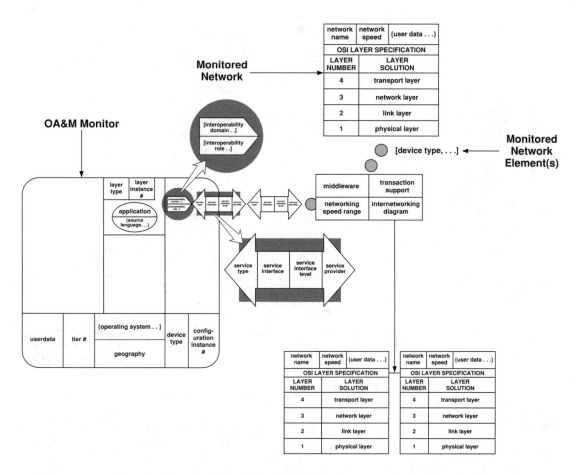

Figure D.1 Simple Network OA&M. With simple network OA&M, the network is included in the Mulciber architecture drawing as a source/sink with the associated OA&M manager(s).

dumb terminal), or a source or sink, as shown on Figure D.2, an MNOD drawing illustrates the network being monitored and the OA&M management of representative elements within the network. In these cases, the ITD types are brouter, router, bridge, hub, and so on. In the event that the object of OA&M monitoring is a communications transport mechanism or multiple communication element, the representative drawings show clusters of related elements.

3. *Level 3: Complete Network Drawing*
   This is the logical end of a Level 2 drawing. Instead of drawing selective or representative elements of the network, one would

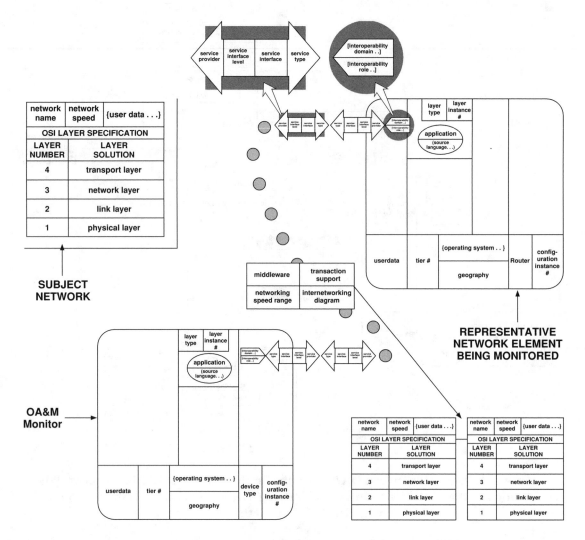

Figure D.2   Mulciber Network OA&M Diagram (MNOD). With an NMOD drawing, the OA&M of exploded and representative network elements is shown.

draw the entire network using the Mulciber conventions. The MNOD drawing would look like just another Mulciber architecture diagram, except it would have the defining network program at the top. As an addition in this case, one might wish to develop a programming notation to identify the different types of transport mechanisms and devices.

E

Maneuverability Analysis

In Section 1.3, we argued that I/T achieves its maximum state of business alignment when it can be used as a tool to both create and exploit favorable marketplace dislocations—and, conversely, to prevent a competitor from executing a dislocation maneuver against you. In this appendix, I would like to present five analytical methods that may be used as part of a strategic planning exercise to use I/T toward that end. In this way, we demonstrate how I/T can be promoted at the strategic planning table as a tool of maneuverability.

1. *METHOD NAME*: SELF VULNERABILITY ANALYSIS (TABLE E.1)

When Used: During the Situational Analysis step of the strategic planning cycle.

Purpose: To forestall a successful maneuver attack against yourself. This method is used to analyze how an opponent may attack you and how you may preempt or defend against her actions.

Discussion: As shown in Table E.1, Self Vulnerability Analysis requires you to coldly assess your vulnerabilities to determine how an astute competitor would attack you and how you could defend against such an assault. The data elements are as follows:

- *Product:* defines the product(s) or service(s) that the company sells that are subject to a competitive threat.
- *Market Segment:* defines the market segment(s) in which this product is sold.
- *Competition:* defines the competitors in the market segment (existing or potential) for the products or services.
- *Center of Gravity:* defines your center of gravity. What advantage or vulnerability could they attack to leave your business highly disrupted?

337

Table E.1
Self Vulnerability Analysis. This analytical method is used to foresee and forestall an attack by a competitor.

Product: _____   Market Segment: _____

Center of Gravity: _____   Gaps: _____ _____ _____ _____

Competitor(s): _____   Marketplace Style: _____

Maneuver Action Cluster	Maneuver Actions	What Will They Attack?	How Will I Defend?	How Will I Use I/T to Defend?

- *Gaps:* define your weaknesses. These are points for your competitors to attack.
- *Marketplace Style:* defines your current marketplace style (e.g., A, Am, M, or Ma).
- *Maneuver Action Cluster:* Maneuver attacks are characterized by a set of sequential and simultaneous actions. This item defines a group of coordinated actions.
- *Maneuver Actions:* Defines from 1 to *n* coordinated actions that a competitor may take against you.
- *What Will They Attack?:* Defines the center of gravity or gap(s) that would be the target of this Maneuver Action Cluster.
- *How Will I Defend?:* Defines a set of 1 to *n* actions that could be taken to either preempt or nullify such an attack.
- *How Will I Use I/T to Defend?:* Specifically identifies how I/T will be used to defend against this Maneuver Action Cluster.

2. *METHOD NAME*: COMPETITOR VULNERABILITY ANALYSIS (TABLE E.2)

When Used: During the Situational Analysis step of the strategic planning cycle.

Purpose: To develop a maneuver attack against your competitors.

Discussion: As shown in Table E.2, Competitor Vulnerability Analysis requires you to assess your competitors' vulnerabilities to determine how you could attack and how you could overcome their defense. The data elements are as follows:

Table E.2
Competitor Vulnerability Analysis. This analytical method is used to design a maneuver attack against a competitor.

The Competitor
Competitor: _____   Product: _____

Center of Gravity: _____   Gaps: _____ _____ _____ _____

Marketplace Style: _____

Yourself
Product: _____

Marketplace Style: _____

The Marketplace
Market Segment: _____

Maneuver Action Cluster	Maneuver Actions	What Will I Attack?	How Will I Attack?	How Will I Use I/T to Attack?

- *Competitor:* name of the competitor.
- *Competitor's Product:* defines the product(s)/service(s) that the competitor sells that you wish to attack.
- *Competitor's Center of Gravity:* defines the competitor's center of gravity. What advantage or vulnerability could you attack to leave your competitor highly disrupted?
- *Competitor's Gaps:* define the competitor's weaknesses. These are points for your attack.
- *Competitor's Marketplace Style:* defines the competitor's current marketplace style (e.g., A, Am, M, or Ma).
- *Your Product:* defines the product(s) or service(s) that you sell against the competitor.
- *Your Marketplace Style:* defines your current marketplace style (e.g., A, Am, M, or Ma).
- *Market Segment:* defines the market segment(s) to which the products are sold.
- *Maneuver Action Cluster:* Maneuver attacks are characterized by a set of sequential and simultaneous actions. This item defines a group of coordinated actions.
- *Maneuver Actions:* Defines from 1 to *n* coordinated actions that you may take.
- *What Will I Attack?:* Defines the center of gravity or gap(s) that you will target on this Maneuver Action Cluster.
- *How Will They Defend?:* Defines a set of 1 to *n* actions that they could take to either preempt or nullify such an attack.
- *How Will I Use I/T to Attack?:* Specifically identifies how I/T will be used to enable this Maneuver Action Cluster.

3. *METHOD NAME*: CUSTOMER'S VULNERABILITY ANALYSIS (TABLE E.3)

When Used: During the Situational Analysis step of the strategic planning cycle.

Purpose: To understand how your product can help your customer defend against an attack by her competitors. By linking your product to your customer's marketplace defense strategy, you improve your value-added position with your client.

Discussion: As shown in Table E.3, a Customer's Vulnerability Analysis requires you to assess your customer's vulnerabilities to determine how your customer could be attacked and how you could help to preempt or nullify an attack. The data elements are as follows:

Table E.3
Customer's Vulnerability Analysis. This analytical method
is used to analyze the vulnerability of a key customer to an attack
by her competitors.

Your Customer

Customer: _____ Product: _____

Center of Gravity: _____ Gaps: _____ _____ _____ _____

Marketplace Style: _____ Market Segment: _____

Yourself
Product: _____

Market Segment: _____

The Competition
Competitor(s): _____

Maneuver Action Cluster	Maneuver Actions	What Will They Attack?	How Will My Product Help Defend?	How Will I Use I/T to Help?

- *Customer:* name of customer
- *Customer's Product:* defines the product(s) or service(s) that the customer sells that use your product.
- *Customer's Center of Gravity:* defines the customer's center of gravity. What advantage or vulnerability could be attacked to leave your customer highly disrupted?
- *Customer's Gaps:* define the customer's weaknesses. These are points for competitive attack.

- *Customer's Marketplace Style:* defines the customer's current marketplace style (e.g., A, Am, M, or Ma).
- *Customer's Market Segment:* defines the market segment(s) to which the products are sold.
- *Competitor:* name of the competitor.
- *Your Product:* defines the product(s) or service(s) that you sell to the customer.
- *Your Market Segment:* defines the market segment in which you sell your product.
- *Maneuver Action Cluster:* Maneuver attacks are characterized by a set of sequential and simultaneous actions. This item defines a group of coordinated actions.
- *Maneuver Actions:* Defines from 1 to *n* coordinated actions that competitors may take against your customer.
- *What Will They Attack?:* Defines the center of gravity or gap(s) that the competitors will target on this Maneuver Action Cluster.
- *How Will My Product Help Them Defend?:* Defines a set of 1 to *n* actions that the customer could take to either preempt or nullify such an attack.
- *How Will I Use I/T to Help?:* Specifically identifies how I/T will be used to enable a defense.

4. *METHOD NAME*: CUSTOMER'S COMPETITOR VULNERABILITY ANALYSIS (TABLE E.4)

When Used: During the Situational Analysis step of the strategic planning cycle.

Purpose: To understand how your product can help your customer attack her competitors. By linking your product to your customer's marketplace growth strategy, you improve your value-added position with your client.

Discussion: As shown in Table E.4, a Customer's Competitor Vulnerability Analysis requires you to assess your customer's competitor's vulnerabilities to determine how your customer could attack and how you could help to formulate an attack. The data elements are as follows:

- *Customer:* name of customer.
- *Customer's Product:* defines the product(s) or service(s) that the customer sells that use your product.
- *Customer's Marketplace Style:* defines the customer's current marketplace style (e.g., A, Am, M, or Ma).

Table E.4
Customer's Competitor's Vulnerability Analysis. This analytical method is used to design a customer's maneuver attack against a competitor.

Your Customer

Customer: _____   Product: _____

Marketplace Style: _____   Market Segment: _____

Yourself
Product: _____

Market Segment: _____

The Competition

Competitor(s): _____   Marketplace Style: _____

Center of Gravity: _____   Gaps: ___ ___ ___ ___

Maneuver Action Cluster	Maneuver Actions	What Will Customer Attack?	How Will My Product Help Attack?	How Will I Use I/T to Help?

- *Customer's Market Segment:* defines the market segment(s) to which the products are sold.
- *Competitor:* name of the competitor.
- *Competitor's Center of Gravity:* defines the customer's center of gravity. What advantage or vulnerability could be attacked to leave your customer highly disrupted?
- *Competitor's Gaps:* define the customer's weaknesses. These are points for competitive attack.
- *Competitor's Marketplace Style:* defines the customer's current marketplace style (e.g., A, Am, M, or Ma).

- *Your Product:* defines the product(s) or service(s) that you sell to the customer.
- *Your Market Segment:* defines the market segment in which you sell your product.
- *Maneuver Action Cluster:* Maneuver attacks are characterized by a set of sequential and simultaneous actions. This item defines a group of coordinated actions.
- *Maneuver Actions:* Defines from 1 to n coordinated actions that your customer may take against her competitor.
- *What Will Customer Attack?:* Defines the center of gravity or gap(s) that the customer will target on this Maneuver Action Cluster.
- *How Will My Product Help Them Attack?:* Defines a set of 1 to n actions that the customer could take to develop such an attack.
- *How Will I Use I/T to Help?:* Specifically identifies how I/T will be used to enable the attack.

Note: This method and the prior method can be redone by substituting yourself for the customer and your supplier for yourself. In this way, you will be able to analyze the entire value chain by asking: How can I help my customer attack and defend? How can I attack and defend? How can my supplier(s) help me attack and defend?

5. *METHOD NAME*: INFUSING STRATEGIC MOVES WITH MANEUVERABILITY (TABLES E.5–E.8)

When Used: During the Strategy step of the strategic planning cycle.

Purpose: To modify a proposed set of strategic actions with additional traits that will both make the actions more maneuverable and incorporate the use of I/T.

Discussion: However you get there, you will reach the point in the Strategy step of the strategic planning cycle where a set of strategic actions has been developed. This four-step analytical method is used to alter the proposed strategic moves to infuse them with the spirit of maneuverability and to ensure that I/T capabilities are incorporated. The function of each step is as follows:

Step 1: Strategic Action Clustering (Table E.5)

This step groups the proposed actions into logically related clusters of actions that were naturally intended to be executed sequentially or simultaneously as a coordinated thrust. The data elements are as follows:

Table E.5
Strategic Action Clustering. This analytical method is used to group the proposed strategic actions into related groups.

Cluster	Action 1	Action 2	Action 3	Action n

- *Cluster:* assigns a name or number to a selected cluster of proposed strategic actions.
- *Action* n: a proposed strategic action.

Step 2: Cluster Categorization (Table E.6)

This step categorizes the clusters. The data elements are as follows:

- *Cluster:* the name or number of a strategic action cluster.
- *Market Scope:* identifies whom you are challenging with this cluster. Is it the market leader, the market challenger, an also-ran, or a niche player?
- *Force:* identifies how much of your resources you will be deploying in support of this cluster.
- *Status Quo or Radical:* Is the thrust of the cluster an incremental change to the market, or are you attempting a radical action?
- *Competitive Threat:* How will the competition interpret this action?

Table E.6
Cluster Categorization. This method is used to categorize the strategic action clusters.

Cluster	Market Scope	Force	Status Quo or Radical	Competitive Threat	Center of Gravity or Gaps	Geography	Customer Satisfaction
C1							
C2							
C3							
Cn							

- *Center of Gravity or Gaps:* What center of gravity or gaps will be attacked?
- *Geography:* Where will you be attacking?
- *Customer Satisfaction:* How will this cluster increase customer satisfaction?

Step 3: How Will They Respond? (Table E.7)

This step attempts to anticipate the response level of the competition. The data elements are as follows:

- *Cluster:* the name or number of a strategic action cluster.
- *Willingness:* Will the cluster be viewed as a sufficient threat to warrant a response, and if so, to what degree?
- *Ability:* Will they have the capability to respond?
- *Speed:* How fast will they be able to respond?
- *How Respond:* What set of actions will they take in response?

Step 4: Maneuverability Design (Table E.8)

Given the more complete understanding of the nature of your actions and the possible competitive response to them from the prior three steps, this step attempts to amend your actions with additional actions that infuse maneuverability traits and the use of I/T. The data elements are as follows:

- *Cluster:* the name or number of a strategic action cluster.
- *Will:* How can I reduce their will to respond?
- *Ability:* How can I design the actions so that it will very difficult for them to respond?

Table E.7
How Will They Respond? This analytical method is used to anticipate the response of your competitors.

Cluster	Willingness to Respond	Ability to Respond	Speed of Response	How Respond
C1				
C2				
C3				
Cn				

Table E.8
Maneuverability Design. This analytical method is used to amend your current set of strategic actions with additional actions that infuse maneuver and I/T.

Cluster	Will to Respond	Ability to Respond	Speed	Surprise	Punch/ Force	Psychology	Barriers	Customer Satisfaction	I/T Usage
C1									
C2									
C3									
C*n*									

- *Speed:* How can I infuse speed into the actions?
- *Surprise:* What can I do that is unexpected?
- *Punch/force:* How much punch or force would be necessary to deliver a decisive blow?
- *Psychology:* What can be added to my actions to dispirit my competitors?
- *Barriers:* What barriers to response can I build into my actions?
- *Customer Satisfaction:* What can I add to my actions to excite my customers?
- *I/T Usage:* How can I use I/T to accomplish the preceding?

In using these analytical methods, as is true with using any strategic planning methods, one must always remember that what counts is not mindless filling in the blanks but the depth of thought, sensitivity, and insight applied to the analysis. Methods are only as good as the understanding and thinking process that accompanies their use.

Index

About the Author

Mr. Bernard H. Boar is an accomplished author in the field of strategy and information technology. His most recent books are *The Art of Strategic Planning for Information Technology: Crafting Strategy for the 90s* and *Implementing Client/Server Computing: A Strategic Perspective*. His book *Application Prototyping: A Requirements Definition Strategy for the 80s* is now recognized as the seminal work on the subject. Mr. Boar has been published in *CIO Journal, Computerworld, Journal of Systems Management, Journal of Business Strategy, Auerbach*, and *The Handbook of Business Strategy*. He is a frequent speaker at leading industry conferences on I/T strategy, I/T management, and client/server computing. He holds an M.B.A. from the Baruch Graduate School of Business and a B.S. in Computer Science from the City College of New York. Mr. Boar is a member of both the Strategic Planning Forum and the Strategic Management Society. He serves as an information technology strategist, architect, and consultant for AT&T Bell Laboratories QUEST in Holmdel, New Jersey. He is reachable at the internet e-mail address of boar@attmail.com.